Troilus and Cressida

ARDEN EARLY MODERN DRAMA GUIDES

Series Editors:
Andrew Hiscock, University of Wales, Bangor, UK and
Lisa Hopkins, Sheffield Hallam University, UK

Arden Early Modern Drama Guides offer practical and accessible introductions to the critical and performative contexts of key Elizabethan and Jacobean plays. Each guide introduces the text's critical and performance history, but also provides students with an invaluable insight into the landscape of current scholarly research, through a keynote essay on the state of the art and newly commissioned essays of fresh research from different critical perspectives.

A Midsummer Night's Dream, edited by Regina Buccola
Doctor Faustus, edited by Sarah Munson Deats
King Lear, edited by Andrew Hiscock and Lisa Hopkins
Henry IV, Part 1, edited by Stephen Longstaffe
'Tis Pity She's a Whore, edited by Lisa Hopkins
Women Beware Women, edited by Andrew Hiscock
Volpone, edited by Matthew Steggle
The Duchess of Malfi, edited by Christina Luckyj
The Alchemist, edited by Erin Julian and Helen Ostovich
The Jew of Malta, edited by Robert A. Logan
Macbeth, edited by John Drakakis and Dale Townshend
Richard III, edited by Annaliese Connolly
Twelfth Night, edited by Alison Findlay and Liz Oakley-Brown
The Tempest, edited by Alden T. Vaughan and
Virginia Mason Vaughan
Romeo and Juliet, edited by Julia Reinhard Lupton
Julius Caesar, edited by Andrew James Hartley
The Revenger's Tragedy, edited by Brian Walsh
The White Devil, edited by Paul Frazer and Adam Hansen
Edward II, edited by Kirk Melnikoff
Much Ado About Nothing, edited by Deborah Cartmell and
Peter J. Smith
King Henry V, edited by Karen Britland and Line Cottegnies

Further titles are in preparation.

Troilus and Cressida

A Critical Reader

Edited by
Efterpi Mitsi

THE ARDEN SHAKESPEARE
LONDON • NEW YORK • OXFORD • NEW DELHI • SYDNEY

THE ARDEN SHAKESPEARE
Bloomsbury Publishing Plc
50 Bedford Square, London, WC1B 3DP, UK
1385 Broadway, New York, NY 10018, USA

BLOOMSBURY, THE ARDEN SHAKESPEARE and the Arden Shakespeare logo
are trademarks of Bloomsbury Publishing Plc

First published in Great Britain 2019
Paperback edition published 2020

Copyright © Efterpi Mitsi and contributors, 2019

Efterpi Mitsi and contributors have asserted their right under the Copyright,
Designs and Patents Act, 1988, to be identified as the authors of this work.

For legal purposes the Acknowledgements on p. viii constitute an extension of this
copyright page.

Cover design: Irene Martinez Costa
Cover image taken from the 1615 title page of *The Spanish Tragedy* by Thomas Kyd

All rights reserved. No part of this publication may be reproduced or transmitted
in any form or by any means, electronic or mechanical, including photocopying,
recording, or any information storage or retrieval system, without prior permission
in writing from the publishers.

Bloomsbury Publishing Plc does not have any control over, or responsibility for, any
third-party websites referred to or in this book. All internet addresses given in this
book were correct at the time of going to press. The author and publisher regret
any inconvenience caused if addresses have changed or sites have ceased to
exist, but can accept no responsibility for any such changes.

A catalogue record for this book is available from the British Library.

A catalog record for this book is available from the Library of Congress.

ISBN: HB: 978-1-3500-1419-0
        PB: 978-1-3501-7870-0
        ePub: 978-1-3500-1418-3
        ePDF: 978-1-3500-1417-6

Series: Arden Early Modern Drama Guides

Typeset by RefineCatch Limited, Bungay, Suffolk

To find out more about our authors and books visit www.bloomsbury.com
and sign up for our newsletters.

CONTENTS

Series Introduction vii
Acknowledgements viii
Notes on Contributors ix
Timeline xii

    Introduction   1
    Efterpi Mitsi

1 The Critical Backstory: The Reception of *Troilus and Cressida* through the Ages   13
    Kinga Földváry

2 The Performance History   53
    Francesca Rayner

3 The State of the Art   87
    Johann Gregory

4 New Directions: The Decay of Exemplarity in *Troilus and Cressida*   107
    Rob Maslen

5 New Directions: 'What Art Thou, Greek?': Greeks and Greece in *Troilus and Cressida*   129
    Miklós Péti

6 New Directions: '[B]its and Greasy Relics':
   The Politics of Relics in *Troilus and
   Cressida*   147
   Vassiliki Markidou

7 New Directions: Scenes of Repossession:
   Greek Translations and Performances of
   Troilus and Cressida   165
   Paschalis Nikolaou

8 'Degrees in Schools': Learning and Teaching
   Strategies   189
   Richard Stacey

Appendix: Theatre Resources   211
Notes   215
Select Bibliography   261
Index   275

SERIES INTRODUCTION

The drama of Shakespeare and his contemporaries has remained at the very heart of English curricula internationally and the pedagogic needs surrounding this body of literature have grown increasingly complex as more sophisticated resources become available to scholars, tutors and students.

This series aims to offer a clear picture of the critical and performative contexts of a range of chosen texts. In addition, each volume furnishes readers with invaluable insights into the landscape of current scholarly research as well as including new pieces of research by leading critics.

This series is designed to respond to the clearly identified needs of scholars, tutors and students for volumes which will bridge the gap between accounts of previous critical developments and performance history and an acquaintance with new research initiatives related to the chosen plays. Thus, our ambition is to offer innovative and challenging guides that will provide practical, accessible and thought-provoking analyses of early modern drama. Each volume is organized according to a progressive reading strategy involving introductory discussion, critical review and cutting-edge scholarly debate. It has been an enormous pleasure to work with so many dedicated scholars of early modern drama and we are sure that this series will encourage you to read 400-year-old play texts with fresh eyes.

Andrew Hiscock and Lisa Hopkins

ACKNOWLEDGEMENTS

I wish to thank the series editors, Professors Andrew Hiscock and Lisa Hopkins, for giving me the opportunity to edit this volume on *Troilus and Cressida*, a play that has always intrigued me, and for guiding me through its publication. I am indebted to the anonymous reviewer whose insightful comments and suggestions helped improve this volume. I would also like to acknowledge the valuable assistance of the editorial and production team at Bloomsbury, especially Emily Hockley, Susan Furber and Lara Bateman for their guidance from the early to the latter stages of the project.

Most of all, I am grateful to have had the opportunity to collaborate with such an excellent group of contributors from the UK, Greece, Hungary and Portugal. At every stage of this project, they have been enthusiastic, cooperative and professional and I wish to thank them for generously offering their intellectual engagement and scholarship.

Thanks are also due to my home institution, the National and Kapodistrian University of Athens, for its continued support of my research, to my colleagues at the Department of English Language and Literature for providing a stimulating environment for teaching and research, and to my students who have been an inspiration in thinking about the play.

I wish to thank the Oregon Shakespeare Festival and the Colorado Shakespeare Festival for generously allowing us to use photographs from their productions of *Troilus and Cressida*, in 2012 (directed by Rob Melrose) and 2016 (directed by Carolyn Howarth) respectively.

Finally, my greatest debt is to my family and friends for their encouragement and love. I would especially like to thank my husband, Dimitris, who has always been there for me, 'the strong base and building of my love'.

CONTRIBUTORS

Kinga Földváry is Senior Lecturer in the Institute of English and American Studies at Pázmány Péter Catholic University. Her main research interests include Shakespearean drama, problems of genre in film adaptations of Shakespeare's plays, early modern chronicles and chorographies, particularly William Harrison's *Description of England*, and twentieth- and twenty-first-century British literature.

Johann Gregory is a Research Associate at Cardiff University, where he has also taught English literature for several years. He has had essays published on early modern drama, as well as on John Taylor the Water Poet (1578–1653). His latest publication is a journal article on '"Nature's Fragile vessel": Rethinking approaches to material culture in literature', in *Cahiers Élisabéthains: A Journal of English Renaissance Studies* 94, no. 1 (2017): 37–56.

Vassiliki Markidou is Assistant Professor in English Literature and Culture at the Department of English Language and Literature, National and Kapodistrian University of Athens. She has published a number of articles on representations of early modern religious, national and cultural identity, with particular reference to the Ottomans, spatial and temporal palimpsests, and seventeenth- and eighteenth-century women's writing. She has co-edited (with Alison Findlay) *Shakespeare and Greece* (The Arden Shakespeare, 2017) and (with Apostolos Lampropoulos) the second volume of the electronic journal of comparative literary studies *Synthesis*, entitled *Configurations of Cultural Amnesia* (2010).

Rob Maslen is Senior Lecturer in English Literature at the University of Glasgow. He is the author of *Elizabethan Fictions*

(1997), *Shakespeare and Comedy* (2005), and *The Shakespeare Handbook* (2008); he has edited Sir Philip Sidney's *Apology for Poetry* (2002) and Mervyn Peake's *Collected Poems* (2008), and co-edited Thomas Dekker/Thomas Middleton's *News from Gravesend* for the Oxford Middleton (2007) and Mervyn Peake's *Complete Nonsense* (2011).

Efterpi Mitsi is Professor in English Literature and Culture at the Department of English Language and Literature, National and Kapodistrian University of Athens. Her research and publications are on word and image relations, classical receptions and on travel literature in early modern England. Her most recent publication is *Greece in Early English Travel Writing, 1586–1682* (2017).

Paschalis Nikolaou is Assistant Professor in Literary Translation at the Department of Foreign Languages, Translation and Interpreting of the Ionian University, Corfu. His most recent publication is *The Return of Pytheas: Scenes from British and Greek Poetry in Dialogue* (2017). He has edited *12 Greek Poems after Cavafy* (2015), and co-edited *Translating Selves: Experience and Identity between Languages and Literatures* (2008), *The Perfect Order: Selected Poems 1974–2010* by Nasos Vayenas (2010) and *Richard Berengarten: A Portrait in Inter-Views* (2017).

Miklós Péti is Associate Professor in English Literature and Culture at Károli Gáspár University of the Reformed Church. His research is mainly focused on the reception of the ancient classics in early modern English literature and culture. Recently he has been working on a series of articles about classical allusions and self-fashioning in the works of authors such as Spenser, Marlowe, Milton and Pope.

Francesca Rayner is Assistant Professor at the Universidade do Minho, where she teaches undergraduate and graduate courses in theatre and performance. Her research has centred on the cultural politics of Shakespearean performance with a particular focus on Shakespearean performance in Portugal.

She has published widely in national and international journals and is currently working on a book on post-revolutionary performances of Shakespeare in Portugal. Her most recent publication is *Contemporary Portuguese Theatre: Criticism and Performance (2010–2016)* (2017).

Richard Stacey is currently University Teacher in English 1500–1700 at the University of Glasgow. He has published on Shakespeare, and is currently working on a monograph which explores the relationship between politics and regionalism in early modern drama.

TIMELINE

26 April 1564	William Shakespeare is baptized in Stratford-upon-Avon, son to John and Mary Shakespeare.
27 November 1582	A marriage licence is issued to William Shakespeare and Anne Whateley (Hathaway) of Temple Grafton.
26 May 1583	Susanna, William and Anne Shakespeare's first child, is baptized.
2 February 1585	The twins Hamnet and Judith Shakespeare are baptized.
1592	Robert Greene's *Groatworth of Wit* calls Shakespeare an 'upstart crow'.
1593	Shakespeare's narrative poem *Venus and Adonis* is his first ever published.
1594	The Lord Chamberlain's Men, a theatre troupe that includes actor Richard Burbage and comic Will Kemp, performs with Shakespeare in their group.
11 August 1596	Burial of Hamnet Shakespeare.
4 May 1597	Shakespeare buys the New Place, one of Stratford's largest homes.
1599	Opening of the Globe theatre. *Julius Caesar* is performed at the Globe for the first known time on 21 September according to Thomas Platter's diary.
7 February 1603	*Troilus and Cressida* is entered into the Stationers' Register by James Roberts. The entry implies that the play was performed by the Lord Chamberlain's Men but it was certainly not printed.

1609	*Troilus and Cressida* is entered into the Stationer's Register by Richard Bonian and Henry Walley. Publication of a Quarto edition in two versions, with the only significant difference in the title page. Both title pages refer to the text as a history, one claiming that it was acted by the King's Majesty's Servants, while the other version states that the play has never before been acted on the public stage.
1613	The Globe theatre burns to the ground to reopen in 1614.
23 April 1616	Death of Shakespeare, his burial recorded in the Stratford Holy Church Register two days later.
1623	Publication of Shakespeare's plays in the First Folio edition. 'The Tragedie of Troylus and Cressida' is placed between the histories (after *Henry VIII*) and tragedies (before *Coriolanus*).
1679	Adaptation by Dryden published under the title *Troilus and Cressida, or Truth Found Too Late*. The adaptation is performed at the Duke's Theatre in London, undergoing four more London revivals until 1734.
1709	Nicholas Rowe's edition of Shakespeare's plays places *Troilus and Cressida* in the middle of Volume IV of the six-volume edition, between *Henry VIII* and *Coriolanus*.
1725	Publication of Alexander Pope's edition of Shakespeare, sorting tragedies into 'Tragedies from History' (volume V) and 'Tragedies from Fable' (volume VI), with *Troilus and Cressida* belonging to the latter group. Pope attributes the anachronism of Hector quoting Aristotle in the play to the blunders of the first publishers.

1733	Publication of Lewis Theobald's edition of the plays. Theobald refutes the way Pope attributed the anachronism to the printers, considering it a commonly accepted practice among dramatists.
1765	Publication of Samuel Johnson's edition. His detailed textual footnotes to the play present a critical reading of both the Quarto and Folio texts.
1815	Publication of August Wilhelm Schlegel's *Lectures on Dramatic Art and Literature* in English; Schlegel categorizes *Troilus and Cressida* as a historical drama while considering it a generic oddity.
1880	Algernon Charles Swinburne's *A Study of Shakespeare* groups together *Troilus and Cressida*, *Measure for Measure* and *Pericles* as tragi-comedies.
1896	Introduction of the term 'problem plays' in Frederick Boas *Shakspere and his Predecessors* to refer to *All's Well That Ends Well*, *Measure for Measure*, and *Troilus and Cressida*, adding also *Hamlet* to this category.
1912	Directed by William Poel at King's Hall in London.
1930	G. Wilson Knight's *The Wheel of Fire* dedicates a whole chapter to *Troilus and Cressida*.
1935	First radio version produced for the BBC. Many more will follow in 1946, 1952, 1959, 1964, 1980 and 2005.
1938	Directed by Michael Macowan for the London Mask Theatre Company at the Westminster Theatre in London.
1946	Publication of Una Ellis-Fermor's *The Frontiers of Drama* that places *Troilus and Cressida* among the extraordinary rather

	than the minor plays in the Shakespearean canon.
1951	Publication of E.M. Tillyard's *Shakespeare's Problem Plays*.
1956	Directed by Tyrone Guthrie at the Old Vic.
1961	Jack Landau's 1961 *Troilus and Cressida* at Stratford, Connecticut sets the play in the American Civil War in the year of its centennial.
1960	Directed by John Barton at Stratford in collaboration with Peter Hall. Barton directed the play again in 1968 and in 1976, emphasizing male sexuality.
1965	Directed by Joseph Papp for the New York Shakespeare Festival at the Delacorte Theatre in Central Park.
1971	Adrian Hall's production for the Providence Trinity Square Repertory Company draws parallels with the ongoing Vietnam War.
1972	Directed by the Romanian director David Esrig for the Munich Bayerisches Staatsschauspiel Residenztheater.
1977	Directed by Terry Hands for the Vienna Burgtheater.
1981	Directed by Jonathan Miller for the BBC Television Shakespeare series.
1986	Directed by Dieter Dorn at Münchner Kammerspiele in Munich.
1990	Directed by Sam Mendes for the Royal Shakespeare Company.
1991	Directed by Krzysztof Babicki at Teatr Wybrzeze in Gdansk.
1995	Directed by Mark Wing-Davey for the New York Shakespeare Festival at the Delacorte Theatre.
1998	Directed by Stefan Bachmann for Theater Basel.

2003	Directed by Annie Ruth and Rangimoana Taylor at the Te Whaea Theatre, Wellington Aotearoa/New Zealand.
2006	Directed by Peter Stein for the Royal Shakespeare Company and the Edinburgh International Festival.
2008	Cheek by Jowl production directed by Declan Donnellan.
2009	Directed by Matthew Dunster for the Globe Theatre.
2012	Royal Shakespeare Company and Wooster Group production directed by Mark Ravenhill and Elizabeth LeCompte, with the Wooster Group playing the Trojans and the RSC the Greeks.
2012	Maori production by the Ngakau Toa theatre company directed by Rachel House opens the Globe's World Shakespeare Festival.
2012	Rob Melrose's production for the Oregon Shakespeare Festival located the play within contemporary conflicts in the Middle East.
2013	Directed by Melissa Hillman at La Val's Subterranean in Berkeley, California, as part of a San Francisco Festival that produced thirty-six new plays about the Trojan War.
2016	Directed by Carolyn Howarth for the Colorado Shakespeare Festival, with women actors playing the roles of Agamemnon, Aeneas and Ulysses.

Introduction

Efterpi Mitsi

In the fourth act of *Troilus and Cressida*, as Agamemnon welcomes Hector to the Greek camp, he reflects on the ruin and oblivion wrought by time:

> Worthy of arms! As welcome as to one
> That would be rid of such an enemy –
> But that's no welcome. Understand more clear:
> What's past and what's to come is strewed with husks
> And formless ruin of oblivion;
> But in this extant moment, faith and troth,
> Strained purely from all hollow bias-drawing,
> Bids thee, with most divine integrity,
> From heart of very heart, great Hector, welcome.[1]

The image of the 'wasteful time' of the *Sonnets* persists throughout *Troilus and Cressida*, appearing as 'Injurious Time' (4.4.41) and as 'a great-sized monster of ingratitudes' (3.3.166), a merciless force bringing devastation to humanity.[2] Agamemnon's words add an ironic tone to the proverbial notion of time's oblivion, suggesting, as David Bevington argues, that 'the past gives no meaning to human destiny'.[3] The Greek general explains that Hector's welcome occurs in the present moment in opposition to the past (what has already happened) and the future (what will happen), both compared to 'formless ruin[s] of oblivion', to a landscape strewn 'with husks' and fragments. Although the notion of the forgotten and ruined past may be conventional, Agamemnon's inclusion of the future, of 'what's to come', in the bleak picture is unexpected.[4]

The play's characters, the famous Greek and Trojan heroes, have not fallen into oblivion but are still very much part of the literary tradition of the West, as they were in Shakespeare's own time. Yet, their future, in the play's world, is already past; a collection of literary fragments reflected in the ruins of Troy. Agamemnon and Hector exist as they truly are only in the 'extant moment', the brief moment of truce before the battle in the fifth act; this identity will be inevitably lost in the events lying ahead both within and beyond the play. The constant and often ironic oscillation between the play's present and the future, which is already known to the audience, creates a thrilling and self-reflexive effect. In fact, audiences, both in Shakespeare's time and today, are well aware that an endless number of literary texts sprang from the ruins of Troy. The play itself is an assemblage of the literary fragments of the Trojan War, a translation of the Trojan epic narrative for the stage that questions not only the heroic ethos of its epic characters but also the significance of theatrical representation and role-playing. By summoning multiple sources, classical, medieval, and contemporary, and by drawing on different genres, *Troilus and Cressida* is one of Shakespeare's most complex problem plays, perplexing and even dividing readers and critics over the past 400 years.

At the same time, the 'formless ruin of oblivion' foreshadows the fate of the play itself, which fell into oblivion until the twentieth century. Ever since its first publication, the text has been enigmatic: composed in late 1601, shortly after *Hamlet* and in the context of the so-called 'War of the Theatres', it was first published in 1609, in a Quarto edition with two versions which construct the play as either a reading edition or a performance document, together with a third version in the Folio of 1623.[5] While the 1603 Stationers' entry claims that the play was 'acted by my Lord Chamberlain's men', the first page of the publisher's advertisement added to the revised 1609 Quarto calls *Troilus* 'a new play, never staled with the stage, never clapper-clawed with the palms of the vulgar',[6] leading scholars to debates about the play's early performances and audiences.[7] Another issue which has troubled editors and critics is the relationship between the Quarto and Folio texts and their numerous differences which far exceed simple editorial corrections and revisions.

Following its early performances, *Troilus and Cressida* had to wait until the early decades of the twentieth century to be rediscovered by theatre practitioners and audiences. As Francesca Rayner argues in Chapter 2 of this book, 'the problematic history of *Troilus and Cressida* in performance might be rewritten less as a history of absence than as a peculiarly modern one'. Due to its belated or deferred beginnings, the play has been considered one of Shakespeare's most 'modern' ones, whose modernity, especially after the Second World War, developed into its main strength. In one of the most violent centuries in the history of humanity, the staging of *Troilus and Cressida* provided theatre practitioners and theatregoers with the opportunity to reflect on the absurdity of war, with the Trojan War paralleling a series of international conflicts, ranging from the Great War to the Cold War and Vietnam, to Bosnia and the Middle East.

The appeal of the play for modern theatre directors has to do not only with its anti-heroic perspective but also with its gender and sexual politics. The play speaks to a range of issues that riveted the twentieth century. During the 1960s, directors like John Barton emphasized male homosexuality within a classical setting which nonetheless reflected the sexual revolution and socio-political change unsettling western societies in that period.[8] Thus, *Troilus and Cressida* rose from neglect and oblivion to popularity, becoming identified with an irreverent attack on the conventional ideas of heroism and honour, of loyalty and love. Its modernity arises from the conflict between past and present through the subversion of conventional interpretations of classical literature and the demystification of great heroes and grand narratives, pertinent to periods witnessing crises of the systems of values and beliefs, such as the 1960s and the past decade. From the demonstrations against the Vietnam War, the Prague Spring and the radicalism of May 1968, to the early twenty-first-century conflicts in the Middle East, events that provided the framework of several productions, *Troilus and Cressida* continues to engage theatre practitioners and audiences in its depiction of decay and disease in the context of an endless and pointless war – a war that has gone on for so long that the enemies have almost forgotten what they are fighting for.

A similar uncertainty, if not obscurity, characterized the criticism of *Troilus and Cressida* from the centuries following its publication until the mid-twentieth century. The play's mysterious textual history and generic instability perplexed editors and critics, who disagreed for a very long time on every aspect of the play from its form and meaning to its virtues and defects. Older scholarship was confused by *Troilus and Cressida*'s hybridity and ambiguity regarding both its genre, which is inspired by epic poetry, chronicle, romance, and satire, and by its relation to the Troy story, including its medieval and Elizabethan transformations and significations. As Kinga Földváry shows in Chapter 1, the debate surrounding the play begins from Dryden's and Johnson's reflections on its strangeness of form and content, continues among Romantic critics and culminates with the late nineteenth- and early twentieth-century critical attempts to find a term to describe its genre. It was only in the late nineteenth century that Frederick Boas coined the term 'problem plays' to describe a group of Shakespeare's plays, *Measure for Measure*, *All's Well That Ends Well* and *Troilus and Cressida*,[9] which contain both comic and tragic elements, creating a meaningful generic category not only for *Troilus* but also for those other plays that defied traditional classification.

At the same time, Boas and other Victorian critics were shocked by the play's cynicism and satirical perspective on the Trojan War, which had been one of the most popular narratives in England since the Middle Ages. Seven books of Homer's *Iliad* had been translated by George Chapman a few years before the publication of *Troilus and Cressida*, which often echoes Chapman's translation while undermining the Chapmanesque style. For the epic plot, Shakespeare also draws on William Caxton's *Recuyell of the Histories of Troye* (1474) and John Lydgate's *Troy Book* (1513) and for the love story of Troilus and Cressida, which is not mentioned in Homer, he borrows from Chaucer's poem *Troylus and Criseyde* (1385–7) and Robert Henryson's *Testament of Cresseid* (1532), a dark and powerful continuation of the tale ending with Cressida's tragic fate as a leper and outcast.[10] Thus, *Troilus and Cressida* incorporates the entire tradition of the 'Matter of Troy', a cycle of stories repeated and reinvented by medieval poets that reaches the Renaissance to be assimilated again in the works of dramatists and poets.[11] For Shakespeare's audience, the events of the play, leading to Cressida's betrayal and Hector's death, would have been anticipated from the very beginning. Therefore, Agamemnon's words as he welcomes Hector to the Greek camp assume an ironic tone as everyone knows that Troy will inevitably fall. A few lines later when Ulysses foretells the future, the fall of the walls and towers of Troy, Hector refuses to accept it:

> I must not believe you.
> There they stand yet, and modestly I think
> The fall of every Phrygian stone will cost
> A drop of Grecian blood. The end crowns all,
> And that old common arbitrator, Time,
> Will one day end it.
>
> (4.5.221–6)

Hector refers to the proverbial *Finis coronat opus* to claim that Troy will survive the Greek siege although it will eventually succumb to the inescapable devastation of time itself as it destroys humans, monuments and kingdoms.

Troilus and Cressida survived the critical neglect and discomfort during the eighteenth and nineteenth century, although it was not until the mid-twentieth century that critics acknowledged the play's qualities and emphasized its position among the most interesting rather than among the negligible plays in the Shakespeare canon. In its transition from obscurity to popularity, *Troilus and Cressida* has inspired literary critics to interpret it in a variety of ways. As Johann Gregory shows in Chapter 3 on 'The State of the Art', the interpretive approaches in the past 25 years range from the examination of the play's early modern publications and audience, considering whether the play was written for an elite audience at the Inns of Court, or as a play for a broader audience at the Globe, to the investigation of its historical, political and theatrical context. Critics have also read its language in relation to that of trade and economics and foregrounded its semantic instability. Other important issues include the metatheatrical quality of the play and the ways in which gender is represented and performed. In addition, recent readings have focused on masculine gender negotiations, homosociality and emulation while ecocriticism has used *Troilus and Cressida* to think about humanity's place in the world.

The power of the play to create divergent meanings and 'to test audience expectations, even as it eschews a final moral, message or perspective', as Gregory argues, is explored in the four 'New Directions' essays in this book. Chapters 4 and 6 (Rob Maslen and Vassiliki Markidou) take the historicity and significance of Troy in late Elizabethan England a step further, connecting the play with political, moral and religious issues. The legend of Brutus, the great-grandson of Aeneas who had travelled from Rome to England to found Troynovant had persisted in England since the Middle Ages. Geoffrey of Monmouth's *Historia Regum Britanniae* (dated 1135) claimed a Trojan origin for the British monarchy and people, initiating a national mythology that explains the anti-Greek bias of

Shakespeare's contemporaries. This foundation myth was still considered factual in the Elizabethan period, with Elizabeth tracing her origin in Troy despite the Tudors' Welsh or ancient British descent. As Frances Yates explains, '[w]hen the Tudors ascended the throne of England, so runs the myth, the ancient Trojan–British race of monarchs once more resumed the imperial power and brought in a golden age of peace and plenty'.[12] Yet, in spite of Shakespeare's contemporaries' investment in the Trojan heritage, toward the end of Elizabeth's reign, the myth was becoming less convincing. Markidou argues that Troy itself had turned into a sacrosanct relic in Elizabethan England, and thus the target of Shakespeare's acerbic play which 'punctures venerated early modern myths' through the ambivalent references to relics. Maslen, on the other hand, is particularly concerned with the writing of the past in early modern England and 'with the function of history as theorized by the humanist education system that shaped Shakespeare's mind, such as he and his early audiences would have approached this particular story with a strong sense of their own complicity with the notoriously non-exemplary dispositions of the ancient Trojans and Greeks'.

Shakespeare's cynical and irreverent treatment of the Trojan legend, undermining both its mythical glory and heroic warfare, was probably one of the reasons the play was unsuccessful in its own time, as Troy still was a focus of value for many Elizabethans. According to Heather James, the play's 'self-conscious mishandling of the Troy legend's cultural ambition cuts, perhaps, too deeply into the skins of late Elizabethan audiences', especially as the language of the decay and disease reminded them of 'their own diseased body politic'.[13] The play also probably failed for political reasons, as the controversial Robert Devereux, Earl of Essex, executed for treason in 1601, was often compared to Achilles.[14] In fact, Chapman's translation of the seven books of the *Iliad* was dedicated to 'the most honored now living Instance of the Achilleian vertues eternized by divine Homere', the Earl of Essex, transformed into an exemplar of virtue and bravery.[15]

Moreover, Achilles' refusal to fight in the beginning of the play reminded Shakespeare's contemporaries of Essex's withdrawal from the court in 1597 after believing that Elizabeth had favoured his rivals, and then again in 1598.[16] Nonetheless, *Troilus and Cressida* re-enacts an ambiguous world shared by Greek and Trojan heroes to criticize not only contemporary national politics and anxieties but also, as Maslen shows in Chapter 4, the use of classical literature and myth for propagandistic historical moralizing. At the same time, this criticism extends far beyond Elizabethan England, as evidenced by modern and contemporary performances as well as by translations; as Paschalis Nikolaou argues in Chapter 7, the translations of *Troilus and Cressida* in Modern Greek suggest the blind spots that exist in the way Greeks understand their own ambiguous relationship with antiquity.

Before *Troilus and Cressida*, Shakespeare had incorporated the Trojan War in *The Rape of Lucrece*, published in 1594 and dedicated to Henry Wriothesley, Earl of Southampton, who was one of the conspirators in Essex's rebellion. The poet shows Lucrece, after her rape by Tarquin, contemplating 'a piece of skilful painting made for Priam's Troy';[17] in this lengthy ekphrasis, Lucrece recalls the suffering caused by the abduction of Helen and mourns for 'Troy's painted woes' (1492), identifying her own violation with the sack of Tory (1544–7).[18] Drawing on Virgil's famous description of the fall of Troy in the *Aeneid* (1.441–93), when Aeneas views the events depicted on the temple of Juno in Carthage, *The Rape of Lucrece* invokes another text's ekphrasis to reflect on imitation and on the relation between verbal and visual art. Similarly, the fall of Troy reappears in *Hamlet* 2.2.384–455, when one of the players is asked to recite Hamlet's favourite part of Aeneas's speech to Dido, the slaughter of king Priam by Pyrrhus, which alludes to *Aeneid* 2.506–58. Both passages are self-reflexive, using the fall of Troy not only to emphasize the painter's and actor's skill of bridging the gap between past and present but also to re-read the epic myth.

From Lucrece's rage against the pictorial representation of the treacherous Sinon, 'tear[ing] the senseless Sinon with her nails' (1564), to the debased Greek and Trojan heroes of *Troilus and Cressida*, Troy highlights the contradiction between the heroes' epic world of honour and the reality of their flaws, their pettiness, deceit, pride and lust. The final scene between Hector and Achilles gives the final blow to the tradition of classical heroism, presenting Hector, the noblest among the Trojans, pursuing a Greek for his suit of armour (5.6.28–32) while Achilles, the bravest among the Greeks, orders his soldiers to slaughter Hector when they find him unarmed, showing a total lack of principles and honour. As Miklós Péti argues in Chapter 5, the Greeks in *Troilus and Cressida* are in 'a permanent crisis of identity', which is particularly striking in those scenes of the play where Shakespeare echoes Homeric episodes, such as the council scene in Book 2 of the *Iliad*.

Moreover, the action of *Troilus and Cressida* depends on self-reflexive moments of theatricality mirroring the pictorial or verbal reconstructions of the fall of Troy in *The Rape of Lucrece* and *Hamlet*.[19] In Act 1, Scene 3, Ulysses describes Patroclus's performance in Achilles' tent, a pageant of mocking impersonations of the Greek generals. Patroclus's pageant threatens the Greek army, deferring the action of war, and echoes the performance itself of *Troilus and Cressida* as well as its irreverent treatment of the matter of Troy. Although Ulysses castigates Patroclus's parody of the Greek leaders, he also stages his own spectacles, such as the provocation of Ajax and Achilles, aiming at stirring the latter out of his inertia. Using theatricality to his own advantage, Ulysses compares performances to trade transactions and draws attention to the connection between theatricality and deception: 'Let us, like merchants show our foulest wares, / And think perchance they'll sell' (1.3.360–1).

The startling metadramatic effect of *Troilus and Cressida* is reinforced by Thersites, the observer and commentator within the play, who uncovers the emptiness and corruption of the other characters, setting off a Brechtian detachment.[20] Thersites strips both Greeks and Trojans from their heroic glamour and incites the audience to question what happens on-stage and challenge the assumptions about the legend of Troy. He also constantly watches the actions of all participants and comments on their 'performance'. From the very beginning of the play, characters are never alone on stage but always observed by others, as is evident in the lovemaking and seduction scenes: in Act 3, Scene 2, Troilus and Cressida are watched by Pandarus, and later in 5.2, when Cressida meets Diomedes she is spied on by Troilus and Ulysses, all of whom are also secretly watched by Thersites. As the lovers are scrutinized by other characters, the audience is reminded of its own gaze and consumption of stage plays and is led to the emotional detachment necessary for rethinking love, honour and heroism. Theatricality is thus crucial in foregrounding the questions posed by *Troilus and Cressida*, the interconnected themes of war, love, time and disillusionment which continue to be of great interest in our own age.

It is those questions which this book aims to explore. It opens with an account of the play's critical backstory by Kinga Földváry, discussing the most important editions and scholarship from the Quarto and Folio publications to the mid-twentieth century. This chapter also highlights the twentieth century's rediscovery of the play's virtues, showing how modernist and feminist critics like Wilson Knight and Una Ellis-Fermor have highlighted previously unappreciated aspects of the play. This paves the path for Francesca Rayner's examination of the performance history of the play, focusing on its re-emergence from obscurity in the twentieth century, largely as a result of its ambiguous representation of war in a century that witnessed two devastating world wars. Rayner discusses the performances of *Troilus and Cressida* in relation to a number of issues, such as war, homosexuality and sexual liberation, the engagement with Jan Kott's influential reading of the play as a text informed by the cruelty of the grotesque,[21] gender and postmodern eclecticism, and concludes with the play's current global presence. In the next chapter, 'The State of the Art', Johann Gregory surveys the recent critical research on *Troilus and Cressida* from the historicist, Marxist and feminist readings of the play in the 1980s and 1990s to the most recent presentist and ecocritical approaches.

The critical and performance history of *Troilus and Cressida* follow four chapters of original approaches to the play, offering new responses to its iconoclastic nature and key themes, ranging from Elizabethan politics and the uses of antiquity to questions of cultural translation, with particular attention paid on the play's 'Greekness'. In the first of these, 'The Decay of Exemplarity in *Troilus and Cressida*', Rob Maslen discusses the way in which Troy and the Troilus and Cressida story were used as exempla in sixteenth-century English culture, particularly in the fields of rhetoric and poetry, and how Shakespeare criticizes this tradition of writing and learning from history. In the second, '"What Art Thou, Greek?": Greeks and Greece in *Troilus and Cressida*', Miklós Péti reconsiders the representation of Greeks in the play, arguing that it challenges both 'ancient and early modern commonplaces about Hellenic characteristics'. In the third, '"[B]its and greasy relics": The Politics of Relics in *Troilus and Cressida*', Vassiliki Markidou focuses on the complex representations of relics in the play which combines relic worship and sexuality in an irreverent and iconoclastic way. In the fourth, 'Scenes of Repossession: Greek Translations and Performances of *Troilus and Cressida*', Paschalis Nikolaou reflects on translation by examining the play's translations and performances in Greece, which, as he contends, 'reclaim' the play and enact a kind of return to the linguistic and cultural space that first gave rise to its story.

Finally, Richard Stacey, in '"Degrees in Schools": Learning and Teaching Strategies', situates the text in the classroom, exploring the ways in which the play can be taught. Stacey focuses on the teaching resources currently available on *Troilus and Cressida*, from scholarly guides and online databases to theatre resources. He also explores different approaches and techniques which can be used to stimulate discussion in class, such as close-reading exercises which emphasize rhetoric and metaphor as well as performance-based strategies. This chapter also offers a bibliography and an appendix of theatre resources for readers wishing to research further on the above issues.

Although, as Cressida emphasizes during her vows to Troilus, 'waterdrops have worn the stones of Troy, / And blind oblivion swallowed cities up, / And mighty states characterless are grated / To dusty nothing' (3.2.181–4), Shakespeare's play has vanquished oblivion; rising from the obscurity of its past, it continues to address the present and the future.

1

The Critical Backstory

The Reception of *Troilus and Cressida* through the Ages

Kinga Földváry

It would be an understatement to claim that *Troilus and Cressida* is a controversial play. It is not only controversial in its theme and moral message, or its effect on audiences, but even in its dramatic structure and textual history, therefore it should come as little surprise that the play has troubled readers and viewers, critics and scholars, performers and academics alike throughout its history of more than 400 years. Coleridge struggled with its description, 'scarcely knowing what to say of it',[1] Hazlitt declared it 'loose and desultory',[2] Swinburne found in the play proof that 'some cynic had lately bitten [Shakespeare] by the brain',[3] and Mark van Doren went as far as considering it 'Shakespeare's revenge upon mankind'.[4] It is equally true, of course, that *Troilus and Cressida* has never been and is not now without its own ardent fans: David Bevington confesses in his introduction to the new Arden Shakespeare edition of the drama that for him, 'the play is remarkably tender, sad and personal, in the midst of its unsparing depiction of brutality'.[5] Such a statement may sound surprising as hardly any critical voices have been raised in appreciation of the play's tenderness, although many were eager to remark on its brutality. And yet, it is not too hard to convince ourselves why it is indeed a heart-breaking play, a drama of young love gone all too wrong, a catastrophe of thwarted hopes and ambitions – not to mention the whole universal tragedy of the Trojan war in the background, which only adds to our presentiments of impending doom and disaster that threatens to bring down all of civilization as we know it.

The truth is, *Troilus and Cressida* continues to fascinate us, for all its obvious and undeniable inconsistencies. It displays not only the usual Shakespearean queries of when it was written, where and how it was first performed, and which of the Quarto texts is more authoritative – after all, we are acquainted with such problems from our dealings with practically every single play in the canon. Nor is *Troilus and Cressida* the only drama whose classification makes it problematic; for more than a century now, it has had a comfortable position among a whole group of similarly troublesome plays whose (retrospectively applied) generic label, the 'problem play', reflects on the difficulty of their categorization, as they 'do not fit snugly into any of the major classifications'.[6] In fact, all of these issues would simply offer challenges that Shakespeare scholars are more or less familiar with, but what opens onto a particularly dangerous minefield is the diversity of critical opinion that the play has attracted over the past 400 years. Is it a bad play, even one of the worst, or does it display the most tangible proof of Shakespeare's genius? Should any part of the narrative be taken at face value, or is irony its governing device? Did Shakespeare fail to do his homework in the classics, or did he consciously alter what he found in his sources, to highlight new aspects of the same old story? Do the inconsistencies point to a different author's hand, or are these interpretative cruxes similar to those we can find in the rest of the canon? Questions like these feature in nearly all accounts, and as the following summary of the play's critical history intends to show, it was not until the mid-twentieth century that general critical opinion has settled into acknowledging the play's remarkable qualities and appreciating them over its weaknesses.

Creation and first texts

There are a number of reasons why *Troilus and Cressida* has the dubious honour of being 'ranked among the most controversial of Shakespeare's plays',[7] one of these reasons being the drama's somewhat puzzling early publication history. The general consensus concerning the play's creation usually points towards the very beginning of the seventeenth century, around the years 1602 or 1603, right after *Hamlet*, and before, or at least close to, the two other plays also labelled as 'problem plays': *All's Well That Ends Well* and *Measure for Measure*.[8] Internal evidence, thematic concerns, a remarkable similarity between *Hamlet* and *Troilus*, together with the equally noticeable difficulties of categorization with the other two make the dating more or less likely and as convincing as it is possible. The play was entered into the Stationers' Register twice, first conditionally in 1603 by James Roberts, 'to print when he hath gotten sufficient aucthority for yt', and then again in 1609 by Richard Bonian and Henry Walley.[9] The 1603 entry implies that the play was performed ('as yt is acted by my lo: Chamberlens Men'),[10] yet what seems certain is that James Roberts did not print *Troilus and Cressida* in 1603.

The next entry in 1609, however, was followed by the publication of a Quarto edition – or, more precisely, two versions of the same, with the only significant difference in the title page ('one issue with *two states of issue*'[11]). While both title pages refer to the text as a history (the second one as 'The Famous Historie of Troylus and Cresseid'[12]), the printer's/publisher's preface (that David Bevington calls 'an enigmatic publicity blurb'[13]) attached to the revised version consistently refers to the play as a comedy. The two titles are also at odds as regards the past accessibility of the play: one making the typical claim to a previous performance: 'as it was acted by the Kings Maiesties seruants at the Globe';[14] while the publisher's preface in the later version states that the play has never before been acted on the public stage, or more precisely, that it had never been 'clapper-clawed with the palms of the vulgar' ('A Never Writer', lines 2–3).[15] The exact meaning of the words has often been disputed, whether it actually means no previous performance, or simply no performance on a public stage, but rather in one of the Inns of Court (a theory proposed by Peter Alexander in 1928[16]), or even at one of the universities.[17]

The First Folio of 1623 does not do much to dispel the above listed textual uncertainties; indeed, it adds to them by giving the title as 'The Tragedie of Troylus and Cressida', but placing the play in an odd position within the volume: between the histories (after *Henry VIII*) and tragedies (before *Coriolanus*). At the same time, the play is missing from the Catalogue (i.e. the table of contents), suggesting a later insertion into the volume, most probably as a result of the printer Jaggard's late acquisition of the rights for publication from the copyright holders (although some scholars dispute the authority of this hypothesis[18]). There is also evidence to suggest that had it not been for this last-minute arrangement, which resulted in Jaggard's printing the play on a separate quire of paper, it would have been placed after *Romeo and Juliet*, among the tragedies,[19] and in a much less ambiguous position genre-wise. There are a few surviving copies of F1 which do not include the play at all, and a few others, among them one in the Folger Library, have the leaf with the last page of *Romeo and Juliet* on one side, and the first page of *Troilus* on the other.[20] As it is, however, the practically liminal placement proved to be prophetic – no single genre category seems able to lay absolute claim to this play, and it was only the late nineteenth-century critics who came up with the most satisfactory terms we have used ever since to describe the problematic nature of the small group of dark tragicomedies where *Troilus and Cressida* seems to find its best place.

The differences between the Quarto and Folio texts are numerous, and not all can be explained as simple editorial emendations; indeed, the relationship between the two versions – which one should be seen as a revision of the other? – is still often debated. David Bevington in his 'Preface' even recommends publishing the two versions separately,[21] in order to highlight the thousands of differences between them, yet he also remarks that these 'come down for the most part to individual word choice',[22] rather than missing or reassigned speeches or even whole scenes, as is the case with *Hamlet* or *King Lear*. Even so, there are several major differences; apart from the above-mentioned printer's epistle found only in the revised Quarto, the Folio includes a Prologue to the play, although this can be seen as an example of 'padding', inserted by the editors 'to fill up the extra white space'.[23] On the other hand, 'the textual peculiarities surrounding Pandarus' final speech'[24] continue to be regarded as the most problematic textual cruxes of the play.

Dryden's interpretation

While the 1603 entry in the Stationers' Register together with at least one of the Quarto title pages explicitly claim that the play was on stage in the author's lifetime, there is no evidence of later performances for nearly 300 years. Nonetheless, although *Troilus and Cressida* was apparently not performed again until the end of the nineteenth century, the story of the tragic love affair of the young Trojan couple did not remain completely unknown to theatre audiences until then. In fact, the first detailed analysis and critical commentary on the play came together with John Dryden's 1679 adaptation published under the title *Troilus and Cressida, or Truth Found Too Late*, which was also performed a few times. There is some critical disagreement over whether it was 'poorly received' or had 'some popularity',[25] but it certainly never achieved the fame or significance that Nahum Tate's *Lear* or other Restoration adaptations of Shakespeare's work did. As the editor of Dryden's work notes: 'Like most of the plays produced near the end of the 1670s which caused no notable scandal in political, social, or literary life, Dryden's *Troilus and Cressida* appears to have engendered nothing in the way of contemporary commentary or theatrical gossip.'[26] This is, however, not entirely true, as the first edition had already occasioned a few critical writings, some of which made references to the Shakespearean original, but even more of them praised Dryden's more refined version.

As the title page of the first edition shows, Dryden's adaptation of *Troilus and Cressida* was performed at the Duke's Theatre in London,[27] which later came to be known as the Dorset Garden Theatre.[28] The play was subsequently published, together with a whole set of paratexts, all offering some commentary on either the original or the adapted version (or both): a Dedication to the Earl of Sunderland, followed by a long Preface to the play, including what can be regarded as an independent essay on 'The Grounds of Criticism in Tragedy', and finally 'A Prologue Spoken by Mr Betterton, Representing the Ghost of Shakespear'. This first edition also included a commendatory poem by English clergyman and poet Richard Duke, who appears to have been a friend of Dryden's,[29] and had translated some of the classics for him. In his poem he praises Dryden for his *Troilus and Cressida*, claiming that the poet 'found it dirt but ... have made it gold'. Shakespeare's work seems to be criticized for its structural inconsistencies rather than any other (moral or aesthetic) shortcomings, with Duke implying that before these efforts, 'A dark and undigested heap it lay, / Like *Chaos* ere the dawn of infant Day'. True, the genre requires the praise of the addressee over his forerunners, but it is interesting that when Duke suggests that the burning of Troy was worth the price if 'three such mighty names' could sing its story, the list does not even include Shakespeare's, let alone Chaucer's, and only lauds the efforts of Homer, Virgil and Dryden himself.

As the introductory essay and the rest of the paratexts make it clear, Dryden's intention was to amend the play's imperfections, mostly as regards a proper tragic finale, therefore he chose to rewrite the last act completely, to punish Cressida, and finish off all who do not deserve to survive a tragedy. Dryden's approach is also characteristic of the performance practice of the age, in which the literary production of previous eras functioned as raw material from which new authors picked what they considered morally or aesthetically suitable for their own audiences, and added what they thought was lacking. As Emma Smith observes: 'These adaptations are themselves works of criticism, often, in prefatory material and epilogues, explicitly so.'[30] Dryden's words in the Preface in fact gave voice to a line of criticism prevalent both in England and on the continent for much of the seventeenth and eighteenth centuries: the 'beauty-and-faults criticism' that Michele Willems describes in connection with Voltaire's attitude towards Shakespeare:

> On the one hand, critics were intent on checking Shakespeare's conformity to their prescribed models (and the French were not the only ones to judge by the book of rules), hence the censuring of what they perceived as 'irregularities'. On the other hand, they admired some isolated beauties such as fine speeches or moral thoughts, hence their selective approach to the plays, a constant of Shakespearean criticism on both sides of the Channel.[31]

Harping on anachronisms – *Troilus and Cressida* in eighteenth-century editions

While the eighteenth century may not have been the age that saw Shakespeare's *Troilus and Cressida* on the stage, it was certainly the period when scholarly editions of the completed dramatic *oeuvre* of Shakespeare began to appear, displaying a gradually increasing awareness of the multifaceted nature of editorial work. The earliest editions attached no detailed textual notes or commentary to the plays, but took pains in their general prefaces to shape Shakespeare's appreciation for the reading public. Nicholas Rowe's 1709 edition is well known for being not only the first one in the century, but also the first one graced with the editor's name, printed in practical and illustrated octavo size, and this edition also includes an account of Shakespeare's life by way of a preface. The Preface makes a single reference to *Troilus and Cressida* in the list of peculiar or outstanding characters from the plays, where Rowe remarks on Thersites in *Troilus*, and Apemantus in *Timon* being 'Master-Pieces of ill Nature, and satyrical Snarling'.[32] Rowe's editorial interventions are subtle but often motivated by conviction rather than evidence; still, they were accepted as authoritative by Pope and several other successive editors, as Lewis Theobald remarks with no little outrage in his own version, which will be discussed below. The position of the play itself within the collection follows the order of the Folio editions: it is placed in the middle of Volume IV of the six-volume edition, between *Henry VIII* and *Coriolanus*, and described as a tragedy, but no critical commentary is offered on it (or any other play, for that matter).

Alexander Pope, editor of the second eighteenth-century collected edition, also confines his treatment of the drama to his general preface, where he first refers to the play as evidence of Shakespeare's learning and knowledge not only of the classics but also 'the Ancients of his own country',[33] that is, Chaucer as well as Henryson who wrote a darker version of 'Cresseid's' story. The Preface also makes it clear that Pope took pains to consult the earliest available editions, as he is already aware of the problem of the two contradictory title pages of the Quarto of *Troilus*. He mentions these to prove his claim that Shakespeare may not have been involved in the actual publication of his plays, as the inconsistencies and misprints seem more characteristic of the carelessness of the press than the author himself. Interestingly enough, 'those palpable blunders of Hector quoting Aristotle' convince him not of 'Shakespear's want of learning' but 'the blunders and illiteracies of the first Publishers of his works'.[34] (The offending lines are Hector's chastising Paris and Troilus for being like 'young men, whom Aristotle thought / Unfit to hear moral philosophy' in 2.2.166–7.) Even though Pope appears to have a realistic view of Shakespeare's general education, allowing for faults and dramaturgical irregularities as well, such blatant anachronisms clearly do not fit his image of the Genius of Shakespeare. While Rowe made no mention of the same issue in his prefatory essay, he also seems to have been troubled by the blunder, as he simply corrected the offending name Aristotle to 'graver Sages'[35] in the text, a correction Pope preserved. Another interesting aspect of Pope's work is that he refines Rowe's (and the Folio editors') genre divisions, sorting tragedies into 'Tragedies from History' (Volume V) and 'Tragedies from Fable' (Volume VI), with *Troilus and Cressida* clearly belonging to the latter group, together with *Cymbeline*, *Romeo and Juliet*, *Hamlet* and *Othello*.

Lewis Theobald in the preface to his 1733 edition revisits the question of the anachronism in *Troilus*, and with scathing irony refutes the way Pope attributed it to the printers, considering them 'the Effect of poetic Licence, rather than of Ignorance in our Poet'[36] – a licence he claims Pope used even more often in his own editorial interventions. Theobald's resentment of the way Rowe and Pope treated the issue also brings to light his surprisingly modern editorial concerns when he demands an authoritative explanation for such drastic changes in the text. Theobald's work is also pioneering in the amount of explanatory footnotes, and the infamous reference to Aristotle gets a note of nearly two-and-a-half pages, practically a short essay with copious examples not only from Shakespeare but from other classics to show how poets' and dramatists' awareness of historical chronology can often be found wanting; yet, this appears to have been a commonly accepted practice, 'upon a Supposition that their Audience were not so exactly inform'd in Chronology'[37] to notice such forward leaps in time.

A lesser-known editor, Sir Thomas Hanmer does not mention *Troilus* in the preface to his 1743–4 edition, and his only interesting editorial comment is added in the form of a footnote to the beginning of the play, referring to the controversy of the play's early performance and publication history. He also mentions Dryden's claim that the play may be among Shakespeare's earliest ones, which he refutes, suggesting that the Preface of the play points to its being 'one of his last; and the great number of observations, both moral and politick, (with which this piece is crowded more than any other of his) seems to confirm that opinion'.[38]

Notwithstanding Theobald's undeniable merits in establishing the principles of modern editorial practice, no eighteenth-century account of Shakespeare's reception could be complete without reference to the work of Samuel Johnson, whose editions (1765, 1773, 1778), notes and critical commentary have been reprinted in diverse collections and included in plenty of later editions, defining the plays' interpretation for generations. Precisely because of the many forms in which he commented on the plays, it is not easy to form a true impression of his opinion, as his laborious and scholarly, cold-headed editorial work seems often at odds with some of the frequently quoted notes which display a much wider range of emotions, from passionate dislike to something near admiration. However, as Edward Tomarken notes, 'in fact the combination of scholarly, textual analysis and interpretive, evaluative commentary is characteristic of Johnson's criticism'.[39]

Johnson's well-known Preface contains no other reference to *Troilus and Cressida* than a passing invocation of the anachronism issue with Hector's Aristotelian quotation, and there is little in his 'stricture' (defined in his *Dictionary* as a 'slight touch upon a subject, not a set discourse'[40]) added to the play that could allow us a glimpse into his thoughts on the work. What his detailed textual footnotes establish, however, is the careful critical reading of both the Quarto and Folio texts and all previous editions, offering explanation when the meaning seems obscure, suggesting possible varieties of reading, disagreeing with unjustified earlier emendations, and sometimes freely admitting that he does not understand some word or phrase. On the very last page, two short paragraphs reveal his general observations, beginning with the oft-quoted summary statement that: 'This play is more correctly written than most of Shakespeare's compositions, but it is not one of those in which either the extent of his views or elevation of his fancy is fully displayed.'[41] As a result of the abundance of Shakespeare's source material, he can find nothing particularly inventive in the plot, but remarks on the characters' diversity, particularly the detestable features of Pandarus and Cressida, and the 'powerfully impressed' comic characters, which 'seem to have been the favourites of the writer'.[42] What the stricture does, however, is respond to Dryden's preface to his adaptation in several ways,[43] and through his respectful but critical reading of Dryden's work, placed alongside earlier editors' emendations, we may be able to understand his view of the role of the editor. As Tomarken argues, 'Johnson uses Dryden as a literary critical touchstone because the coherence of his drama derives from an artistic goal, an assessment and interpretation of *Troilus and Cressida*.'[44]

For all his editorial care, Johnson does not display a desire to provide an analysis of the play, and this general lack of interest in the drama seems to characterize his contemporaries throughout the eighteenth century. The question that incites the most heated debate is that of Shakespeare's learning: whether it is possible to find factual errors in the canon and still consider him a genius, or whether the anachronisms (particularly Hector's reference to Aristotle) and the arbitrary use of literary and historical sources should force his readers to reconsider their appreciation of him. The lack of critical consensus on these matters may suggest that critics trusted their own gut reactions more than the work of earlier commentators, and a difference of opinion simply justified their efforts in producing yet another commentary on the already much-debated work. At the same time, it is also true that most critical work on

Shakespeare in the eighteenth century is written in the form of prefaces or notes to collected editions, neither of which is a format inviting in-depth analysis. Apart from speculations on the playwright's genesis, a few characters are described in greater detail, but *Troilus and Cressida* does not have any character of Falstaffian scope who could invite such endeavours, and the most respectful references are the ones where little is said about the rather disturbingly odd play.

One editor, however, who is often praised for the way he relied on earlier editors' findings was Edmund Malone, whose 1790 edition of Shakespeare in Andrew Murphy's opinion 'can be seen essentially as the culmination of the eighteenth-century editorial tradition'.[45] Malone's work is founded on evidence rather than hypothesis, as he always aims at objectivity, rather than editorial speculation. Whenever possible, he gives priority to the earliest available textual variant, but this does not mean that he never uses later versions or even emendations suggested by previous editors; in fact, his (and Edward Capell's) work had 'established the importance of the First Folio text in the transmission of Shakespeare's plays'[46] by the end of the century. Malone's overall opinion and interpretation of *Troilus and Cressida* is hard to establish, since it is scattered in footnotes, many of which simply show his agreement or doubt in relation to earlier editors' work. Yet his insistence on authenticity, and his understanding of earlier editorial procedures, together with the quality of his own work as an editor all contributed to what Emma Smith calls a 'textual paradigm shift',[47] and paved the way for nineteenth-century textual criticism.

The nineteenth century – moralizing and psychology at home and abroad

As D. Nichol Smith points out in his 'Introduction' to a collection of *Eighteenth-century Essays on Shakespeare*, for all the work done by the great editors of the eighteenth century, their efforts were either ignored or despised by the following generations. As he observes, 'The early nineteenth century was too readily convinced by Coleridge and Hazlitt that they were the first to recognize and to explain the greatness of Shakespeare.' One reason for this, as Smith argues, may have been the fact that Pope and Johnson, even though they were ready to acknowledge and praise Shakespeare as 'the glory of English letters', also 'ventured to point out, in the honesty of their criticism, that Shakespeare was not free from faults; and it was this which the nineteenth century chose to remark'.[48] Shakespeare's appreciation clearly underwent a radical turn with the advent of Romanticism, as the nineteenth century was more forgiving with regard to unusual formal aspects when counterbalanced by equally unprecedented heights of passion – but the time was yet to come when *Troilus and Cressida* was truly appreciated for its own sake. The two central concerns of the first half of the nineteenth century are, on the one hand, an interest in the psychological realism most readers observe and enjoy in Shakespeare's plays, and on the other hand, the uncovering of moral intentions behind the changed depiction of a story familiar from classical antiquity.

The nineteenth-century interest in Shakespeare's work, partly rooted in the Romantics' appreciation for the genius clearly at work in him, is well documented in the writings of the poets and theoreticians of the age, both in Britain and on the continent. While *Troilus and Cressida* captivated neither the German nor the English Romantics in quite the same way as *Hamlet* or several other plays did, even the occasionally no more than passing references to the play imply that their lack of enthusiasm often stems from the generic oddities and the difficulties of classification of the drama. On the whole, the Romantics seem to find themselves at a loss when confronted with the play – after all, it presents the loftiest of source materials turned into a story of debasement all around, without many redeeming features in the moral conclusion. German critics, in particular, seem to be troubled by the contrast between the theme's classical ancestry and Shakespeare's rather sarcastic treatment of it. Indeed, the awareness of (and occasional antagonism between) English and German authors in the age testifies to an active intellectual community bridging the English channel; it is notable how in the 1830s Heinrich Heine, among others, claims the Germans' superior skill in understanding Shakespeare, as opposed to Swinburne's sarcastic end-of-century comments on German critics who pretend to know everything better than the English.

Among early nineteenth-century critics, the first significant mention of the play is by August Wilhelm Schlegel in his *Lectures on Dramatic Art and Literature*, where most of his critical writings on Shakespeare can be found. The *Lectures* include several general approaches to the topics commonly discussed by his contemporaries: Shakespeare's life and times, learning, anachronisms, character and style, together with the fundamental knowledge of humanity displayed by Shakespeare's genius. His criticism may be dismissed as conventional but, to be fair to him, one must acknowledge the fact that his lectures were meant to be popular and accessible to a general audience. Besides, he also had the intention of marketing the new complete set of translations, partly undertaken, partly supervised by himself and Ludwig Tieck, and therefore in his lectures he took pains to discuss at least briefly every single play by Shakespeare. Yet his judgment is, on the whole, more positive than that of his contemporaries, possibly as a result of his different textual approach, according to Christine Roger and Roger Paulin: 'Much of Augustan disapproval (like Johnson's) had of course been elicited by individual loci: Schlegel hardly discusses the text. In the discussion of the individual plays, his own preferences emerge.'[49]

Troilus and Cressida is considered in the lecture on what he calls historical dramas, in between the Roman plays and the English history plays, but it is treated as a generic oddity, together with *Timon of Athens*. Schlegel summarizes the difficulty of categorization and his own attitude towards the play in the following way: '*Timon of Athens*, and *Troilus and*

Cressida, are not historical plays; but we cannot properly call them either tragedies or comedies. By the selection of the materials from antiquity they have some affinity to the Roman pieces, and hence I have hitherto abstaned [*sic*] from mentioning them.'[50] When he does mention *Troilus*, it is not for any in-depth analysis, but a general appreciation in which he emphasizes Shakespeare's ironic treatment of the material: 'The whole is one continued irony of that crown of all heroic tales, the tale of Troy.'[51] He does not accuse Shakespeare of intentional indignity towards Homer, but finds the various other sources responsible for the often comic and disrespectful representation of the characters and their motivations. Still, he notices and acknowledges the poetic and rhetorical beauties and insights in characterization that the play abounds in, and even finds the drama entertaining on the whole:

> In a word, Shakespeare did not wish, in this heroic comedy, where every thing, from traditional fame and the pomp of poetry, seems to lay claim to admiration, that any room should be left for esteem and sympathy, if we except, perhaps, the character of Hector; but in this double meaning of the picture, he has afforded us the most choice entertainment.[52]

Partly motivated by 'some little jealousy' of the 'foreign critic' and his work, William Hazlitt published his *Characters of Shakespeare's Plays* in 1817, only two years after the first complete English translation of Schlegel's *Lectures*. In his Introduction, Hazlitt acknowledges the efforts not only of Schlegel but even a number of lesser-known authors who engaged in the critical reading of Shakespeare's characters. He quotes Lessing at length to prove Shakespeare's superior literary achievement, but also in an effort to defend the reputation of the Bard and his *oeuvre* from the less-favourable criticism of Johnson, clearly outraged at the lack of enthusiasm displayed by someone who is 'neither a poet nor a judge of poetry'.[53] Barely restraining himself from improprieties, he announces: 'Dr. Johnson's Preface to his edition of Shakespear looks like a laborious attempt to bury the characteristic merits of his author under a load of cumbrous phraseology, and to weigh his excellences and defects in equal scales, stuffed full of "swelling figures and sonorous epithets".'[54] Still, when it comes to *Troilus and Cressida*, Hazlitt can find little more to say than Johnson did; he starts out by criticizing the drama for its apparent structural inconsistencies: 'This is one of the most loose and desultory of our author's plays: it rambles on just as it happens', but he acknowledges its richness of detail, finding 'a prodigious number of fine things'[55] in it, together with some examples of characters, particularly 'Cressida and her uncle Pandarus [who] are hit off with proverbial truth'.[56] Hazlitt emphasizes the poetic richness of Shakespeare's language, and illustrates his opinion with copious quotations from the play,[57] in a clear attempt to confirm Shakespeare's position among classical authors of high culture, rather than among the – apparently inferior – class of theatrical artisans: 'the poet's genius was not confined to the production of stage effects by preternatural means.'[58] At the same time, his main interest in *Troilus* lies in the dramatic characters, partly as a result of their plausibility (or lack thereof), and above all, their moral positions. He declares that 'Troilus himself is no character: he is merely a common lover',[59] Hector's character 'is made very amiable',[60] 'Cressida and Pandarus are very amusing and instructive',[61] but also original when compared to the Chaucerian sources. The chapter concludes with a lengthy comparison of Chaucer's and Shakespeare's treatment of the story, which Hazlitt explains with reference to 'the different genius of the two poets'.[62] (Interestingly, earlier critics appeared to have no interest in such a comparison, and referred to Chaucer simply as a source for Shakespeare's work.) This different artistic temperament allows Shakespeare a mixture of styles: 'In Shakspeare the ludicrous and ironical are constantly blended with the stately and the impassioned';[63] and whereas Chaucer 'arrived at truth through a certain process; Shakspeare saw everything by intuition',[64] which clearly stands for the highest possible praise in the era of Romanticism.

After Schlegel, the other German literary giant of the nineteenth century, Johann Wolfgang von Goethe, also mentions the play, although only in a passing reference in his posthumous essay 'On the Parody of the Ancients' ('Über die Parodie bei den Alten', written in 1824, but published only in 1833). In the course of the discussion of Euripides' play *Cyclops*, he makes a comparison between the *Iliad* and Shakespeare's *Troilus*, and while the references are too brief to merit the name of analysis, his comments show that he was observing the play first and foremost as an adaptation. In this context, he appreciates the original elements Shakespeare's reworking added to the ancient story, and also notes the play's reflection on its own age and characters. For him, 'it requires just as profound a sincerity, just as decided a talent, to depict for us similar personalities and characters with so light a touch and so lucid a meaning, and represent them for a later age with all the human traits of that age, which thus sees itself reflected in the guise of the ancient story'.[65] He consequently describes the play as 'neither parody nor travesty', but rather a 'happy transposition',[66] although I believe that the phrase ('glückliche Umformung'[67] in the original) refers more to a successful adaptation rather than to a cheerful or comic tone that the English translation may suggest.

Samuel Taylor Coleridge, the English contemporary Schlegel most often finds himself compared to, approached individual Shakespearean plays with a different method, focusing more on textual interpretation than the German Romantic master. *Troilus and Cressida*, however, did not find particular favour with Coleridge – in his 1833 note on the play he seems practically stupefied by the impossibility of classifying it either among the fictitious or the 'proper ancient histories', and then runs off on a tangent to describe several other tragedies rather than having to discuss this troublesome play, as in his opinion, 'there is no one of Shakspeare's plays harder to characterize'.[68] What most of his notes on the play perform is a series of attempts at trying to find not only the proper genre label, but also the intention, the main plotline, and the dominant belief system informing the narrative. Interestingly, while he finds in the play 'the flesh and blood of the romantic drama', he also believes that Shakespeare's intention was 'to translate the poetic heroes of paganism into the not less rude, but more intellectually vigorous, and more *featurely*, warriors of Christian chivalry'[69] – an observation not often shared by contemporary readers, who find some of the ancient heroes presented either faithful to their Homeric forms, or in an ironic/sarcastic light, devoid of virtues, rather than endowed with new Christian ones. Charles Lamb seems nonplussed by some heroes at least, and the only explanation he finds is Shakespeare's not having read the *Iliad*: 'If he had read it, could he mean to *travesty* it in the parts of those big boobies, Ajax and Achilles?'[70]

The German poet Heinrich Heine was offered a contract in 1838 for a volume of 45 portraits of Shakespeare's female characters, to accompany a collection of English steel engravings, previously published in Berlin.[71] This visual approach – the poet 'sees himself in the role of gatekeeper who opens the gates of an imaginary gallery of portraits for his public and guides them through it'[72] – is tangible in his *Notes on Shakespeare's Heroines* (1838), but he does not conceal his analytical instinct, or his classical erudition either. Heine's introduction is in fact extremely useful for his account of the German (together with the French) reception of Shakespeare's work. In his treatment of the heroines in *Troilus*, he emphasizes Shakespeare's realistic depiction of the heroes of antiquity, which in his view comes at the price of their idealized heroism; as he claims, Shakespeare 'divests the heroes of their bright armour and brings them before us in absurdly homely gear'.[73] He also goes to great lengths to describe the ways in which the play defies generic classification, and claims this quality to be the sign of Shakespeare's genius. What is surprising, however, is not only his admission that *Troilus* is the play where we can witness Shakespeare's method best (seeing that it is an adaptation of well-known classical material), but that in his focus on female characters, he includes Cassandra and Helen as well as Cressida in the volume. Since his interest in the play is motivated by his knowledge of the Homeric source, his slight disappointment is unsurprising when he states that 'Shakespeare has not given more attention to beautiful Helen than to Cassandra',[74] who 'only utters a few unimportant words; to him she is but an ordinary prophet of evil running through the cursed town with her cry of woe'.[75] However, what Heine finds lacking in Shakespeare, he substitutes by comparisons, embellishing the stories from Schiller's poetry and the story of Johannes Faustus. By way of justification, he refers to the same age-old rivalry that motivated Hazlitt's work as well; Heine appears to be convinced, just like Schlegel, that 'Germans have entered into the mind of Shakespeare better than Englishmen'.[76]

Only a year after Heine's writing, his compatriot, the German philosopher Hermann Ulrici, dedicated a longer essay to the play; but whereas for Heine, Shakespeare's novel approach seems to be motivated by a desire to create a more truthful representation of conflict and character, Ulrici in his 1839 essay finds the reinterpretation to serve a fundamentally moral purpose: to satirize the antique lifestyle for its 'decidedly immoral element'.[77] Another mid-nineteenth-century German author, the literary and political historian G.G. Gervinus, also displays an interest in moral issues in his 1849–50 commentaries on Shakespeare, although he does not comment on the immorality of the whole story (only that of Cressida). Quite the contrary, he remarks on the 'absence of a moral cause in both Greeks and Trojans'[78] and concludes that Shakespeare's intention must have been 'to degrade the whole subject by a caricatured representation'.[79] While Gervinus uses almost the same metaphor as Heine does for Shakespeare's psychological realism in depicting his characters: 'they wear their everyday-dress instead of that of festal pomp',[80] the conclusion they draw is different. What Heine finds more associated with Melpomene, the muse of tragedy, even if here she 'dances the *Cancan* at a ball of *grisettes*, with shameless laughter flitting across her pallid lips, and with death in her heart',[81] for Gervinus, the title heroes' love affair seems to be approached 'from its comic side',[82] and in fact, 'is of little worth in itself', since it 'creates throughout no real effect on the mind'.[83] He does acknowledge the masterful style and vitriolic criticism of 'this polemic comedy',[84] but the conclusion he draws is one full of uncertainty – he fails to find the proper target of Shakespeare's criticism, either in Homer and his world, or the later chivalric sourcebooks, and ends on a general note of dissatisfaction (with the comfortable knowledge that his uncertainty is shared by 'the warmest admirers of Shakespeare').[85]

Towards the end of the nineteenth century, the poet Algernon Charles Swinburne, another devoted admirer of Shakespeare, also undertook to present his views on the whole of the Bard's *oeuvre*, including a few apocryphal writings, mostly *Edward III*, in his *A Study of Shakespeare* (1880). There is one particular reason why his description of Shakespeare's 'Third period: Tragic and Romantic' is enlightening, although he cannot find it in his heart to like the three plays he groups together (*Troilus and Cressida, Measure for Measure* and *Pericles*), since he sees in them 'humour and reality supplanted by realism and obscenity; an exchange undeniably for the worse'.[86] At the same time, he points out the stylistic connections between them, and he believes that the 'singular little group of two or three plays not accurately definable at all but roughly describable as tragi-comedies'[87] is united in 'an all but absolute brotherhood in thought and style and tone and feeling'.[88] Clearly dissatisfied with 'tragi-comedy' as a term, though, he keeps attempting to define the undefinable genre of the plays, sometimes referring to *Troilus* as a 'quasi-tragedy'[89] and claiming *Measure for Measure* 'in its very inmost essence a tragedy'.[90] *Troilus*, 'this ... mysterious and magnificent monster of a play',[91] he finds evoking the most controversial and contrary responses: 'This wonderful play, one of the most admirable among all the works of Shakespeare's immeasurable intelligence, as it must always hold its natural high place among the most admired, will always in all probability be also, and as naturally, the least beloved of all.'[92] The use of superlatives in this statement may be a consequence of his own radical Hellenism, and his preference for the more relaxed moral and cultural standards of ancient Greece to those of Christianity; in fact, his criticism often serves to support his argument by claiming that Shakespeare also 'believed in a godless universe',[93] just like himself. Still, his generally positive evaluation of *Troilus* is all the more remarkable for having little critical precedent; in fact, as the play's performance history tells us, until the late nineteenth century, it seemed to attract little or no attention by theatres or critics for its own sake. Swinburne's praise may possibly be attributed to the loftiest of Hellenic sources, Homer's *Iliad*, rather than representing a generally accepted recognition of *Troilus* on its own right – and as if to prove us right, Swinburne qualifies his admiration by finding in the play 'too much that Swift might have written when half inspired by the genius of Shakespeare'.[94]

Looking back on the first three centuries of the play's critical history, the character who fares worst from such mixed praise must definitely be Cressida – not that Ajax or Achilles, or even Patroclus, get any positive criticism, but it is usually the playwright who has to shoulder the blame for their wretched characters, or the 'abomination'[95] in the friendship between the latter two that Shakespeare disgraced the stages with. The eponymous heroine of the drama, however, is either 'the portrait of a vehement passion ... contrasted with the profound affection presented in Troilus',[96] or a plain strumpet, as in Heine's view; at least that is implied by the description that she is 'spoken of as a strumpet by Thersites the eavesdropper, who is rude enough always to call things by their names'.[97] G.G. Gervinus declares her to be 'without depth, an adept at double-entendre, and indelicate in her expressions', indeed not 'so much a coquette by profession as by nature';[98] Swinburne sees in her portrayal the study 'of an utterly light woman, shallow and loose and dissolute in the most literal sense, rather than perverse or unkindly or unclean'[99] – and yet, G.B. Shaw apparently thought Cressida 'to be most enchanting', even to the extent that he claimed at an 1884 meeting of the New Shakespeare Society that 'Shakespear was indulgent to women, and he thought Cressida to be Shakespear's first real woman'.[100]

Also characteristic of the Victorian era is the attempt at explaining every change of mood or style, the dominance of certain genres over others with reference to the author's biography – and in this context, *Troilus and Cressida* is a logical consequence of 'the corrupt condition of morals' that 'could hardly fail to leave some mark on a disposition which, just at this time, was susceptible and irritable to the highest degree' – no wonder therefore that during this period 'his melancholy was prone to dwell upon the darkest side of life' and he shows 'a sickly tendency to imbibe poison from everything'.[101] At least this is how Danish critic and scholar Georg Brandes explains the disillusioned atmosphere of the play to which he dedicates four chapters in his three-volume work of biographical criticism published in 1898. This tendency to explain thematic features within the *oeuvre* by reference to the socio-historical context or the personal emotions of the author became increasingly popular around this time, and can be seen as justification in particular for the generic oddities of the problem plays themselves. Such an approach encourages the critic to make comments like 'never had he been so downcast and dispirited, never had he felt so keenly the emptiness of life'[102] – and to explain Shakespeare's interest in 'a plot which chimed in with his mood',[103] 'stuff for a tragi-comedy of right bitter sort'.[104] As Brandes explains, the story of Helen and Menelaus could no longer excite the author, as it is practically over before the play begins; but in other legendary sources 'he found, in miniature, the plot whereon the whole war turned. Cressida, a rejuvenated Helen; Troilus, the simpleton who loved her, and whom she betrayed; and round about them grouped all those archetypes of subtlety, wisdom, and strength'.[105] He takes it thus for granted that the Trojan war and its heroes are well known to all and sundry, and as the playwright stumbled upon the story in a sarcastic mood, the result can be seen in this strangest of plays, *Troilus and Cressida*.

Still, before dismissing the work of Brandes as an example of psychologizing fantasy, we must mention that he also took pains to examine all pre-Shakespearean versions of the narrative, from the single reference to Troilus in Homer's *Iliad*, through the various medieval retellings, pointing out the elements that later found their way into Shakespeare's work. The explanation he offers for the sarcastic turn the story took in Shakespeare's hands is none other than the misery the author must have felt over his disappointment in his lady-love, the Dark Lady of the sonnets – 'and his wrath over wasted feelings and wasted time and suffering, over the degradation and humiliation of its self-deception, and ultimately the treason itself, seeks final and supreme relief in the outburst, "What a farce!" which is in itself the germ of *Troilus and Cressida*.'[106] Not only is Cressida's degradation explained by the Dark Lady, but Brandes also supports the theory first suggested by Scottish critic William Minto in 1874 that the Rival Poet of the sonnets was none other than Chapman, Homer's translator. Thus, 'in all probability it was the grief Shakespeare felt at seeing Chapman selected by Pembroke' which motivated him to present 'the *Iliad*'s most beautiful and most powerful elements . . ., but only to profane and ridicule all'.[107] Another cause for Shakespeare's bitterness is 'the undoubted stupidity of the English public'[108] – although, if truth be told, here it is hard to distinguish between the biographical critic's conviction of the Elizabethan English playwright's supposed contempt for the middle classes and the Danish author's general derision for the 'Land of Spleen'.[109]

The moral element that characterized much of nineteenth-century criticism appears here as well, although with a slightly different twist: Brandes is disappointed to see that in Shakespeare 'the Christian conception of faithlessness in love has replaced the old Hellenic innocence and naïveté'[110] – the contemporary moralist rewriting of the Homeric narrative is obviously seen as a corruption of innocence, rather than a refinement of morality. He goes as far as explicitly casting aside G.G. Gervinus's moralizing comments, claiming that 'Shakespeare most certainly was never so moral as this moralizing German critic (and what German critic is not moralizing) would have him to be. It is not a sense of the ethics of Homer, but a feeling for his poetry that is lacking.'[111] Thus the late nineteenth-century Scandinavian critic, who acquired a reputation for his theoretical writings that associated him with Henrik Ibsen and other realist and naturalist writers of his age, could still not find it in his heart to appreciate the down-to-earth human characters of Shakespeare's play.

Twentieth-century reception

Priscilla Martin begins her introduction to her 1976 collection of critical essays with the statement that 'Until this century *Troilus and Cressida* was one of the least popular of Shakespeare's plays',[112] and thus we are right in expecting a radical change with the advent of modernity, first in the drama's critical interpretation, then in the form of a revival on the stage. This changed attitude began to be felt already in the final decades of the nineteenth century, with the renewed efforts of certain critics to define the play's genre. William B. Toole describes the end of the nineteenth century as the first prominent stage in the critical history of the problem plays; he finds this starting point in 'the classification, based on biographical inferences, suggested by Edward Dowden in 1889',[113] although in the first edition of his work in 1875, Dowden declares that he is 'unwilling to offer any criticism of the play of *Troylus and Cressida* [sic] until I see my way more clearly through certain difficulties respecting its date and its ethical significance'.[114]

Rather than Dowden's work, possibly the most significant turning point in the reception of *Troilus and Cressida* (along with its fellow dark comedies) is generally seen in F.S. Boas's

1896 volume *Shakspere and his Predecessors*, which deals with Shakespeare's work in a chronological framework, focusing not only on the connections within the *oeuvre*, but also the plays' relations to each other. Boas has achieved lasting fame mostly for the categorization of the comedies, and for the term he introduced to describe the most elusive group: the 'problem plays'. He places *All's Well That Ends Well*, *Measure for Measure* and *Troilus and Cressida* in the same group with *Hamlet*; although noting the tragic ending of the latter that distinguishes it from the others, he finds the general atmosphere of the four plays sufficiently similar to justify calling them a separate group among Shakespeare's dramas. As a result of the unsatisfactory ending that characterizes the plays, he declares: 'Dramas so singular in theme and temper cannot be strictly called comedies or tragedies. We may therefore borrow a convenient phrase from the theatre of to-day and class them together as Shakespeare's problem-plays.'[115] This sensitivity to the modernity of the plays is what Boas shares with many later critics, and that connects him more to the twentieth century rather than to his late Victorian contemporaries. For him, the 'theatre of to-day' is mostly the drama of Henrik Ibsen, or even the early work of G.B. Shaw, and although many of Boas's critics observed that his use of the term is not only uneven, but markedly different from the contemporary theatrical genre (where it referred to plays 'dealing with problems confronting not a single individual but contemporary society as a whole'),[116] the phrase still stuck and has remained in use until the present day. Notwithstanding the many discrepancies between later authors' use and interpretation of the term, Boas's summary of the plays' conclusion is still often used as a reference point. As he observes: 'at the close our feeling is neither of simple joy nor pain; we are excited, fascinated, perplexed, for the issues raised preclude a completely satisfactory outcome'[117] – not to mention the fact that post-war critics turned to the plays with a renewed interest precisely for their representation of social ills that felt more than familiar after modernism. Interestingly enough, G.B. Shaw, who may have been in the best position to identify with these plays, had Boas been right, also observed the connection to Ibsen, and, what is more, he remarked on the modernity of the plays, saying that 'in such unpopular plays as *All's Well*, *Measure for Measure*, and *Troilus and Cressida*, we find [Shakespeare] ready and willing to start at the nineteenth century if the seventeenth would only let him'.[118] This surprising modernity, a somewhat anachronistic quality of the plays continues to be mentioned as the most probable reason for the centuries-long neglect, but also for the rediscovery of the plays at the beginning of the twentieth century.

After the late nineteenth-century attempts at grouping and labelling the long-neglected bunch of plays into meaningful categories, the turn of the century brought possibly the single most influential writing on Shakespearean drama for a long time: A.C. Bradley's 1904 lectures on *Hamlet*, *Othello*, *King Lear* and *Macbeth*. Even though Bradley's focus is on the great tragedies, several of his comparative remarks and even a few footnotes make enlightening comments on *Troilus* as well. In a note attached to his lecture on *King Lear*, while he steers clear of the question of 'how far Shakespeare's works represent his personal feelings and attitude, and the changes in them',[119] he refers to a supposed order of writing the plays, claiming that during the same years when the great tragedies were born, Shakespeare

> wrote ... certain 'comedies', *Measure for Measure* and *Troilus and Cressida* and perhaps *All's Well*. But about these comedies there is a peculiar air of coldness; there is humour, of course, but little mirth; in *Measure for Measure*, perhaps, certainly in *Troilus and Cressida*, a spirit of bitterness and contempt seems to pervade an intellectual atmosphere of an intense but hard clearness.[120]

He does not refer to Boas, but the grouping of the plays reflects an awareness of the similarities between the three plays' stylistic and thematic qualities that had made Boas devise the term 'problem play'. Bradley also remarks that in certain plays the reader is aware of 'a partial suppression of that element in Shakespeare's mind which unites him with the mystical poets and with the great musicians and philosophers', claiming that 'in one or two plays, notably in *Troilus and Cressida*, we are almost painfully conscious of this suppression; we feel an intense intellectual activity, but at the same time a certain coldness and hardness, as though some power in his soul, at once the highest and the sweetest, were for a time in abeyance'.[121] These short and scattered comments are hardly sufficient to establish a radically new assessment of the play, but they show that Bradley appears to have left behind the predominantly moralizing attitude that characterized the majority of Victorian critics.

This intellectual distance from the subject is what the British poet and critic Arthur Symons also emphasizes in his 1907 critical comment in *Harper's Monthly Magazine*, observing that: 'Here, more than anywhere else in Shakespeare, we get the comedy of pure mind, with its detachment from life, to which it applies an abstract criticism.'[122] It is hard to decide whether he means the above as words of praise or contempt, as he goes on to argue that 'To write drama from a point of view so aloof is to lose most of the material of drama and all dramatic appeal', and that this approach is inimical to a natural realism: 'We must apprehend wholly by the intelligence, never by the feelings.'[123] Strangely enough, while Symons begins his critical comment with the argument that the play is clearly the work of either several hands, or shows signs of (rather careless) authorial revision from more than one periods in Shakespeare's dramatic career, he then goes on to describe it as 'a kind of *Don Quixote*, in which it is even more difficult to disentangle the burlesque from the serious element'[124] (a comparison to the Spanish classic often made by the late Victorian aesthetic movement).[125] Finally, evoking Swinburne's words from 1880, he implies that the author's mouthpiece, his chorus must be Thersites, 'in this morbid, almost Swiftian consciousness of the dung in which roses are rooted'.[126] In fact, the short essay gives the impression that the critic was struggling to find a point of entry from which to approach the play – he mentions its early publication history, ponders on questions of authorship, refers to the difficulties of generic classification, and even attempts to place it in the author's career based on its predominantly ironic tone. Then he gradually warms to his topic to such an extent that he ends with the summary judgment, claiming that through his vital immensity, Shakespeare 'can give us in a single play, as in *Troilus and Cressida*, a complete philosophy, which will prove sufficient for the use and fame of more than one great writer who is to come after him; and can then go on his way, creating new aspects from which to see life, as nature itself leads the way for him'.[127]

Revival in the 1930s

The 1930s brought another resurgence of interest in the problem plays, and this revival continued throughout the century, as if trying to make up for the resentful silence in which the works were shrouded for so long. As the following pages will illustrate, the bulk of twentieth-century research has indeed strengthened the position of the plays in the canon – Michael Jamieson refers to this modern 'revaluation so radical as to amount to a rediscovery' – but this reappraisal is also accompanied by a questioning of 'the aesthetic validity and critical usefulness of regarding these plays as a group'.[128] For all the efforts of the turn-of-the-century critics, the real success in championing 'the re-instatement of the problem plays ... since 1929 in a changing climate of opinion'[129] must be attributed to G. Wilson Knight and his 1930 volume *The Wheel of Fire*, an extremely influential collection of essays, again primarily focusing on Shakespearean tragedy, but with a whole chapter dedicated to *Troilus and Cressida*. Although acknowledging his debt to, and respect for, Bradley's *Shakespearean Tragedy*, the volume takes a conscious effort to move beyond the character-based criticism so dominant in the previous century and in turn-of-the-century critical writings. What Knight offers is a focus on pattern and theme, on overarching unities rather than particularities, and despite his theatrical experience as actor and director, he is not concerned with performative aspects of the plays, claiming that 'the literary analysis of great drama in terms of theatrical technique accomplishes singularly little'.[130] In connection with *Troilus*, he emphasizes 'the peculiar dualism that persists in the thought of this play', not simply that of the two 'primary values, love and war', but also observing how 'the root idea of *Troilus and Cressida* is the dynamic opposition in the mind of these two faculties: intuition and intellect'.[131] His interpretation brings to light the analytical nature of the play's many arguments – a quality that alienated earlier critics; in Knight's approach it finds a place both in the complexity of the play's thought and even in the Shakespearean *oeuvre*. He examines the time metaphor that takes him to 'the core of this play's philosophy. It is the arch-enemy, Time, that kills values.'[132] At the same time, he also shows how the 'time-thinking in this play is inextricably twined with the central love-theme',[133] which has previously often been ignored mostly because of its unsatisfactory conclusion. Knight, however, argues that the play's philosophy and its poetry, its form and its content, are in perfect harmony, and even goes as far as claiming that 'in no play of Shakespeare is there a more powerful unity of idea'.[134]

What is also significant is his attitude to Cressida: the heroine, who has been described as harlot, strumpet, loose and treacherous, sometimes with the excuse of her admitted charm, as in G.B. Shaw's words, now appears for the first time as a character consistent in herself, as 'she lives emotionally'.[135] Moreover, there is the slight implication that she can also be seen as a victim, as an object of the commerce of war (a notion that echoes throughout feminist criticism, particularly after the 1980s). For Knight, 'the handing over of Cressida to the Greeks, which is the pivotal incident of the play, has thus a symbolic suggestion'[136] – and Knight's powerfully expressed appreciation of the drama has also become nearly symbolic in the way it attracted attention and discussion towards this previously neglected play.

Only a year after the first edition of *The Wheel of Fire*, W.W. Lawrence's monograph on *Shakespeare's Problem Comedies* was published, in which he intends to shed light on the plays with the help of a 'study of mediaeval analogues and customs',[137] which he believes will demonstrate 'the continuing vital spirit of an earlier time in the splendidly creative age of Elizabeth'.[138] Nonetheless, even at the time of its publication the volume's shortcomings were mentioned by reviewers, most notably the contradictions between Lawrence's unquestioning reliance on earlier critical tradition, e.g. in connection with certain 'spurious' scenes in *Troilus and Cressida*, and his recognition of the significance of the very same scenes for the interpretation of the play as a whole.[139] Still, his efforts in strengthening the position of the problem plays as valid subjects of critical interest are undeniable, and his comparative work has brought to light many subtle details of the medieval cultural heritage familiar to Shakespeare's audiences.

The early 1930s also saw the publication of a seminal work in the study of Shakespeare's use of poetic images. Caroline Spurgeon's *Shakespeare's Imagery and What it Tells Us*, while not focusing only or even particularly on *Troilus*, argues convincingly how the dominant groups of images in the play, disease and food, run through *Hamlet* as well, strengthening the ties between the two dramas. As she points out, 'The main emotional theme in *Troilus and Cressida* – passionate, idealistic love, followed by disillusion and despair – is pictured with overwhelming vividness, through physical taste: the exquisite anticipation by a sensitive palate of delicious food and wine, and the sick revolt and disgust on finding on one's tongue only "greasy relics" or rotting fruit.'[140] Spurgeon's findings were later expanded by other scholars, and several more detailed investigations into the play's language have shed light on other dominant thematic elements as well, including the imagery of movement or animals, as Kenneth Muir points out in his

1953 lecture, yet her work still has its firmly established place in Shakespeare scholarship.

In the late 1930s, beside the above-mentioned investigations into the play's imagery and themes, O.J. Campbell approached the historical context of the play's creation from a new angle. Similarly to Boas, Campbell sees *Troilus and Cressida* as the product of the age, not because of some supposed depressive period in Shakespeare's private life, but rather explained by the theatrical context. As he argues, in the first years of the seventeenth century, playwrights – mostly Marston and Jonson – were experimenting with the combination of 'old comedy' with a more satirical vein, after the Bishop's edict of 1599, banning formal satirists from pursuing their previously favoured genre. Campbell therefore does not see the play as simply an expression of personal disillusionment but as 'a conscious and successful effort to follow Jonson's lead'. Campbell also argues against G. Wilson Knight's view of Troilus's personality, interpreting the oft-quoted passage ('I am giddy . . .'; 3.2.16–27) not as 'an expression of unsatisfied aspiration or of dismay at "the feared impossibility of actual fruition"' as Knight does, but pronounces Troilus to suggest 'the educated sensuality of an Italianate English roué'.[141] Campbell's analysis of the play against the backdrop of contemporary satirical comedies found many followers, except for his conclusion that the play is intended to be 'ultimately moralistic'.[142]

As we could see on the previous pages, after the long silence, the play has returned to the foreground of critical discourse from the 1930s onwards. It was also taken up by twentieth-century theatres with a vengeance, and the play's relevance for the modernist viewer and critic, recently traumatized by one Great War and on the march toward another, was gradually becoming a commonplace. Already after the First World War this topicality appears, but it is the Second World War that drives the message truly home: the more ironic or sarcastic Shakespeare's presentation of the fall of Troy, the easier it is to believe and identify with it.

Among post-war critics, Una Ellis-Fermor continues the appreciation of the play by including it in *The Frontiers of Drama*, her volume dedicated to 'those rare plays which by a supreme reach of art contrive to break through or transcend what seem their natural limits'.[143] She thus reinforces the position of *Troilus* among the extraordinary, rather than the negligible plays in the Shakespeare canon, and in describing it as a 'great play ... one of the most weighty in the Jacobean period',[144] she determines the tone of much later criticism as well. Her analysis focuses both on matters of form and content, pointing out that 'they collaborate not fortuitously, but intentionally', and in this way 'the form illuminates and interprets the theme'.[145] The key to this acknowledgement is her understanding of the play as rooted in a 'vision of the disjunction and disintegration of civilization',[146] an experience better understood by her generation than any other before them. As she argues, 'our actual experience of disintegration and disruption, so unlike that of any age between, has thrown fresh light upon the nature and foundations of what we call civilization'[147] – in short, the traumatic events of the twentieth century explain why the play has returned to stages and into the focus of critical attention as well.

Not all post-war critics, however, approached the play with the intention of drawing parallels between their own age and the early seventeenth century. G.B. Harrison in his *Shakespeare's Tragedies* (1951) describes *Troilus and Cressida* mostly in terms of its historical topicality, this time with reference to the history of the play's creation. He claims that

> the parallel between Essex, Southampton and Cuff sneering at the old Queen and her ministers was very close to the situation in the play where Achilles, Patroclus and Thersites sneer at Agamemnon, Nestor, Menelaus, Ajax and the rest. It is indeed far closer to the actual events and personalities of these months than to the original story and characters in the *Iliad*.[148]

Harrison also describes *Troilus* as a drama of a personal tragedy: 'the play of a man who is suffering from a queasy soul.'[149] Yet it is hard to say whether the man in question is Troilus or possibly Achilles in this context, as the general sense of disillusionment and 'cynical disgust'[150] that Harrison attributes to Shakespeare are shown to be universal, rather than familiar only to the twentieth-century.

The 1950s also saw renewed efforts to classify and label the problem plays as a genre, with one of the last major breakthroughs being E.M.W. Tillyard's study of *Shakespeare's Problem Plays*, after which 'the full-length interpretation and evaluation of the plays as works of art'[151] became the critical norm. Tillyard, while satisfied with none of the phrases in circulation, accepts the advantages of the term 'problem play' for want of a better one, recognizing 'that the plays make a group and that a common name is needed'.[152] He also includes *Hamlet* in his study, based on its connections to *Troilus and Cressida* in particular, implying not so much a return to the grouping first suggested by F.S. Boas, but rather providing evidence of the ongoing debates concerning the problem plays' position within the Shakespearean canon, and even the actual plays that may (or may not) belong to this problematic class. The debate has certainly not settled after Tillyard's work; Ernest Schanzer in his controversial 1963 study of *The Problem Plays of Shakespeare* shows his dissatisfaction with earlier classifications, and instead of *Troilus* and *All's Well*, places *Julius Caesar* and *Antony and Cleopatra* next to *Measure for Measure*, in order to define the term 'more narrowly and precisely than has been done in the past'.[153] In other cases, we can witness constantly evolving definitions even within the critical *oeuvre* of individual scholars. Northrop Frye, for one, first raises his voice against Tillyard's classification in *A Natural Perspective*,[154] his 1965 study of the comedies and romances; then he discusses *Troilus and Cressida* both in *Fools of Time*,[155] his 1967 volume on the tragedies, and in his investigations in a series of lectures in 1981, which later formed the basis of *The Myth of Deliverance: Reflections on Shakespeare's Problem*

Comedies. True, Frye argues that the play does not fit into any of the traditional generic categories (though such '"fitting" is not the point of generic criticism'),[156] but in his treatment of the play, he also ends up commenting 'that this play is about us, if not about the aspect of us that we want to put on exhibition'.[157]

On this note of self-identification with the meaning of the plays, we have already noted how characteristic this attitude has become in twentieth-century criticism. It may be the case that the post-war anxiety made the problem plays appear more significant than they really are, or simply enhanced those features that alienated earlier critics. At the same time, it is also easy to agree with the remark of William B. Toole, who claims in the Introduction to his 1966 monograph that the past three decades of criticism emphasized not so much the plays' modernity but rather a 'more acute understanding of the social, historical, literary, and intellectual milieu, the cultural complex, in which they are rooted'.[158] Whatever the case, the newly found topicality is undeniably a recurring theme in the writings of several post-war critics. Kenneth Muir in his 1953 Stratford lecture also refers to the increase in the number of *Troilus* performances: 'If the play has now become relatively popular on the stage, and if modern critics have come to appreciate it more in the study, we may suspect that audiences and critics have been taught by two world wars and by changes in society to see what Shakespeare was trying to do.'[159] M.C. Bradbrook in her 1958 analysis of the way Shakespeare uses the Chaucerian source material in *Troilus* also remarks that 'the Sack of Troy was to the sixteenth century the highest secular symbol of Disaster, the Great Crash; it was what 1914 was to writers of the twenties and thirties'.[160] Curiously, Bradbrook does not mention her own wartime experience, but the references to the twentieth-century historical and economic catastrophes make it clear that she finds ways to connect the Trojan story to her own recent past. But the best-known volume that associates the absurdity of the play with the experiences humanity gained by the mid-century is without doubt Jan Kott's *Shakespeare Our Contemporary*. Unsurprisingly, *Troilus and Cressida* features heavily in the Polish critic's writing, who describes it with the adjectives 'amazing and modern', claiming that it 'is from the outset a modern play, a sneering political pamphlet'.[161] Interestingly, Kott finds this modernity in the play's metaphorical references to early modern politics – 'Troy was Spain, the Greeks were the English',[162] but also in terms of his own age, as in the cynicism of Cressida, whom he describes as 'a teen-age girl of the mid-twentieth century'.[163] Joyce Carol Oates focuses on one contemporary theme, pinpointing the play's representation of a variety of infidelities, together with the discrepancy between essential and existential elements of human life as signs of its modernity.[164]

Moving forward in time, it becomes increasingly difficult to make general comments on trends in Shakespeare studies, as th unqualified acceptance of *Troilus* as a mature and valuable work resulted in its receiving previously unprecedented critical attention. A few focal points appear from time to time, though; among others, we can observe the intention of finding evidence for the play's conscious organization with reference to the rest of the Shakespearean *oeuvre*, a theme already tangible in G.W. Knight's interpretation, and even more in the work of Ellis-Fermor and Muir. Muir makes frequent use of the Sonnets and longer poems, beside the plays, to exemplify the imagery of time and the ways it is employed by Shakespeare, but he emphasizes 'three other groups of images of greater importance':[165] those of sickness, movement, and animals. Moreover, he qualifies G.W. Knight's conclusions regarding the centrality of the values of love and war in the play, but he goes against O.J. Campbell's and Ellis-Fermor's utterly disillusioned readings. Evoking T.S. Eliot's words on the metaphysical poets, he declares:

> The most remarkable thing about the play is perhaps the way in which the poet managed to fuse thought and feeling, to unify an extraordinary mass of materials, and to counter

the sense of chaos and disruption, not so much by the sense of order implicit in the artistic form, as by his establishment of the values denied or corrupted in the action.[166]

The post-war decades were a particularly prolific period in Shakespeare studies, which brought forth a number of the best-known critical writings that have laid down the foundations of what we consider the modern interpretation of Shakespeare's work. Even though Michael Jamieson rightfully observes, regarding twentieth-century criticism on the problem plays, that 'while the study of texts and sources has advanced, research has unearthed no new fact about the original date of writing or the circumstances of first performance of any of the plays',[167] this does not mean that critical interest in *Troilus and Cressida* would have waned. Among the most seminal works, A.P. Rossiter's *Angel with Horns*, a collection of lectures originally delivered at Cambridge, argues for the play's interpretation within a predominantly Jacobean context; the literary background evoked here is not the satirical comedy of Marston and Jonson, as in O.J. Campbell's earlier work, but the metaphysical poetry of the early seventeenth century. In this light, Rossiter sees *Troilus* 'concerned with the questioning of values in the new and sceptical atmosphere generated from the decay in the worlds of Spenser and the Petrarchan sonneteers',[168] a newly disillusioned world which he associates with John Donne's *Anatomie of the World* and its depiction of universal decline. Published a few years later, Willard Farnham's essay also finds some of the play's imagery comparable to Donne's, but in his examination of the two sides of Troilus's character (the lover, bound to fall, and the warrior, allowed to prevail, although in an ultimately ironic manner), he connects Troilus to famous Elizabethan, rather than Jacobean, heroes, Marlowe's Tamburlaine and Faustus, arguing that 'His vision of infinite will or boundless desire matched with human action fated to suffer indignity by confinement or slavery is of their kind.'[169]

In the following few decades, there is practically no self-respecting Shakespeare scholar who does not offer his or her bit to enrich the dialogue forming around the play. As the bibliographical overview of new scholarship in the 1967 volume of *Shakespeare Survey* observes, from among the problem plays, in that year (and I believe in several others as well), it is *Troilus and Cressida* 'which appears to be stimulating the hardest thinking'.[170] In-depth studies treating some aspect of the play include R.A. Foakes's 1963 essay[171] that argues for the complementary nature of tragedy and comedy in the play, together with Nevill Coghill's interpretation of the play as being originally the tragedy of Hector.[172] Throughout the 1960s and 1970s, we can find investigations of source, form and structure (e.g. Norman Rabkin's essay on '*Troilus and Cressida*: The Uses of the Double Plot'),[173] meaning and interpretation; a variety of critics examine performance traditions informing the play's creation, but there are also a number of the quasi-philosophical close readings of the text characteristic of the post-war era. David Kaula finds a religious quality in Troilus's imagery,[174] R.J. Kaufman talks of the play as 'Shakespeare's strangest contribution to [the] literature of preliminary devaluation'[175] comparable to the writings of Ibsen, Nietzsche, Conrad and the like. While the opposition of reason and passion has often been mentioned as central to the play, in Kaufman's view here 'Shakespeare questions most drivingly the existential sufficiency of reason as an ordering force'.[176]

Anne Barton's 1962 volume on the theatrical metaphor in Shakespearean drama, *Shakespeare and the Idea of the Play*, includes a short chapter on 'Dark Comedies and *Troilus*' that not only highlights the 'general darkening of plot and subject-matter characteristic of the "problem comedies" and the great tragedies',[177] but also emphasizes the significance of the theatrical imagery in *Troilus and Cressida*. She shows how the player metaphor has undergone a radical change when compared to earlier writings in Shakespeare's career, and here it is associated 'with hollow pretension, negation and pride', besides expressing 'part of that great theme of disorder so important in the play as a whole'.[178] Focusing on another aspect of the play's language, T. McAlindon and Mark Sacharoff conducted a lengthy debate in 1969 over several rhetorical features in the play. Their point of contention was whether, as McAlindon claims, these could qualify as errors in decorum, which even 'have a dramatic purpose, being used by Shakespeare to focus attention on the graver maladies that afflict the Greeks and Trojans',[179] or are simply neologisms, 'daring innovations (coinages, catachreses) or poetic ornamentation and extravagance somewhat beyond, but not different in kind from, the stylistic level of the great tragedies',[180] as Sacharoff maintains. Whichever may be true – and however the play's Shakespearean audiences perceived these linguistic elements, the discussion certainly testifies to the power of the play to invite debate and open ever more areas of research, which is possibly the clearest evidence of its merits.

After the enthusiastic research that characterized the post-war decades, the 1970s appear a period of dearth, and it is indeed the 1980s when fresh theoretical approaches will again succeed in encouraging new research concerning *Troilus* as well. As Johann Gregory's chapter on current critical debates illustrates, the continuity in scholarship is practically unbroken, as many of the questions that have been troubling readers and viewers since the first appearance of the play still provoke lively discussion, but from time to time, previously dormant trends gain momentum and energize the field. Feminist criticism comes into full bloom from the 1980s, although Cressida's character has already inspired countless earlier writings. R.A. Yoder in her 1972 article makes a renewed claim for a contemporary reading of the play, arguing that one can only truly appreciate it after 'cubism and atonality, . . . fascism and Freud',[181] but also disillusionment in social institutions and ruling classes, the Vietnam War and the countercultures of the flower generation create a context where the drama becomes easier to understand: 'There is no doubt, *Troilus and Cressida* gives back our own world.'[182] In fact, this is the only tentative conclusion that I feel entitled to draw at the end of this long but inevitably incomplete survey: *Troilus and Cressida* still defies simplifying or generalizing attempts, and in the same way as its plot feels unfinished, its conflict unresolved, and the play indeed belonging to a 'perpetual present',[183] it keeps inspiring its readers, and so the critical history goes on, not only until the present time, but into the unconfined infinite.

2

The Performance History

Francesca Rayner

Early modern performance

Theatricality is not only keenly present but also the subject of some suspicion in the early editions of *Troilus and Cressida*. In a second version of the 1609 Quarto, the prefatory note boasts of a play 'never staled with the stage, never clapper-clawed with the palms of the vulgar'.[1] It entreats its audience to 'refuse not, nor like this the less, for not being sullied, with the smoky breath of the multitude'.[2] These remarks distance the play from the physicality of public performance and appear to privilege a more select readership. As such, they reverse the priorities of the first 'state' of the 1609 Quarto which advertised the play as having been 'acted by the King's Majesty's servants at the Globe'.[3] These inconsistencies may be the result of appealing to different theatre audiences. Law students at the Inns of Court or audiences at the Court, for instance, might have responded positively to an accent on their exclusivity and their distinctiveness from audiences at public theatres like the Globe.[4] The inconsistencies might also suggest that performances of the play were politically controversial or unpopular with theatre audiences. In this sense, the second 'state' of the Quarto was attempting to find a new readership for the play which could compensate for its lack of success or too evident topicality in the public theatre. Despite such speculation, however, there is no evidence of a production of Shakespeare's *Troilus and Cressida* between the Stationer's Entry in 1602/3, which details the play as having been performed by the Lord Chamberlain's Men, and the twentieth century.[5]

The texts themselves are suffused with theatricality of different kinds and satirical comments on these performances. At the heart of the play is a parodic performance that is cast as a direct threat to Greek attempts to win the war. Rather than fight the Trojans, Achilles prefers to remain in his tent and applaud the pageants of Patroclus as he parodies the physical and verbal characteristics of the Greek generals. The *Oxford English Dictionary* defines 'pageant' at this time as '*fig.* Something empty or insubstantial; a delusion; a specious display or tribute'.[6] Yet the effects of such pageants in *Troilus and Cressida* are anything but insubstantial. Ulysses chastises Achilles for his interest in such 'imitation' which extends to the very top of the Greek command: 'Sometime, great Agamemnon, / Thy topless deputation he puts on, / And, like a strutting player, whose conceit/Lies in his hamstring, and doth think it rich / To hear the wooden dialogue and sound / 'Twixt his stretched footing and the scaffoldage, / Such to-be-pitied and o'erwrested seeming / He acts thy greatness in' (1.3.151–8). Through such comments, the actor playing Ulysses also parodies overacting on the early modern stage in an implied contrast between a lack of stagecraft in rival companies and the greater abilities of Shakespeare's men, or between the stage and the page. While Achilles maintains that it is his love for the Trojan Polyxena that prevents him going into battle, it is the concern that Achilles and Patroclus's imitative games might spread through the Greek camp that particularly concerns Ulysses. Emulation is a key word in *Troilus and Cressida* and its combination of male envy and rivalry seems at the beginning of the play to have paralyzed the Greek warriors rather than spurred them on to victory. As Ulysses points out, the camp is struck down by 'pale and bloodless emulation' (1.3.134). To counter this, Ulysses is not above participating in such pageants himself. The taunting of the vain and proud Ajax by the Greek generals is staged like the imitations the Greek generals apparently deplore, and in an attempt to provoke Achilles out of his lethargy the generals pass by Achilles' tent and pretend cattily to ignore him in yet another satirical pageant. Ulysses makes use of this snub to remind Achilles that heroic deeds are soon forgotten and encourages him to fight. Rather than eliminate theatricality, therefore, Ulysses uses it to his own advantage to encourage the Greeks towards more appropriately masculine military activity rather than a theatrical passivity associated with effeminacy.

If the pageant is a theatrical form associated with an emulous Greek masculinity, the return of the Trojans from battle resembles a military fashion parade. The warriors are surveyed by Cressida and Pandarus who comment on their physical attributes as they pass over the stage. The parade culminates in Pandarus's exaggerated praise of Troilus, emphasizing both how 'his sword is bloodied, and his helm more hacked than Hector's' and more generally 'how he looks and how he goes!' (1.2.224–6). Hecuba and Helen are also watching the parade, making this a form of male performance primarily for female consumption. If the Greek Achilles simply refuses to fight and prefers theatrical entertainments in his tent, there is a sense on the Trojan side that the warriors fight to appear more masculine in the eyes of the women who watch them. It is an appropriate form of theatricality for a royal house which elevates the value of keeping Helen over the loss of human life her rape has brought in its wake.[7]

When Cressida reaches the Greek camp, these two forms of theatricality collide. While she is used to a more mocking relationship with the Trojan men, such a strategy turns out to be disastrous in the Greek camp. She deals with the kisses she receives from the other Greek generals in the camp lightheartedly and explicitly teases Menelaus, but her encounter with Ulysses reveals the tension between these rival modes of performativity. Cressida entreats him to beg for a kiss and Ulysses refuses to engage in such a humiliating performance. Immediately afterwards, he produces a speech of utter contempt for Cressida and for women in general (4.5.55–64). The gesture and the speech illustrate how the performative liberties that Cressida has been used to in Troy are deliberately misunderstood in the patriarchal structure of the Greek camp where women are noticeable for their absence.

Restoration performance

During the Restoration, *Troilus and Cressida* was performed only in Dryden's adaptation *Troilus and Cressida, or Truth Found Too Late*, written for the Duke's Theatre, London, in 1679. Dryden was interested primarily in the stage possibilities of a sentimentalized, occasionally titillating, love plot rather than the vicissitudes of war, but he also tidied up these scenes so there was 'no leaping from Troy to the Grecian tents' as he found in Shakespeare's *Troilus and Cressida*.[8] A notable performative feature of the adaptation is the way it brings Shakespeare himself onstage. In a cameo appearance, Shakespeare's ghost appears in the play's Prologue in the person of the actor-manager Thomas Betterton. Dryden makes use of Shakespeare's ghost to castigate the playwrights of the period, whose plays are notable only for their 'dulness'.[9] Both Shakespeare and Dryden are cast as writers of quality drama in adverse circumstances where mediocrity is the norm, and the Prologue thus functions as a cue for Dryden to position himself as a Shakespearean successor. Dryden pretends humility to the Shakespearean play through the figure of Shakespeare's ghost: 'In this my [Shakespeare's] rough-drawn play, you shall behold / Some master-strokes, so manly and so bold / That he who meant to alter, found 'em such / He shook, and thought it sacrilege to touch'.[10] Yet the very existence of the adaptation belies this humility and positions Dryden judiciously within a Shakespearean lineage.

In the first performances of the play, Betterton played Shakespeare's ghost as well as Troilus. However, in the 1709 revival at Drury Lane, Betterton played Thersites. This suggests that even in Dryden's adaptation, the question of where to find a starring role for an actor in the play remained a problematic one. Betterton also seems to have had a hand in some of the changes introduced in the adaptation as Dryden acknowledged that his expansion of the scene between Troilus and Hector in 3.2 was 'hinted to me by Mr. Betterton'.[11] The expansion of the role of Andromache might similarly have been to make use of Mrs Betterton's stage talents for sentimentality as well as to reinforce Hector's heroism in deciding to go into battle despite the pleas of his wife. Somewhat surprisingly given the sentimentalist premise of the adaptation, Dryden kept Thersites and Pandarus, perhaps through a savvy awareness that both roles would be theatrical crowd pleasers. The Epilogue is spoken by Thersites rather than Pandarus and is an opportunity for Dryden to rail *à la* Thersites against undiscriminating audiences and inept playwrights. He suggests caustically that: 'Those Ophs [Oafs] shou'd be restraind, during their lives / From Pen and Ink, as Madmen are from knives',[12] once again reinforcing his own status as a dramatist with a better quality of writing for the stage. Dryden's adaptation underwent four more London revivals until 1734, suggesting that even with his major alterations, the stage popularity of the play might have been temporarily achieved but was by no means permanently assured.

Contemporary performance

1 Referencing war

Jeanne T. Newlin discussed preparations for a production by John Philip Kemble at the end of the eighteenth century in which Kemble was to play Ulysses. This nuanced notions of a 'darkened stage' with no productions of Shakespeare's *Troilus and Cressida* between the period of Shakespeare's lifetime and the twentieth century.[13] However, Kemble's project never reached the stage and *Troilus and Cressida* as a play for performance only came into its own in the twentieth century. This was largely as a result of its anti-heroic perspective on war in a century which saw two devastating world wars.[14]

In Britain, the approach of the First World War prompted one of the first significant twentieth-century productions. In 1912, William Poel staged the play at King's Hall in London and the production later travelled to Stratford in 1913. Poel's approach stressed the absurdity and bitterness of war and the kind of damaging compromises it forces on those caught up in war. His cutting of Ulysses' speech on order and degree (1.3) reinforced this anti-war perspective. As with Poel's other attempts to recreate the performance conditions of the Elizabethan theatre, the play was performed on a bare stage where onstage spectators in Elizabethan costume witnessed the action. The Greeks were dressed as Elizabethan soldiers while the Trojans were more sophisticated courtly figures. Poel himself played a cockney Pandarus and Thersites was played as an Elizabethan clown. In the Stratford performances, while the idea of the clown was maintained, Thersites was played by an actress (Elspeth Keith) rather than an actor. Women also played the smaller roles of Aeneas, Paris, Helenus and Alexander. Cressida (Edith Evans) was played as significantly older than Troilus and her accommodation to the Greeks in the Greek camp was presented as just one more unhappy compromise brought about by war. The play ended with Troilus kneeling in grief over Hector's body while Cassandra wailed and drums were heard in the distance.

The lead up to the Second World War saw Michael Macowan's 1938 London Mask Theatre Company modern dress production at the Westminster Theatre in London. It portrayed a 1930s social elite paying little attention to the realities of war, an approach that was eminently topical given that the play opened as Neville Chamberlain was appeasing the Nazis in Germany. The stylishly-dressed Trojans lounged on settees or drank at the bar, while a louche Pandarus (Max

Adrian) sang a Gershwin-inspired melody to Paris and Helen. In battle, however, the Trojans and Greeks dressed more soberly in khaki and pale blue uniforms. Ulysses (Robert Speaight) stood out among the Greeks as a diplomat in white tennis trousers while Thersites (Stephen Murray) was given a key role in the production as a left-wing journalist commenting sarcastically on events, who recognizes that this class will be incapable of reforming itself and avoiding the drift to war. The figure of Shakespeare's ghost was resurrected once more to deliver the Epilogue.

After the Second World War came a production informed by memories of this war but looking back to a previous one. Tyrone Guthrie's 1956 production at the Old Vic, which later toured to New York, took place during the year of the Suez events and the Hungarian Revolution. Nevertheless, Guthrie's production avoided contemporary parallels as well as attempts at Elizabethan authenticity by setting the play in the late Edwardian period, just before the First World War. Guthrie justified the relocation of the play by arguing that while it was impossible in the late 1950s to think of war as sport, in the period leading up to the First World War, this was a widely-held view within a male elite for whom it held out the promise of honour and status.[15] The atmosphere of war was present throughout, with military flags, drums and guns filling the stage. However, the characters seemed unconcerned with the war around them and more interested in maintaining the elegance and privileges of their class. Guthrie did not try to reconfigure Cressida's behaviour in the Greek camp but he did place her relationship with Diomedes in context in order to explain why Cressida chooses to seek his protection. Her actions were seen to be understandable considering the precarious situation in which she found herself. Nevertheless, most of the characters in the play were presented as objects of ridicule rather than compassion. As with Macowan's earlier production, the only exception was Thersites (Clifford Williams), a drunken war correspondent looking on scornfully at the events taking place and those responsible for them. He spent his time setting up his camera on a tripod and writing in his notebook as if wishing to capture the mood of the times. Guthrie's production was significant for the way in which it sought to find a meaningful performance setting for the play's dramatic wars that also enabled him to integrate an anti-war perspective into the production.

Jack Landau's 1961 *Troilus and Cressida* at Stratford, Connecticut, also set the Trojan wars in a different period, in this case the American Civil War in the year of its centennial. The Trojans were the Southern Forces while the Greeks were the Northerners and Priam and Agamemnon were made to look like Generals Robert E. Lee and Ulysses S. Grant respectively. Such relocation was not, however, without its critics. They focused on anachronisms such as the substitution of guns for swords as well as the highly romantic costumes and settings. Howard Taubman suggested that the performance setting was more reminiscent of contemporary cinematic culture than Shakespeare. He complained that: '[w]hen the shooting begins, when cannon are deployed and rifles pop, when soldiers roar across the stage giving off Rebel yells, the production achieves a noisy silliness worthy of Westerns, but not of Shakespeare.'[16]

Nevertheless, relocations of the war continued to mark subsequent productions in order to increase the topicality of the play for audiences. Adrian Hall's 1971 production for the Providence Trinity Square Repertory Company pointed to parallels with the ongoing Vietnam war, with the front end of a destroyed military truck sticking up from the stage floor and camouflage netting hung over the audience. Yet, the production's aesthetics were more eclectic than this contemporary setting suggested. The production began with a dumb show of Paris with Hera, Athena and Aphrodite in drag, presented as an overseas servicemen's show with Pandarus as MC. At the end of the production, Hector sat on the stage stripped to the waist while the Myrmidons threw sponges covered in blood at him over the heads of the audience. Such eclecticism illustrates some of the difficulties in updating the play's wars to a more contemporary context where notions of warfare and honour are markedly different from the early modern or classical periods.

After a long period of uneasy peace, attention has focused once more on finding topical parallels with contemporary wars in the twenty-first century. Rob Melrose's 2012 production for the Oregon Shakespeare Festival located the play within contemporary conflicts in the Middle East. The production was part of a season which also staged *Henry V* and *Romeo and Juliet* and provided a contrast with the problematic heroism of the former and the more straightforward presentation of love and desire in the latter. Melrose chose to set his *Troilus and Cressida* in a Middle-Eastern country that brought to mind contemporary Baghdad after the 2003 invasion by US forces. The events were staged against a sweeping panorama of sand with the ruins of Babylon and Assyria set alongside contemporary architecture. Melrose wanted to reference a war that audiences would instantly recognize and that remained a divisive issue at the moment it was being performed. He also felt that such an immediately recognizable context would bring out the satirical and political humour of the play. The Greeks wore camouflage like US Special Forces. The Trojans were a royal family from a contemporary Middle-Eastern country, while Cressida (Tala Ashe) was a wealthy member of that family whose wit and sexuality left her caught uneasily between Western and Eastern notions of appropriate behaviour for women (Figure 1). When the troops were not fighting, Achilles (Peter Macon) bought drugs from Thersites (Michael Elich) who was outfitted like a private contractor, while Helen (Brooke Parks) partied with Paris in the Trojan's pool. The production stressed the idea that war corrupts everything around it and that this inevitably inflects the experience of the lovers.

Melissa Hillman's 2013 production at La Val's Subterranean in Berkeley, California, was part of a San Francisco Festival that produced thirty-six new plays about the Trojan War. The modern-dress costumes featured fatigue uniforms, bullet-proof vests and military boots with two types of camouflage that

FIGURE 1 *Tala Ashe (Cressida) and Bernard White (Calchas) in the 2012 Oregon Shakespeare Festival's* Troilus and Cressida, *directed by Rob Melrose. Photo by Jenny Graham. Courtesy of the Oregon Shakespeare Festival.*

distinguished Greeks from Trojans and reminded audiences once more of contemporary wars in Iraq and Afghanistan. Sounds of gunfire, graphic fight choreography and stark lighting all reinforced the sense of a violent war fought against an unforgiving landscape. The Greeks were portrayed as vicious and unsympathetic and the hooded Myrmidons were ninjas in black gowns who murdered Hector (Carl Holvick-Thomas) with their knives. The role of the Trojan Antenor, who is traded for Cressida in the play, was played by the director's son (Jonah McClellan). He recited the Prologue as a cellphone selfie video and reappeared throughout the production, reminding audiences of the consequences of foreign wars from Homer's *Iliad* right up to contemporary wars in the Middle East. The play ended with a silent tableau focused around this minor, voiceless character in the play to emphasize the collateral damage of war on those not directly involved in the fighting.

2 Homosexuality and sexual liberation

Troilus and Cressida in post-Second World War Britain is intimately connected with the name of John Barton. Barton directed three productions of the play at Stratford in 1960, 1968 and 1976; the first in collaboration with Peter Hall and the last in collaboration with Barry Kyle. Although part of a season of comedies, the 1960 production took place in the context of the sexual revolution and political humiliation around the Suez events, and reflected this atmosphere of social and political change. The production was notable for its ability to translate the play into concrete theatrical images that made the language of the text clear for the audience. The central image was an octagonal sand pit that worked to deconstruct the play's lofty discourses on honour. When Hector (Derek Godfrey) was murdered, for instance, his body was dragged through the pit in an avowedly anti-heroic gesture. Behind the sand pit, there was a large blood-red curtain. The battle scenes took place in smoke, an effect which made the Greeks and Trojans seem trapped in a cloud. The production included Eric Porter as a wily Ulysses and a highly sexual Dorothy Tutin as Cressida. Pandarus was played by Max Adrian, who had played the same role in the 1938 Macowan production. His much older Pandarus here moved from an eagerness to bring the lovers together at the beginning of the play to disgust with the consequences at the end.

While its clarity made this production the most artistically successful of the trilogy, it is the 1968 production which is most often remembered as a frontal assault on the conventional notions of honour, truth and love which the play itself interrogates. It was staged one month before homosexuality was decriminalized and during the same year as revolutions in Paris and Prague and mass protests against the war in Vietnam. The action unfolded on a bare stage with a black background. Against this background, Barton anticipated decriminalization by presenting the Greeks and Trojans almost naked onstage, emphasizing the ways in which the Trojan War constitutes an erotic experience and love becomes a battleground. Reinforcing the emphasis on male sexuality in comic form, Thersites (Norman Rodway) wore a phallic codpiece, with a grinning mouth from which a tongue/penis could be extracted. Achilles (Alan Howard) was played as overtly homosexual and keenly sinister. At one stage he wore a blond wig and glittery nightdress pretending to be Helen. On meeting Hector, he opened his nightdress and taunted him with his body. For Stephen Orgel, looking back on the production in 2006,

> It was certainly the most beautiful *Troilus and Cressida* I have ever seen, and it assumed that the norm of beauty was male – indeed, the role of Helen, the most beautiful woman in history, was cut. It also assumed, for the men in the audience, a degree of universal homosexual desire, and it is difficult to imagine that this was not the source of much of the critical outrage it generated. If you admitted that you liked it, what were you admitting?[17]

Helen Mirren as Cressida had a nude scene to complement the focus on male nudity in the production. However, while the near-nakedness of the men signified a daring evocation of male homosexuality within a distancing classical framework, Cressida's nudity tended to reinforce her vulnerability and isolation. As Carol Chillington Rutter has pointed out, Barton, like many directors of the play, ran 4.2 into 4.4 and cut 4.3.[18] The cutting of this scene removes the twelve lines that enable Cressida to change clothes before reaching the Greek camp. As a result, she arrives in more revealing night attire, reinforcing the tendency to sexualize the role rather than question the framework in which Cressida's sexuality is presented in the play.

In Barton's 1976 production, Francesca Annis as Cressida became a scantily-dressed Greek courtesan at the moment of her arrival in the Greek camp, once more rendering the actress vulnerable to Ulysses' scornful assessment of her sexual availability. When she left with Diomedes, she revealed a courtesan's mask on the back of her head as if to hammer home the point. Unlike the clarity of the 1960 production, this production lacked a larger organizing focus. The stage images were reminiscent of Barton's earlier productions but added little to them beyond a greater concern with the play's ambiguities. The sexual radicalism of the 1968 production was also less radical in 1976. Thersites (John Nettles) once more wore a mouth-shaped codpiece with a dangling red tongue/ penis. Paris led Helen by a golden chain around her throat in a somewhat empty performance gesture and she also appeared as a life-sized doll in the Greek camp at various moments of the play. She was finally taken up by Diomedes who carried her to Calchas's tent to watch his seduction of Cressida.

In 2006, Peter Stein directed a production for the Royal Shakespeare Company and the Edinburgh International Festival that was an explicit homage to Barton's 1968 production. However, while near-naked actors onstage had been radical in the 1968 production, they were no longer so in 2006. For Paul Prescott, such decisions were emblematic of the production opting for caricature over clarity in setting and characterization. Yet Prescott praised David Yelland's Ulysses for his authoritative verse-speaking and noted some original touches in the production. These included the scene between Cressida (Annabel Scholey) and Diomedes (Richard Wills-Cotton) where Thersites (Ian Hughes), Troilus (Henry Pettigrew) and Ulysses were placed above the audience in the theatre, making them voyeurs on the action taking place below. Less innovative was the addition of a plea for forgiveness by Cressida followed by Troilus's rejection and death at the hands of the Myrmidons. As Prescott notes: '[i]t is not uncommon for Cressida to be bought on as a mute presence haunting Troilus's final seconds of stage time, but here her vocal request for forgiveness pushed the production toward a sentimental finality alien to the letter and the spirit of the original.'[19]

3 The influence of Jan Kott in Europe

Luchino Visconti's lavish 1949 production in Italy and Roger Planchon's innovative 1964 French production illustrated the concern with finding an effective stage setting and a modern-sounding translation for the play in post-Second World War European productions. The Polish critic Jan Kott's reading of *Troilus and Cressida* in *Shakespeare our Contemporary* as an 'amazing and modern' tragicomedy informed by the cruelty of the grotesque has also had a major influence on European post-war productions.[20] His understanding of Thersites as a wise and bitter fool amongst buffoons and clowns lacking self-knowledge has been particularly influential as has his sense of Cressida as a woman who is contemporary because she 'defends herself with irony' until she 'realizes the world is too vile and cruel for anything to be worth defending'.[21]

In 1972, the Romanian director David Esrig staged *Troilus and Cressida* at the Munich Bayerisches Staatsschauspiel Residenztheater in Germany. Esrig was invited to Germany after the success of his 1965–6 Bucharest revival of the play in a translation by Florian Nicolau which had also played in Paris. This earlier production had strongly farcical overtones and included cabaret elements, while the characters moved around the stage in animal-like movements. The German production commissioned a new translation of the play to complement the director's radical approach. The tone of this later production was primarily parodic and incorporated clowning, circus techniques and gymnastics. As such, it emphasized the grotesque rather than the tragic features of the play. Esrig later recreated *Troilus and Cressida* at Israel's Habima national theatre in 1979, the play's first performance in Hebrew. According to Avraham Oz, it was a 'rough and cynical' production of the play which centred on Thersites (Shlomo Bar-Shavit) as the wise fool.[22] Esrig divided the performance space into several distinct areas. In between them, models of the Trojan walls, Pandarus' house and the lovers' bed floated, while Priam (Shime'on Finkel) rose from a hidden trapdoor on his throne for the Trojan council in 2.2. The production referenced contemporary East–West relations with the Greeks in Cossack furs and the Trojans in clown-like clothes and hats. However, as Oz points out, the possibility of referencing a conflict closer to home in the Middle East was thus lost. It was a predominantly comic production and, in its preference for the grotesque, it downplayed the more sinister aspects of the play. Achilles (Karol Markowitz), for instance, was a giant fool accompanied by a diminutive Patroclus (Ezra Dagan), while Achilles shouted his final lines over Hector's corpse surrounded by childlike Myrmidons.

In 1977, the British director Terry Hands directed a production of *Troilus and Cressida* for the Vienna Burgtheater in a new translation by the theatre's dramaturg Rudolf Weys. Hands was interested in Jan Kott's sarcastic approach to the play where heroes are made to appear ridiculous in order to stress an anti-war perspective on the play. The emphasis here was on language rather than spectacle, although visual elements were also memorable. At the back of a black stage, for instance, there was a golden tree-of-life symbol which turned red during the battle scenes. The Trojans wore elegant, fur-trimmed leather costumes decorated with gold jewellery while the Greeks wore simple black costumes as if to suggest a greater sense of purpose. According to Wolfgang Riehle, Hands stressed the characters' self-destructiveness but balanced this with a focus on the role of art as a counterpoint to this destruction.[23] The early modern armour, for instance, was decorative and richly ornamented and the battle scenes were characterized by a high degree of stylization. Of the cast, Riehle singled out Andrea Jonasson in particular for the way in which she conveyed Cressida's various registers in her performance.[24]

This European experience influenced Hands' return to the play in 1981 when he directed the play for the RSC in a production characterized by satire and rough irony. Hands aimed for a clear and non-prescriptive approach to the play, although the way in which the warriors on both sides were made into buffoons and the women were all whores encouraged a cynical interpretation of the play. The action took place against carpeted black walls and barbed-wire surrounds and Pandarus ended the production impaled unhappily on the barbed wire. The cushioned halls of Troy contrasted with the desolate, littered plain of the Greeks but both sides seemed to have arrived at a state of exhaustion after the protracted war. David Suchet's Achilles dressed in a red skirt with rouged nipples to coax Hector into his tent, yet at other moments he could exude a concentrated ferocity. Joe Melia was a surprisingly likeable Thersites with a light, sardonic touch who also spoke the Prologue. Carol Royle's Cressida was sexually-aware and mocking while Helen (Barbara Kinghorn) was groped sexually by a group of men which also included Paris. Hands's satirical approach to love and war influenced approaches to the play in the 1980s and early 1990s in Britain as Barton had done in the 1960s and 1970s but his more European sense of stage spectacle was less often influential.

At the beginning of the 1990s, Jerzy Limon and Wladyslaw Zawistowski produced a modern, refreshing translation of the play for the Polish Teatr Wybrzeze production in Gdansk directed by Krzysztof Babicki. Anna Maria Rachel's stage design made use of the whole of the theatre. At the back of the stage were two railway freight cars. From time to time, the doors opened to reveal parts of the action inside the carriages. Sometimes the carriages were removed altogether to reveal an oasis of green behind glass. A naked Patroclus (Miroslaw Krawczyk) massaged Achilles' (Jerzy Gorzko) muscles in this space and the lovers' sexual encounter was also staged here. In front of the cars, the stage itself was empty and the audience was separated from the stage by a narrow platform from which wooden steps rose to a balcony.

Before the play began, Cassandra (Dorota Kolak) knelt in the audience space and gazed into a glass pyramid containing a coiled snake. From the balcony opposite, Pandarus (Stanislaw Michalski) limped down the stairs towards her and the two left the stage. At this moment, music broke the silence and the curtain rose, carrying Troilus (Jacek Mikolajczak) with it. He dropped onto the stage shouting Cressida's name, the first word of the play heard by the audience. The rest of the action proceeded, according to Andrej Zurovski, 'in sudden leaps, in massive condensations of the action, spasms'.[25] The Trojans were a group of velvet-clad musicians who were more interested in making music than fighting. The Greeks were brutish soldiers in high boots and brightly-coloured leather jackets. Nestor (Henryk Sakewicz) was pushed around the stage in an invalid chair with a bedpan underneath while Achilles and Patroclus wore white to reinforce their distance from the battle. Jerzy Lapinski's Thersites was a twisted figure dressed in army breeches and a smoking jacket. He was the archetypal wise fool out of both inclination and necessity, railing against a world reduced to physical needs and his cynicism about a world in decay was central to a production caught between laughter and horror. A bored Paris (Kryzysztof Gordon), for example, slept in a chair and told Helen (Joanna Bogacka) he loved her with a yawn.

Against this atmosphere of casual cynicism, Joanna Kreft-Baka as Cressida gave a nuanced performance as a child beginning to awaken to adult feelings and desires. After their sexual encounter, the two lovers tenderly washed each other under the onstage showers to the sound of soft music. However, when Cressida reached the Greek camp, she became aware of the new significance of her sexuality and her precarious position in the camp. Her scene with Diomedes (Krzysztof Matuszewski) suggested she was the new Helen as she lay on the ground with her legs open before him. In a stunning end to the production, Aeneas (Jerzy Nowacki) stood between the railway carriages on a large pile of tyres. Both he and Troilus used shovels to build a funeral pyre from the tyres. Pandarus came down the steps, cursed the world's corruption and fell dead on the ruins of Troy. High above, Troilus stood on the funeral pyre as the lights faded. The ending suggested, for Zurowski, an 'epitaph for a dead age', with a trumpet sounding gloomily in the darkness, echoing the death of the Communist regime and the transition to a capitalist economy.[26]

4 Gender and performance

In the North American context, it was Joseph Papp's darkly comic 1965 production in New York that best caught the mood of the contemporary culture and that set the stage for a reassessment of the role of Cressida. Thersites (Joseph Bova) was at the centre of the performances and his caustic perspective on events dominated the production, yet Papp also reversed the conventional hierarchy between Troilus as the true idealist and Cressida as the epitome of falseness. In keeping with his view of Cressida as the victim in the relationship, Papp directed the scene where Cressida (Flora Elkins) is kissed by the Greeks as a sexual assault and this view of Cressida as the victim of the men around her became more pronounced in later productions that sought to recast the role in explicitly feminist terms.

After the Barton trilogy in the 1960s, a kind of macho homosexuality had become the norm in Britain and an equation between sexual liberation and nudity for the female characters had gone unchallenged. In the 1980s, however, actresses influenced by the women's liberation movement began to question the terms in which Cressida was presented onstage. The seminal feminist performance of the role was Juliet Stevenson's sympathetic portrayal of Cressida in Howard Davies's 1985 production of the play at Stratford. Stevenson rejected Davies's notion of a performance focused on the three-way relationship between Troilus (Anton Lesser), Cressida and Pandarus (Clive Merrison) and attempted to create a more independent, self-aware Cressida. Davies had updated the play to the Crimean War where the action took place in a battered mansion. However, despite the Victorian setting and costume design, Davies had Stevenson arrive in the Greek camp in her nightdress. Stevenson countered her physical vulnerability with a highly effective put down later in this scene where she snapped her fingers and ordered Ulysses (Peter Jeffrey) to kneel. However, for her scene with Diomedes (Bruce Alexander), the need to sexualize Cressida once again played against Stevenson's understanding of the role. As Carol Chillington Rutter has noted, she 'entered looking like a blowsy Carmen, hair down and bunched to dangle over one ear, peasant blouse lowered off her shoulders', and she ended the play emotionally damaged by her experiences with men.[27] The degree of difference that separated Davies and Stevenson's views of the role revealed the pressures that feminist debates within the RSC were putting on productions where male directors continued to sexualize and/or demonize Cressida.

In the 1990s, questions of gender continued to mould British productions of the play. In Sam Mendes' bleak but carefully-staged 1990 RSC production, Simon Russell Beale's outstanding performance as Thersites deconstructed Barton's heroic masculinity through self-parody. His limping, hunchbacked Thersites was a member of the elite who, through his railing and through disease, had been brought to a state of abjection. His dirty old man's raincoat with its Campaign for Nuclear Disarmament and Gay Liberation badges and leather skull cap tied under his chin reinforced this downward spiral. Nevertheless, he took evident verbal pleasure in taunting the Greeks, using perfect comic timing to suggest an imaginative quest for exactly the right insult at any particular moment. Patroclus (Paterson Joseph) at one stage even pageanted Thersites, but he responded in kind with his own superb imitation of Agamemnon (Sylvester Morand). In a multifaceted stage image, Pandarus (Norman Rodway) and Cressida (Amanda Root) paddled together in a pool of shallow water while Paris (John Warnaby) used the water as a mirror. The pool later took on more military overtones as Hector cleaned his sword in it after battle. The versatility of the characters' interactions with the water emphasized the ways in which each character viewed events from their own, often conflicting perspectives. A giant stone-coloured Grecian mask looked down on the action from behind brick walls and bars which pointed to the eventual petrification of even Helen's beauty. The audience were seated on three sides of the smaller Swan theatre, which made Benedict Nightingale comment that the theatre seemed like 'a theatrical debating chamber',[28] and the onstage organization of the debates among the Greeks and the Trojans seemed to explicitly invite reflection from the audience. They suggested a production designed to provoke reflection both on contemporary masculinities and on war.

A New Zealand Drama School production, directed by Annie Ruth and Rangimoana Taylor, was staged at the Te Whaea Theatre, Wellington, Aotearoa/New Zealand in 2003 and linked feminist perspectives on the play with national concerns about bi-culturalism. It relocated the action to the time of the Land Wars (from the 1840s to the 1880s). The Trojans were dark-skinned Maori and the Greeks were the colonizing white Europeans against whom the various Maori tribes united. The politics of bi-culturalism and gender intersected productively on several occasions, emphasizing, for instance, the fact that the white-skinned Helen (Jean Copland) was seen as worth fighting over while the dark-skinned Cressida (Rashmi Pilapitiya) was not. Yet the fact that a Samoan student played Troilus (Louis Sutherland) and a Sri Lankan student played Cressida indicated the production's interest in representing a contemporary society that was not simply bi-cultural but increasingly multicultural.

Women were cast as commanders of both nations, playing Agamemnon (Jodie Hyland), Nestor (Jean Copland), Ulysses (Tahi Mapp-Boren), Priam (Noa Campbell), Calchas (Noa Campbell) and Aeneas (Erina Daniels). Queen Priam and Agamemnon were played as women while others, such as Ulysses, were played as men. Agamemnon was reimagined as a Queen Victoria figure in a satirical portrait of colonial British culture. Yet while regendering on the British/Greek side was essentially parodic, the casting of women as male generals on the Maori/Trojan side challenged the reservation for male Maori elders of the prerogative of public action as women do not have speaking rights in the *marae* (meeting place) to discuss public affairs. The production was mainly in English but used Maori for occasions when a character was supposed not to overhear or to understand what other characters were saying. However, the production stressed the predominance of border crossings between the two camps. This was illustrated first by Helen and Calchas, then by Aeneas' entering the Greek camp with Hector's challenge and Diomedes entering Troy to collect Cressida. Cressida was the next character to cross from the

Trojans to the Greeks before Hector did so to fight Ajax. The production highlighted such border crossings in order to illustrate the futility of a war premised on absolute divisions of race or nation and to point instead to the many instances of cultural mobility across national and ethnic borders in contemporary Aotearoa/New Zealand.

The 2008 Cheek by Jowl production of the play also cast women as central to the production and in the process deconstructed male pride and vanity. Helen (Marianne Oldham) spoke the Prologue surrounded by the evidence of the war and then reappeared throughout the play, enabling the audience to measure the seriousness of war with the somewhat futile character who had given rise to it. Paparazzi followed her and Paris (Oliver Coleman) continually taking photographs. Thersites (Richard Cant) first appeared in drag as a cleaning lady, making sense of Ajax's reference to him as 'Mistress Thersites' (2.1.34) and then returned to entertain the troops in a drag performance. The production highlighted the idealization of men's and women's bodies, particularly the contradictory pull of admiration and envy between men that lies behind notions of military heroism. It illustrated the ways in which self-deception blinds characters to the realities of both love and war by overlapping scenes from the war and love plots. The war here was easy to get into but more difficult to end, like the contemporary wars in Iraq and Afghanistan. The characters wore modern dress and the Myrmidons appeared at the end with sinister gas masks covering their faces that suggested something of the facelessness of modern warfare. However, the battles were fought with swords and shields rather than modern weapons.

In 2016, Carolyn Howarth directed a lively and engaging production for the Colorado Shakespeare Festival which picked up on the play's contrast between long periods of languid inactivity and moments of frenetic activity. It also emphasized common themes in the love and war plots, particularly the promises made and broken, the tarnishing of honour and the ways in which reputation functions as little more than a justification for the killing. Caitlin Ayer's set communicated this deconstructive approach effectively. Above the great gate of Troy, instead of the legendary 'topless towers of Ilium', were towerless tops; worn and rusty peaks of metal that were torn off halfway down, with no supporting foundation.[29] Moreover, the Epilogue was cut from this production so that the play would end with the visual image of Hector hanging from the set's columns in the open-air theatre (Figure 2). Women played a more active role in this production as they were doing in contemporary wars elsewhere. They played the roles of Agamemnon (Kelsey Didion), Aeneas (Lilli Hokama) and Ulysses (Mare Trevathan) as well as the roles that were conventionally gendered female. Andromache's (Paige Olson) plea to Hector (Stephen Cole Hughes) not to fight was given extra poignancy by her pregnancy, while Helen

FIGURE 2 *Troilus (Christopher Joel Onken) stands downstage with sword raised while Achilles (Geoffrey Kent) looks up at a suspended Hector (Steven Cole Hughes) in the 2016 Colorado Shakespeare Festival's* Troilus and Cressida *directed by Carolyn Howarth. Photo by Jennifer M Koskinen. Courtesy of the Colorado Shakespeare Festival.*

(Lindsey Kyler) delivered the Prologue. As for Cressida (Carolyn Holding), the production emphasized the fact that her knowledge of sex and relationships had been gained from her adolescent experiences of war, which made her deeply sceptical about claims of faithfulness. She was controlled and calculating whereas Troilus (Christopher Joel Onken) was played as naïve and immature. Nevertheless, in her scenes with Diomedes (Benaiah Anderson), each time he attempted to leave, a roar emerged from the drunken Greeks that frightened Cressida into calling him back, making sense of her repeated entreaties in the text for him to return.

5 Postmodern eclecticism

David Bevington has referred to *Troilus and Cressida* as 'a perfect vehicle for postmodern angst',[30] and Matt Trueman has argued that the very different registers of the play invite a stylistically eclectic approach in performance: '[t]he tone changes from page to page. It's very modern in that way: collagey and kaleidoscopic. The challenge is not to try and iron that out into one consistent tone, but to try and respond to the play as it shifts.'[31] In several national contexts, there were moves towards such eclecticism during the late 1980s and 1990s, although experiments with developing a postmodern aesthetic for *Troilus and Cressida* have often been greeted with critical derision for not providing a unified interpretation of the Shakespearean text in performance.

Dieter Dorn's excitingly contemporary 1986 Munich production privileged what Dennis Kennedy has referred to as 'mild visual alienations' in order to engage the critical involvement of audiences in the events of the play.[32] The abstract scenography by Jürgen Rose did not suggest a particular place or time. The sides of the stage were differently-coloured cloths and a paper door at the back served for exits and entrances. On the floor, there were flat, raised segments in an irregular pattern. Costumes also did not indicate any particular place or period. The warriors wore battle trousers with bare trunks and tunics. Pandarus and Cressida were dressed in robes with ethnic patterns. This impression of 'vital eclecticism' was reinforced by the Kabuki-style entrances of the actors and sought to convey theatrically the director's interest in the ambivalence of the play's treatment of the themes of love and honour.[33] The production also countered notions that stylistic eclecticism in performance does not lead to a coherent interpretation of the play. Kennedy, for instance, described the play as conveying 'something archaic and passionate, of eruptive ferocity barely restrained, of a primitive culture in its harsh exoticism'.[34]

Stefan Bachmann's playful and postmodern 1998 *Troilus and Cressida* for Theater Basel combined elements of elite and popular culture in a production that resisted humorously the play's grand narratives of love and honour. Agamemnon reminded audiences of Helmut Kohl, while parts of the text were performed in the type of colloquial English spoken outside the theatre by young people. The action took place on a temporary wooden stage in the theatre's lobby to emphasize the temporary nature of the Greek presence outside Troy, while the military outfits had plastic breastplates with the logos hanging out and combined these costumes with jeans and American sportswear. Each scene was engaging and entertaining in its own right rather than part of an overarching narrative. After battle, for example, the Trojans showered together in a parody of male bonding using a shower gel that turned out to be their enemies' blood. Two musicians played an intriguing mixture of Swiss folk music with Tibetan sounds and Australian didgeridoo. Towards the end, Achilles offered Hector a cigarette during the battle before slitting his throat and licking the blood off the knife. As the new millennium approached, this 'vigorous and ironic' production emphasized the growing gap between generations and between elite and popular culture.[35]

A similarly eclectic approach was taken by the British director Mark Wing-Davey's 1995 New York Shakespeare Festival production at the Delacorte Theatre, which walked a fine line between complicity and critique in its treatment of contemporary consumer and media culture. Costumes combined soldiers in camouflage with Greek togas, Japanese kimonos and medieval armour. Cassandra (Catherine Kellner) vacuumed continuously while she prophesied doom. Achilles (Paul Calderon) was a drug-dealer during his time away from battle and Helen appeared throughout on a giant poster. Troilus (Neal Huff) spied on Cressida via a laptop and Ulysses (Stephen Skybell) gave his speech on order and degree to bored Greeks who channel surfed while he spoke. Cinematic representations of past wars were present in the form of clips from *Apocalypse Now* (1979) and *Platoon* (1986). Thersites' (Tim Blake Nelson) obscenities were brought up-to-date to stress his deconstructive take on the events while Pandarus (Stephen Spinella) wore a dildo that responded physically to textual references to dying and groaning. Amid all this stage business, a motorized peacock strutted around the stage in a parody of displays of male vanity.

In the new millennium, Romanian director Silviu Purcarete's postmodern 2005 production for the Katona József Theatre in Hungary had a double row of sinks separating Greeks and Trojans with bunkbeds on each side of the stage.[36] While the sinks enabled the Greeks to undertake everyday domestic tasks such as shaving, washing or brushing their teeth as they debated the war, they also functioned as a front line between the two camps which highlighted the various border crossings in the play. Antenor jumped over the sinks as a dare, was immediately caught, tied to the leg of a bed and hooded like an Abu Ghraib prisoner. Cressida was quite literally handed over the sinks to the Greeks and Thersites attempted unsuccessfully to escape them by climbing over to the Trojan side. Later in the play, the rows of sinks were turned sideways for the battle scenes and the prevailing images of water in the first part of the play were replaced by blood.

The ambitious 2012 RSC and Wooster Group *Troilus and Cressida*, directed by Mark Ravenhill and Elizabeth LeCompte, was almost universally panned by the London theatre critics for the way in which postmodern and naturalistic conventions were combined in the same performance. Paul Taylor in the *Independent*, for instance, called it 'a mass of alienation effects in search of a play'.[37] Some theatre academics, however, were more welcoming of the production's experimentalism. Kara Reilly called it 'a productive friction of postcolonial intertertextuality',[38] while Benjamin Fowler found that it made him 'listen to Shakespeare anew,[39] and Thomas Cartelli suggested that the production posed the fundamental question 'what is a Shakespeare performance a performance of?'[40]

The two companies rehearsed separately. The RSC actors, who played the Greeks, appeared onstage as twenty-first century British troops while the Wooster Group as the Trojans appeared as Native Americans. Kate Valk of the Wooster Group explained that when first reading the Shakespeare play, it felt like a second language for her.[41] The idea of the Native American parallel as a metaphor for this lack of understanding of Shakespearean language resulted from this insight. The RSC sections of the production included an Australian Diomedes and a multicultural cast to complement the Wooster Group's foregrounding of the importance of colonialism in shaping national identity. However, for the London critics and many audience members, the actors seemed to be playing by separate rules. Emphasizing this distinction, a steel wall at the back of the set divided the scenes. The wall was mostly hidden by the wigwam and other onstage objects in the Trojan scenes, while it revolved for the Greek scenes to reveal a minimalist military setting. A steel bed on wheels functioned as Achilles' 'pressed bed' (1.3.162) and later as a military stretcher. For the battle scenes, the wall was projected down the centre of the stage with soldiers and medical staff rushing in and out on either side.

In the RSC sections, Ravenhill queered notions of heroic Greek masculinity. As Thomas Cartelli has suggested, this part of the production was 'queer to the hilt, cynical to a fault, and faultlessly spoken'.[42] The actors playing the Greeks changed in and out of desert combat fatigues and long dresses. Patroclus (Clifford Samuel) wore gold high heels and a matching headscarf while Achilles (Joe Dixon) wore a white towel round his waist as if his tent were a gay sauna. Both he and Patroclus stayed onstage as an asthmatic Ulysses (Scott Handy) gave his degree speech. While queering Achilles has become a standard feature of British performances since Barton, Achilles' grief at losing Patroclus was played here with the same intensity of feeling as that of Troilus losing Cressida. By contrast, Ajax wore a wrestler's outfit complete with Superman cape and exaggerated Styrofoam muscles and struck comic body-building poses throughout the performance. Zubin Varla's Thersites delivered his routines in drag from a wheelchair, reminding audiences of the suffering and bitterness of wounded war veterans. At the end of the play, he climbed out of the wheelchair, undressed and left the Greeks to their own devices. However, this apparently serious focus on twenty-first-century warfare was deconstructed by the weapons used onstage, which included umbrellas, lacrosse sticks, cricket bats and dreamcatchers.

The Trojans had bare chests and feet and wore richly ornamented leggings. The long, dark hair of the men was loosely bound in bandannas, while Cressida and Andromache wore their hair in plaits. They combined the Native American markings on the front of the male actors' bodies with Styrofoam body armour sculpted into Grecian heads and torsos worn from the top of the skull down their backs to create hybrid Greco-Indian warriors. As such, they embodied two foundational national narratives; one dramatic and one performative, one European and the other North American. Smoke rose from an onstage tepee with the aid of a video projection and the Trojan officers assembled in a pow-wow around the campfire. Four small screens at each corner of the stage played clips from a diverse selection of films, including *Atanarjuat, or the Fast Runner* (2001), a film directed by Zacharias Kunuk that retells a thousand-year-old Inuit story, Elia Kazan's gritty 1961 teenage drama *Splendor in the Grass*, and Chris Eyre's *Smoke Signals*, a 1998 film written, directed and acted by members of the contemporary Native American community. The fact that these monitors were blank during the RSC exchanges illustrated a discrepancy between the Wooster's highly visible use of technology and the hidden technical support systems behind the RSC performance.

For this production, the Wooster Group altered its established practice of mashing-up canonical and non-canonical 'texts' in favour of performing the Shakespearean text in flat Northwestern Indian accents and took their cues not from the text they were performing but from footage of the films on the monitors. They seemed to be challenging the audience to do the work of interpretation by themselves instead of relying on the director and actors to do this, or on notions of a transparent meaning in the text which it was the duty of the performance to reveal. This approach, however, contradicted the more obviously interpretative approach of the RSC. Moreover, the Wooster Group's intertexts challenged the values of the Shakespearean play. *Atanarjuat*'s narrative of forgiveness and an end to the killing functioned as a counternarrative to the European myth of the Trojan War, while *Splendor in the Grass* opposed the moralism directed at Cressida with an understanding of the social reasons for female resignation in the Kazan film.

Despite the attempts of theatre academics to explain the choices made by the Wooster Group, the virulence of the criticism directed at the production tended to make the Wooster Group rather than the RSC responsible for the production's supposed disjointedness and many English audience members left the production in the interval. There was less focus on the more productive ways in which the two companies found points of contact between their different performance traditions. The RSC used ritualized movement and choral delivery to echo the ritualistic movements and delivery of the Wooster Group, for example, while Zubin Varla's Thersites spoke most of his speeches into a microphone, creating a parallel with the Wooster Group's externally-focused, technologically-informed delivery of language. However, the production overall tended to illustrate the chasm separating the two performance traditions rather than their possible intersections.

6 A play for global audiences

In the new millennium, a concern with global as well as local and national audiences has characterized productions of the play. In 2009, Matthew Dunster directed a predominantly comic performance for the internationally-focused Globe Theatre. The production was based on an original pronunciation workshop performance of the play in 2005 and something of this earlier experience remained in the diversity of accents within the cast. It stressed the plight of two lovers caught up in a war which necessarily rendered their love precarious and Pandarus's (Matthew Kelly) Epilogue seemed to suggest that he had also been driven mad by what had happened to the two lovers he had struggled so hard to bring together. Cressida (Laura Pyper) was played as a young, impulsive, garrulous woman who gets carried away by her emotions but is also aware of how her impulsiveness might be misconstrued by Troilus (Paul Stocker) and other men. After arriving in the Greek camp, the generals circled her menacingly and forced their kisses on her. Ulysses' (Jamie Ballard) speech on her sexual availability was cut substantially but it was spoken with such vehemence that Diomedes' (Jay Taylor) protection appeared to be a necessity for Cressida. Intriguingly, the actress left the question of whether she acts on an attraction to Diomedes or simply seeks his protection open, refusing to make Cressida's sexuality a 'problem' for the play. However, the audience was encouraged to identify with Troilus, as he moved in close to Cressida during her exchanges with Diomedes and struggled with her unfaithfulness in his speeches downstage near to the audience. In this, therefore, he seemed little different from the other men in the play who sought to make use of Cressida in their power games.

The war consisted of long periods of inactivity broken by random, inconclusive encounters. The Trojans were younger and inexperienced, while the Greeks were older and paralysed by their lack of success in the war. Thersites (Paul Hunter) was played as a physically-challenged clown rather than a bitter detractor within a banal and listless war where the primary motivations of the warriors were revenge and a need to protect their reputations. When the Greeks heard that Hector (Christopher Colquhoun) had been killed by Achilles (Trystan Gravelle), they appeared relieved that this might finally help them win the war. At the end of the production, accompanying Troilus's lines to the Trojan army: 'Let him that will a screech owl aye be called, / Go into Troy and say their Hector's dead' (5.1.16–17), columns of black cloth were released all around the Globe auditorium which sought to collectivize the grief of the ending within a theatrical and social context, but it was a feeling of sad senselessness rather than tragedy that predominated at this moment.

In 2012, the Globe's World Shakespeare Festival was opened by a Maori production by the Ngakau Toa theatre company directed by Rachel House. The production was the vision of actor Rawiri Paratene, who had wanted to bring a Maori-speaking Shakespeare to the Globe and who also played Pandarus in the production. The Globe asked the translator Te Kohe Tuhaka not to translate the play into contemporary Maori but into the classical language used by Maori ancestors, seeking a parallel between notions of Globe authentic practices and a certain linguistic authenticity in translation.

Unlike the 2003 Drama School production which pitted Maori tribes against European colonizers, this production transported the action to the world of the Maori prior to the arrival of the Europeans and focused on a war between two fictional Maori tribes; the Kariki and the Toroi. Characters were given Maori names, such as Toroihi for Troilus (Kimo Houltham) and Kahira for Cressida (Awhina Rose Henari Ashby). The spiritual and social world of the play was also recast in terms of Maori culture and traditions, which also placed a greater emphasis on the play as an ensemble piece rather than a star vehicle for one or two actors. The costumes by Shona Tawhiao incorporated traditional Maori designs, including tattoos and weaving techniques, as well as acknowledging the play's Western origins in the bodices and full satin skirts worn by some of the women. Helen, for instance, resembled a Carmen-like figure with her dress hanging off her shoulders.

The play opened with a powerful *whakaeke* or entrance onto stage, used to deliver the Prologue with a *haka* (dance) and *karanga* (ceremonial call). Such an opening also introduced the characters economically to the audience. Throughout, the production employed Maori traditions, weaponry and instruments. Broad physical comedy, similar to the style adopted by British Globe performers, helped Anglophone audiences to follow what was happening onstage. The long poles used by both sets of warriors, for instance, were used to emphasize both warlike aggression and phallic sexuality. By contrast, the two lovers were played passionately and compassionately. Cressida's scene in the Greek camp was, nevertheless, physically threatening, with the Greek generals circling around her until Diomedes intervened to temporarily protect her. Thersites was played by the actress Juanita Hepi, who played him as a sort of Puck-like figure, mischievous rather than malicious. As Stephen Purcell has noted 'Hepi's Tehiti . . . was able to mimic and pastiche the other characters' masculine behaviour without relinquishing her own gender identity. Her parody of Ahaka's (Ajax's) ultra-macho posturing was acutely observed.'[43] The women characters in the play all returned onstage to watch the final battle, creating a choral lament with musical instruments that reinforced their status as privileged but powerless witnesses of the unfolding tragedy. There were, according to Catherine Silverstone, criticisms in New Zealand of the gay stereotypes in Rangi Rangitukunoa's camp performance of Patroclus, as well as of Paratene's representation of Pandarus as an ageing, meddling queer.[44] Such criticisms pointed to the Maori tradition of a *takatapui* or devoted friend of the same gender which is used by Maori to stand in for English words such as gay or queer. More positively, at the end of the performances, a group of spectators in the yard honoured the song and dance onstage with a *haka* in the yard, using the traditional Maori protocol of call and response, a reaction that pointed to the presence of a significant Maori community in London.

7 Radio, film and television productions

For a play that is difficult to stage because of the long, often static, speeches it contains, radio productions of the play have represented a valid alternative. The BBC produced the play in 1935, 1946, 1952 and 1959. The 1946 production saw Max Adrian repeat his stage success as Pandarus, while the 1952 production starred the stage and screen actor Marius Goring as Troilus. The Canadian Broadcasting Company (CBC) produced the play in 1954, and there was also a German-language production of the play by Radio Bremen in 1961 in a translation by Hans Rothe. As stage productions found new languages for the play in the 1960s and 1970s, the number of radio productions decreased, but the BBC returned to the play in 1964 and in 1980, where Michael Pennington played Troilus. In 2005, a BBC radio version of the play had the Trojan roles played by black actors, including Patterson Joseph as Troilus, Nikki-Amuka Bird as Cressida and Derek Griffiths as Pandarus, while non-black actors played the Greeks. How this distinction played out on radio, however, is hard to assess.

The presence of the play on television has been sporadic. There was an ambitious 1954 BBC TV adaptation of the play by the Marlowe Society's George Rylands and Douglas Allen which was not, however, popular with viewers. In Poland, Lidia Zamkow directed the play for Polish television in 1971 in a translation by Bohdan Korzeniewski, and David Karasik directed a Soviet television version of the play in 1975. Yet the most well-known television production of the play is Jonathan Miller's 1981 English-language production for the BBC Television Shakespeare series. Costumes and setting were

Elizabethan although the chaos of the Greeks' temporary camp was less recognizably so. Miller's approach to the play was mainly text- and language-based. However, there were also some nice comic touches in the production, such as pin-ups of Lucas Cranach's nudes in Ajax's tent and the incomplete wooden leg of the Trojan Horse in the background. The actress Suzanne Burden disagreed with Miller about his view of Cressida as innocent and naïve, seeing her instead as a smart, witty young woman who becomes a victim of male power games, and she found herself estranged from Anton Lesser as Troilus as a result.[45] Pandarus (Charles Gray) was an ageing queer with an eye for younger men, while Thersites was played in drag by The Incredible Orlando (Jack Birkett), who had already played Caliban in Derek Jarman's 1979 film of *The Tempest*. Miller's production has been seen as one of the better ones of the series although it avoided most of the controversial issues raised by the play in stage productions of the same period. In 2008, German television showed a stage version dating back to 1968, directed by Heinrich Koch, once more using Hans Rothe's translation,

Apart from these full-length versions of the play, Stephen Fry and Hugh Laurie included a sketch in the 1982 Cambridge Footlights Revue based on an acting masterclass on Ulysses' speech on time in 3.3. Critics have claimed that Fry's ponderous director in this sketch was a parody of the director John Barton and his consistent engagement with the play. Moreover, in 1988, the highly successful BBC television series *Fortunes of War*, included in Episode 2, set in 1940, an amateur production of the play by English expatriates in Bucharest. Their opening night coincided with the Nazi invasion of Paris and black and white images of this other invasion were intercut with scenes from the theatre production of the play.

Film has not been a popular medium for *Troilus and Cressida*, but there was a somewhat incongruous attempt in the 1970s to recast the play as a rock musical put together by director Joseph Papp, screenwriter Tom O'Horgan and composer Galt Macdermot. The project did not, unhappily, materialize. In 2012, the Japanese director Yukio Ninagawa released a DVD of his all-male stage production of the play, with its stunning set of sunflowers and spectacular, muscular battle scenes, reinforcing a sense of the play as increasingly conceived for global, intermedial audiences in the new millennium. These multiple platforms and new global audiences suggest the continuing possibility of imaginative reconceptions of the play's topicality in the future.

3

The State of the Art

Johann Gregory

This chapter demonstrates the variety of interpretive approaches that have been taken in readings of *Troilus and Cressida* over the past thirty years or so. It explores some of the critical trends in Shakespeare studies in relation to the play, as well as the way the play speaks to larger cultural issues. Critics are still debating the significance of the play's early modern publications and its audience: whether the play should be seen as one written for an elite audience, perhaps at the Inns of Court, or as a play for a more heterogeneous audience at the Globe. New insights have also appeared on the play's historical context and the early modern theatrical scene, as well as thinking on language, gender and critical perspective. The chapter is thematic and inevitably selective; a more exhaustive bibliography is available in the updated Arden edition and from the *World Shakespeare Bibliography Online*.[1]

Critics imagining the play's original audience and theatrical context

The role that the construction of Shakespeare's imagined audience has played in critical readings of *Troilus and Cressida* cannot be overstated.[2] Are the extant texts from Shakespeare's strange Trojan play partially a result of special tailoring for a performance and audience at the Inns of Court? Was the play written for a Globe audience, perhaps in response to other plays in the indoor theatres? Was it ever performed for those at court? These are all questions about Shakespeare's audiences which have troubled scholars concerned with the play's early performance, or else these questions have complicated readings of the play, even when the audience isn't the focus of the research. The problem of locating the play's early audience and imagining playgoers' expectations has also been exacerbated by the Preface to the play published in the 1609 Quarto. This stated that the play was 'never staled with the stage, never clapper-clawed with the palms of the vulgar'.[3]

In 1928 Peter Alexander put forward the theory that the play would not have been appreciated by the usual theatregoers, asserting that '[i]t is unlikely that this play was ever performed to an audience at the Globe'.[4] He suggested that 'Shakespeare may, however, have written the play for some festivity at one of the Inns of Court'.[5] This idea was taken up by W.R. Elton in *Shakespeare's 'Troilus and Cressida' and the Inns of Court Revels*: he argued that the play fitted a 'festive law audience' and that '*Troilus*'s allusions would ... have eluded the capacities of the Epistle's "vulger"'.[6] Alexander may have been taken in by the Quarto epistle's advertising strategy which, in its elitism, is not unlike that of W.R. Elton's view of the Globe audience. Undoubtedly, *Troilus and Cressida* does contain legal language and debating scenes which might appeal to law students, but so do other plays by Shakespeare known to have been performed at the Globe.

Elton suggests that the play's spectators would 'have been such as those who attended licensed and wittily suggestive entertainments, or world-upside-down misrule revels, at London's "Third University", the Inns of Court'.[7] However, the 'wit' of *Troilus and Cressida* is more profound than Elton's revels reading suggests. Anthony Dawson notes in his review of Elton's book that 'to see the play exclusively, or even primarily, in terms of its burlesque appeal to rowdy students seems to me to miss the force of the play's opalescent emotional tonalities as well as its deeply sceptical awareness of the relation between personal desire and philosophical position-taking'.[8] Arguably, the play itself interrogates the theatrical conditions of private entertainments and 'position-taking' in a way that could well be appreciated by an audience at the Globe. If the theory of an early modern performance of *Troilus and Cressida* at one of the Inns of Court is to be countenanced, then, it is likely that it would have been performed in a public theatre as well, just as *Twelfth Night* probably was before being performed at the Middle Temple, one of the Inns of Court, in 1602.

The way that *Troilus and Cressida* treats its audience has divided critics. Some argue that the play is elitist and intended for a private audience; others such as Paul Yachnin suggest that it is hybrid 'populuxe', or at least more open to a mixed audience.[9] Yachnin's populuxe argument rests on the premise that Shakespeare's public theatre audience knew that the Lord Chamberlain's or King's Men performed for royalty and the elite. In this argument, Shakespeare's plays, therefore, offered the public, 'popular' theatregoer a *luxury* enjoyed also by the wealthiest patrons, hence a *populuxe* experience. And yet, the play itself often critiques luxury, commerce and court performance: Shakespeare's *Troilus and Cressida* interrogates performance and audience expectation by producing characters like Thersites who, in Bridget Escolme's words, 'always appears as a spectator, looking on at other performances, expecting, then demanding, that we watch with him'.[10] The warrior-courtiers and the ladies are accused of lechery and luxuriousness: 'How the devil Luxury, with his fat rump and potato finger, tickles these together! Fry, lechery, fry', he exclaims (5.2.57–60).

This understanding of *Troilus and Cressida* as a play with satirical elements is connected to a rich tradition of viewing the play in relation to the satirizing of fellow playwrights, audiences and acting companies during the Poets' War – a dispute between playwrights which became metatheatrically written into several of the plays towards the end of the sixteenth century and the start of the seventeenth. James Bednarz's work has explored this theatrical quarrel in great detail, while almost creating a war of the critics (at least within early modern drama scholarship). The critical debate surrounding the so-called 'War of the Theatres' or 'Poets' War' is such that one critic asked in 2003, 'Are we witnessing a terrible "scholastomachia"?'.[11] Although it is unclear exactly who was thought to have instigated the 'Poetomachia', as Shakespeare's contemporary Thomas Dekker termed it, James Bednarz's *Shakespeare & the Poets' War* is certainly responsible for raising the spectre of the Poets' War again. He shows effectively how *Troilus and Cressida* 'functions as an extension of the Poets' War, sharing in the same themes and techniques that appear in the plays of Jonson, Marston and Dekker.[12] However, while he has been praised for bringing the discussion of the Poets' War – and *Troilus and Cressida*'s role within that – into sharper focus, some of his arguments have met with a certain amount of scepticism and distrust.

As some reviewers acknowledge, there is a history to this distrust, which partly rises from the verve with which nineteenth-century critics (sometimes hastily) sought to find topical allusions to dramatists in early modern plays. In Matthew Steggle's view '[m]uch of Bednarz's book . . . is the set of related and mutually reinforcing factual propositions which build up the argument that Shakespeare's plays contain reference to and personal satire of Jonson'.[13] Steggle argues that Bednarz often 'treats these propositions as if they were fact, without doing justice to the full muddiness of the evidence'.[14] Furthermore, the book's focus on Shakespeare is arguably also disproportionate to the focus that the Poets' War had on Shakespeare. Ken Jackson notes in his review of the book, 'the Shakespearean focus ... seems to inhibit Bednarz from exploring in full the thesis it seems to prove most convincingly: the power of Ben Jonson's art and personality directed the course of early modern drama'.[15] Aside from an argument that rests at times on speculation and very small details, then, Bednarz's book sometimes valorizes Shakespeare at the expense of Jonson, when the latter dramatist was clearly a great innovator to whom Shakespeare was responding in his plays, including in *Troilus and Cressida*.[16] As Edward Gieskes argued, the Poets' War 'participates in the definition of the emergent category of "literature"'.[17] This means that, as well as anticipating audience expectations, Shakespeare's Trojan play is implicitly responding to literary or 'poetic' criticism itself: Ulysses discusses the place of an author when he reads a book in front of Achilles; the whole issue of 'taste', in an aesthetic sense, is explored through the language of cookery and food; centuries of writing on Troy are sent up in this staging; and the play demonstrates an 'in-yer-face' theatre style which continues to surprise audiences and critics.

Historical perspectives on *Troilus and Cressida*

Between the Second World War and the late 1980s, there was a relative paucity of research into the relation of *Troilus and Cressida* to the late Elizabethan period from which the play sprang – partly because there had been such a strong emphasis on the notion of the play being 'amazing and modern'.[18] The notable exception, besides a few source studies that considered the play's Elizabethan audience, was E.A.J. Honigmann, who rehearsed many conjectures about the play's provenance, arguing that it may have been 'too dangerous' to publish and perform due to its 'unintended "Essex allusion"'.[19] Honigmann concerned himself with Elizabethan history in order to make sense of the provenance of the play and its publication. Although critics have often agreed with his dating of the composition of the play in the latter or middle months of 1601, most have not followed the complicated conspiracies he suggested. Historical approaches to Shakespeare's plays were given a new lease of life by new historicists who sought to show how Shakespeare's plays were part and parcel of his era's culture and politics. New historicists such as Eric S. Mallin have argued that the way that *Troilus and Cressida* seems to allude to the Earl of Essex is far from accidental. For Mallin, the play does not simply demonstrate a 'semantic instability', as Lars Engle had commented (discussed below), but shows also a historic political instability as it inscribes its own time at the end of the Elizabethan era.

Although Mallin's case may be at times overstated, he convincingly shows how the play is responding to and engaging with the politics of its own time. He suggests that in this play, Shakespeare 'transforms a de facto Elizabethan policy [of emulous factionalism among the courtiers] and its unforeseen consequences into a central plot complication of the Trojan War story'.[20] Mallin shows how '[b]oth Greek and Trojan camps recollect contemporary political acts and structures; both sides, and their transactions, establish compelling circuits of text and world'.[21] This new historicist take reads *Troilus and Cressida* in terms of its relation to the cult of Elizabeth and ceremonies such as the Accession Day tilts, as well as to the idea of Essex as an Achillean recluse *and* a chivalrous Hector.

Ultimately, for Mallin, the play shows how 'the line between chivalry and criminality was frighteningly thin', and in its fascination with homosocial bonds marks the 'ongoing diminution of Elizabeth's potency'.[22] This new historicist outlook rescues critics from viewing the play as being symptomatic of Shakespeare's dark mood (as some nineteenth-century critics suggested), as purely the result of his satiric method, or as simply part of the 'low' tradition of the infamous couple and their pander. This sensitivity to the historical moment suggests that audiences would have responded to the politics of the play in a context of the Elizabethan court struggles and a *fin de siècle* moment.

Heather James also provides a historical reading of the play, largely agreeing with Mallin, if not always relying on all of Mallin's historical details. She notes how

> [t]he rage mimicked and generated by the play has its roots in the disillusionments of the late Elizabethan period, following the spectacular fall of the earl of Essex, whose ambition and chivalric virtue find their reflection in Shakespeare's Achilles and Hector, respectively.[23]

James provides a sophisticated reading of the historicity of Troy and its literature in late Elizabethan England. She shows how 'Shakespeare endows the world of the play with partial awareness of the multiple sources that constitute the Troy legend as well as the politics and economics that underwrite the continual reproduction of its characters and events'.[24] For James, then, the play is not only inscribed *with* the time, but *inscribes* the time by acting within it, by displaying the *translatio imperii* of the Brutus legend and Troynovant in a different light. James argues that with *Troilus and Cressida*, Shakespeare could hold up a 'resilient mirror ... to socially eclectic audiences'; he 'invites his audiences to be Hamlets, and to study, mull over, appropriate, and act on his play'.[25] James's argument that the play interacts with the audience in theatrical and historical ways puts a new spin on the notion of audience expectation because it sees the play as an invitation, taking part in a cultural poetics that is necessarily political. James's thesis implies that *Troilus and Cressida* should not be seen as a play written by an author expecting an especially intellectual elite audience, but that it engages with ideas that would have concerned and interested 'socially eclectic audiences' in Shakespeare's time.

A number of critics have combined historical approaches with an interest in language to consider the many oaths and vows contained in the play. In *Eternal Bonds, True Contracts*, A.G. Harmon argues that '[t]he contractual elements [of the play] – publicity, value, performance, and contractual tokens, as well as the contractual agent – ... are perverted'.[26] Harmon shows how it is not only characters or state discourses that are corrupt but that this corruption works on a micro-linguistic scale as well as on a macro scale. Emily Ross considered the doomed vows between Troilus and Cressida in relation to customary Elizabethan marriage procedure, while John Kerrigan has studied the significance and importance of the oaths and vows made in the play in a historical context.[27] The work of these critics fits into a broader critical interest in early modern contractual language, and is relevant to larger debates about performative language, religion and legal history.

Shakespeare's Trojan play is an obvious one for critics interested in the dramatist as a reader of literature, and scholars from different critical schools continue to read the play in the light of early versions of the story of Troilus and Cressida. Other sections of this book cover this criticism, but David Bevington's edition of the play also provides a useful chapter on Shakespeare's sources.[28] Those interested in Shakespeare's debt to Chaucer should consult the thought-provoking contributions to a recent book on the two authors' telling of the *Troilus* tale: *Love, History and Emotion in Chaucer and Shakespeare*.[29]

Taken together, the historically-minded critics in this section show that *Troilus and Cressida* does not simply reflect past versions of the Troy story or its own historical context. The play holds the potential to transform the Troy myth, offering a space to critique historiography, mythmaking and the theatre of power.

Attention to language and metatheatre

Critics have found much to say about the language of *Troilus and Cressida*, which is by turns high flung, emotional, sophisticated, dirty and brutal. A number of predominantly Marxist critics have read the play in relation to the language of trade and economics; Raymond Southall suggested that the play 'assesses the weakening feudal relations that had taken place during the sixteenth century by bringing to bear upon a world of romance and chivalry ... the powers of personal and social corruption inherent in the appetitive spirit of capitalism'.[30] Taking this approach a step further, C.C. Barfoot argued that

> *Troilus and Cressida* suggests that we trade in selves just as we trade in words, even as we trade in literature, which we conventionally assume is a transmitter, but not inevitably a transmuter, of value and truth.[31]

This notion that the play engaged with its world, and interacted or transacted with its audience, was taken up in a different way by Joseph Lenz, who considered the 'predominant metaphor for the practice of the theatre in Shakespeare's age [which] was prostitution'.[32] He read the play as acknowledging that, 'like a bawd, [theatre] advertises its product with effeminate gesture and costly apparel; like a prostitute, the motive is the same – money. Thus, the theater is a brothel, a pander, a whore, a way toward debauchery and a site for it.'[33] Arguably, however, Shakespeare's play shows how these traits are not particular to theatre. Other critics, notably Douglas Bruster, Lars Engle and Hugh Grady, have concentrated on the economic language at work within the play itself and early modern culture.[34]

Close to this theme has been the language of identity, with critics like Jonathan Dollimore being influenced by poststructuralism to stress the discontinuities between language and identity in the play.[35] These critics, often using deconstructive approaches, have shown how the play does not only destabilize notions of order and hierarchy, but also shows a crisis with language itself: Gayle Greene comments that

[a]s the questions of order with which *Troilus and Cressida* is concerned reflect the crisis of values in the late Renaissance, so does its concern with language reflect this background of linguistic revolution.[36]

This post-Reformation period was a time of 'a change in attitudes towards language, "dissolving" and "loosing" the bond between word and thing'.[37] This problem of communication was associated with a fall from grace, as Roberta Kwan argued recently in relation to the play.[38] David Hillman has been just one of many critics to emphasize the 'overwhelming citationality of [Shakespeare's] material', while suggesting that in Ulysses' description of Cressida '[h]er faithlessness is figured *as* the faithlessness of language itself'.[39] The distortion of language was also pursued as a theme by Patricia Parker; in her book *Shakespeare from the Margins*, she noted the 'inflation or bloating that affects both bodies and words in *Troilus and Cressida*'.[40] For these critics, the play continually distorts and challenges notions of language as simple communication, often exaggerating and irritating attempts to order language, whether poetically or philosophically.

As Lars Engle observed, it is this 'semantic instability which has made *Troilus and Cressida* a favourite play of deconstructors'.[41] A.D. Nuttall writes that 'in this play Shakespeare is more intellectual, more technically philosophical in the full meaning of the word, than in any other'.[42] Nevertheless, the Hamlet-like intellectual quality of the play is qualified by a resignation or refutation of intellectualism as well, as if overthinking brings its own physical sickness. David Hillman goes so far as to say that the play 'is sceptical about the value of literature, sceptical about the value of philosophy, sceptical therefore about the value of the human as such'.[43] And yet, the play is clearly useful for thinking through philosophical issues, as Andrew Hiscock demonstrates in a recent chapter for *Shakespeare and Hospitality: Ethics, Politics, and Exchange* where he focuses on 'Shakespeare's own theatre of hospitality', and Alex Schulman shows in his reading of the play in relation to Platonism.[44]

The play's debates and complex language are at times also deeply metatheatrical. For Neil Powell, the play's metatheatricality creates the impression that '*Troilus* is a play within a play [where] the audience supplies, and is, the outer audience: hence its peculiar feeling of complicity with the audience'.[45] How the audience is complicit with the performance of the play is a complicated question, but there is still the sense, as Jean-Pierre Maquerlot remarks, that the play is '*foiling* expectation, at all levels of the play's structure'.[46] Troilus exclaims: 'I am giddy: expectation whirls me round' (3.2.16), and yet later in the play his idea of Cressida is suddenly changed. Rolf P. Lessenich noticed how the 'frustration of most of the play's characters is paralleled by the frustration of the spectators, effected through constant ups and downs of expectation and disappointment'.[47] There seems, according to many critics who have studied the metatheatrical quality of the play, to be a deliberate self-consciousness about the play on the part of the characters as represented and arguably on the part of the author too.

Critics such as Linda Charnes have postulated that this frustration of expectations may be because the 'audience ... knows the outcome of this story and expects to get what it pays for', but there may be more to it than that.[48] Eric Byville reads Pandarus's Epilogue as

> the metadramatic parting shot of *Troilus and Cressida* [that] alludes to the play's *failure* to produce pleasure and the disappointment of audience members who came to this 'performance' expecting to be pleased and instead have been disgusted: 'Why should our endeavour be so desired, and the performance so loathed? What verse for it?'(5.11.37–9)[49]

Patrick Cheney argues that in *Troilus and Cressida* Shakespeare can be found 'self-consciously combining a capacious array of dramatic forms', while Gretchen E. Minton labels this self-consciousness the 'metatheatrical anxiety of the play'.[50] Efterpi Mitsi reads this metatheatrical self-consciousness as a response to anti-theatre tracts and Shakespeare's source material.[51] The play's metatheatrically has been a rich space for critics since the play frequently tests the notion that 'all the world's a stage'.

Briget Escolme has provided an important performance-orientated reading of the play, focusing especially on Cressida, where Escolme notes that '[w]e may find ourselves looking at a human being on stage, laughing in comprehension at one moment, the next moment asking "who – or what – is that?" and being asked who we think we are in return'.[52] Being aware of the repercussions of 'staging' characters and expectations helps literary critics to check their expectations of *Troilus and Cressida*. Escolme shows how the metatheatrical can be more than a witty conceit: it is part of the larger significance and experience of the play's performance in the theatre. As Arlin J. Kiken argued in her performance-orientated reading, 'it is a temptation to gather up this complex, seemingly fragmented play with a single clear idea.... But an imposed unity destroys the very complexity that makes the drama so rich'.[53] This is relevant for critics and editors alike. Metatheatrical language and theatrical staging are part of the way the play addresses audience expectations, the *theatrum mundi* theme, and the 'constructed-ness' of identities that we are so familiar with in our own time through the rise of digital social media.

Psychological, feminist and gender criticism

In her reading of the play, Gayle Greene argued:

> That human nature is not 'natural', but is, rather, shaped by social forces and values, is an understanding we have long had in relation to men but one which has been more difficult

to grasp with regard to women. *Troilus and Cressida* may seem the last place to look for such insights, informed as it is with a loathing of humanity, an aversion to sex and the physical, and more misogyny than is usual with Shakespeare.[54]

Countless early critics seem to have followed the other Trojan and Greek characters' readings of the men and women in *Troilus and Cressida*, but Greene takes a more nuanced view. From the 1960s, the tide did begin to turn on the critics who thought that Cressida was simply 'cheap stuff', as Alice Walker put it.[55] Carolyn Asp's 'In Defense of Cressida' argued against critics such as Arnold Stein who had seen Cressida as rather 'underrefined'.[56] Asp suggested that Cressida 'embodies the play's central metaphysical question: is value a quality intrinsic in the object or is it a variable, fluctuating with subjective appreciation and perspectives?'.[57] Besides providing a more sympathetic reading of Cressida, feminist and gender studies of the play have on occasion linked this notion of the characters' perspectives with that of an audience or other critics.

These approaches have especially been interested in the way in which gender distinctions are polarized and collapsed in *Troilus and Cressida*, while others have noted how gender takes on a performative dimension.[58] A number of these performances have been considered in terms of the way that actions are gendered in the ideologies traditionally surrounding love and war, with Barbara Bowen writing a monograph on the play entitled *Gender in the Theater of War*.[59] Considerations of the play especially focused on masculine gender negotiations and homosociality have been provided by Gary Spear, Daniel Juan Gil and Robin Headlam Wells, among others: many of these have focused on the emulation rampant in the play.[60] Alan Sinfield provided a queer reading of the play, seeing 'the sexual potential of various scenarios' in relation to '(what we think of as) homosexual acts'.[61] Together, these critics implicitly raise questions about the ways in which an audience might be expected to emulate the characters in the play, or be repelled by this invitation. All these critics discuss the way that the characters in the play are represented as being concerned about how their relationships are perceived by others.

The way that characters are seen to judge and desire other characters has often been analysed by critics interested in psychological approaches: these have often been poststructuralists using Freud, Althusser and more often Lacan, sometimes linking characters' desires with those of a theatre or reading audience.[62] Thinking on the 'visual pleasure' of the play, Barbara Hodgdon is one of the few feminist critics to ask questions about the possible early audiences for *Troilus and Cressida*, asking rhetorically whether 'a female spectator in the Renaissance [would] share a similar outlook [to a modern one]'.[63] Gayle Greene is representative of many feminist critics who have argued that, 'by showing Cressida in relation to the men and society who make her what she is, [Shakespeare] provides a context that qualifies the apparently misogynistic elements of her characterization'.[64] The topic of desire has been linked to the Trojan matter through Helen of Troy and others for centuries, but in Shakespeare's play this desire is undercut by a more local Elizabethan awareness of the London prostitution scene created through Pandarus's behaviour, Cressida's plight in the Trojan camp and Thersites' commentary on the heroes who 'war for a placket' (2.3.19).

René Girard returns time and again in his writing to *Troilus and Cressida*. In his reading of the rivalries in the play, Girard discerned a 'mimetic desire', rather than a Freudian desire, at work. In this view, desire is incited through someone else's apparent desire. As he put it, '[n]othing incites desire like desire itself'.[65] He reads Pandarus as putting together 'a triangle of desire that will spawn others later on'.[66] Pandarus instigates Cressida's desire for Troilus and vice-versa; Girard not only uses the play to illustrate his theory of mimetic desire: he argues that Shakespeare is 'its theoretician', especially in *Troilus and Cressida*. He suggests that '[n]o play is more clearly designed for the unravelling of a whole range of mimetic phenomena'.[67] The fact that this mimetic desire is *staged* by Shakespeare means that for Girard this play offers a 'theatre of envy'.

Feminist and psychological approaches to the text have helped to highlight the many connections between character expectations and audience expectations, breaking down nineteenth-century notions of a fourth wall in the theatre. Through their attention to gender, these methodologies have implicitly raised the stakes for the way we read the significance of the play in terms of original and present-day audiences, and early modern and present-day concerns.

Troilus and Cressida from the perspectives of presentism and ecocriticism

Partly in reaction to the paradigms of 'purely' historical, theoretical or materialist readings of Shakespeare, a concern with the situation of the critic's perspective coming at least partly from the present has led to a criticism known as 'presentism'. In their introduction to the collection of essays entitled *Presentist Shakespeares*, Hugh Grady and Terence Hawkes began to define presentism by starting 'with what it's not', defining it in opposition to previous orthodoxies.[68] They argued that

> if the alternative [to new historicism and cultural materialism] is to deal with the plays in blissful ignorance of their historical context, to impose on them, as many teachers seem unthinkingly to do, some kind of absurd contemporaneity with ourselves, usually justified by windy rhetoric about the Bard's 'universality', then perhaps historical specificity of some sort is desirable. The new materialism's apparently simple focus on objects is a case in point. Yet inevitably it tends to remain fixed and strangely fixated on objects as such in a practice that threatens to replicate rather than critique what Marx called the fetish of commodities.[69]

For Grady and Hawkes, presentism uses 'crucial aspects of the present as a trigger for its investigations' in a way that warns against fanatically reading a play in relation to its historical context in order to elucidate its meaning.[70] Thus, presentism is an attempt to read texts with an awareness of one's own preoccupations and values, which are often different from those of the original writers, audiences or readers. In the final essay in their book, '*Troilus and Cressida*: The Perils of Presentism', Kiernan Ryan provides a reading of the play from a presentist perspective which is, at the same time, appreciative of both historical difference and the play's ability to 'project a future beyond the one the present is creating for itself'.[71] For Ryan (who could perhaps be described better as a futurist than a presentist), 'the play does not only apprehend the presentness of the past; it also anticipates the pastness of the present'.[72] Ryan's approach, in effect, imagines a *long durée* in which Shakespeare's play is both distanced from, and a part of, the present.

In the opening of his essay, Ryan suggests that 'Dryden's tasteful mutation gives us the measure of the original's delinquency and determination to vex its audience'.[73] If, as Ryan implies, *Troilus and Cressida* does manage to vex more modern audiences, as it may well have its original ones, it would seem that there is something in the matter of the play – something about the way the play addresses expectations – that vexes them. This would not necessarily be because audiences today are the same as they were when the play was written, but because the play's situation, language and plot hold the potential to aggravate different audience members. *Troilus and Cressida* clearly has the potential to generate rich and divergent meanings: critics who have read the play more overtly in relation to their own experience of drama or politics, for example, have often seen the play in a very different light to those who have read the play in relation to its medieval and classical sources. Some critics have read the play with both these sets of expectations in mind. This critical sense of local application *and* of the *longue durée* of the play's Trojan matter is probably analogous to that of early modern audience members; they would have seen the play from their own 'presentist' perspective, while being aware that there was a larger backstory.

A recent book entitled *Shakespeare in Our Time* contains a section devoted to ecocriticism, and, perhaps surprisingly, *Troilus and Cressida*. A growing trend in literary criticism has been a concern with the environmental humanities, and Shakespeare's plays have been a popular site for ecocriticism. The short chapters in the book's section show how the play is full of references to nature and animals. Rebecca Bushnell focuses on the iconography of the bard as nature's poet and one of green pastoral, and shows how this tradition forgets that *Troilus and Cressida*'s 'universe of words, things and humans is fissured'.[74] Steve Mentz focuses on Ulysses famous speech on degree, noting how his speech on order and chaos is shot through with sea imagery: 'Supplementing natural harmony with oceanic dynamism transforms a speech about stable hierarchy into a complex vision of multiply entangled systems. Recognizing the speech's invocations of ocean-flavoured nature unsettles the green pastoralism that has long dominated ideas about natural order.'[75] Similarly, Karen Raber reads the addled egg in Cressida's description of Pandarus's tastes to suggest that 'Disrupted "natural" processes of procreation raise the spectre of nature as a trickster, an infanticidal cannibalizing player in a cosmos that won't reliably reproduce either sameness or difference'.[76] These invigorating ecocritical readings demonstrate that Shakespeare's play can be used to think about our place in the world and the way this world is described and used, rhetorically and physically.

What to expect: 'Shakespeare's neglected masterpiece'

A.P. Rossiter commented that '[m]uch of the effect of the play depends on expecting what you do not get'.[77] The propensity of the play to generate 'a dazzling variety of response[s]', as Anne Barton put it, may well be the very nature of language and performance.[78] Nonetheless, the mixed critical reception that *Troilus and Cressida* has received over the centuries suggests that this play was built with the understanding that people would put their own expectations into it, and that soon enough these expectations would be teased and teased out. The fear of undecidability concerning the author's intentions that critics such as Hazlitt seem to exhibit is not unlike that suggested by Michel de Montaigne in relation to his cat: 'When I am playing with my Cat, who knowes whether she have more sporte in dallying with me, than I have in gaming with hir?'[79] Reading the reception of *Troilus and Cressida*, it is as if some critics and audiences fear their tastes and expectations are being teased by Shakespeare. When the play is considered in relation to the early modern scene, there is reason to believe that Shakespeare *was* involved in a cat-and-mouse game with his contemporary poets and audiences in a 'poetomachia' concerning literary tastes and expectations of theatre, although this doesn't mean that he only had one particular audience in mind.

Shakespeare's engagement with expectation means that the play obliquely *critiques in advance* the way it will be valued by audiences and critics. The play's Prologue says that the play leaves its reception to 'chance', but *Troilus and Cressida* is more controlled in its initial management of expectations than the Prologue would have audiences believe. Slavoj Žižek suggested that '*Troilus and Cressida* [is] Shakespeare's neglected masterpiece, his weirdest play, effectively a postmodern work *avant la lettre*'.[80] To see the play as a masterpiece rather than a failure is to recognize that, despite the language of failure that pervades the play, the text still holds the potential for insight and a sense of purpose in its dramatic affects: it holds the potential to test audience expectations, even as it eschews a final moral, message or perspective by seeming at times purposeless and fragmentary.

Characters in the play do not explicitly discuss audience expectation in the obvious way that characters in the induction scenes of Ben Jonson's plays explicitly do, for example; however, *Troilus and Cressida* foregrounds the importance and predicament of expecting – awaiting, looking out. Although many critics have thought that the play is bent on simply disrupting audience expectations, the play is also about audience expectations and about criticism, including literary criticism.

4

New Directions

The Decay of Exemplarity in *Troilus and Cressida*

Rob Maslen

Shakespeare wrote *Troilus and Cressida* in late 1601, after the execution for high treason of the national hero Robert Devereux, Earl of Essex, in the protracted final days of Elizabeth I.[1] With the death of Essex, a phase of Shakespeare's life came to an end. When the Earl staged his abortive coup in February of the same year, one of his co-conspirators was Henry Wriothesley, Earl of Southampton, to whom Shakespeare had dedicated his major poems *Venus and Adonis* (1593) and *The Rape of Lucrece* (1594).[2] Another co-conspirator, from one point of view, was Shakespeare himself, since the company of actors for whom he wrote most of his plays – the Lord Chamberlain's Men – had staged a performance of a play about Richard II, who was deposed and executed after a successful fourteenth-century insurrection, the day before the Earl made his bid for power.[3] After that performance

Shakespeare stopped writing English history plays for over a decade. Thus, it is hardly surprising if the ancient Greek history play he wrote in or around the following year has an air of sardonic retrospection, replacing the triumphalist rhetoric of *Henry V* – his last English history play of the 1590s, which refers to Essex as the heroic 'General of our gracious Empress' (5.0.30)[4] – with the language of disease, decay and obfuscation.

Troilus and Cressida, therefore, can be seen as Shakespeare's long farewell to English history, and in particular to the history of England under Elizabeth Tudor. It concerns itself with the question of the 'indirect, crook'd ways' by which the past gets written, and with the function of history as theorized by the humanist education system that shaped Shakespeare's mind.[5] Its chief target is the humanist doctrine of exemplarity: the claim that you can derive general principles or rules by which to govern your actions from particular examples, that is, from exemplary individuals or episodes discoverable among the disconnected fragments and wilful distortions of conflicting historical narratives.[6] I would like to suggest that the topic of historical exemplarity was already implicit in his choice of subject – Troilus, Cressida, the war over Helen – and that for various reasons he and his early audiences would have approached this particular story with a strong sense of their own complicity with the notoriously non-exemplary dispositions of the ancient Trojans and Greeks.

In Tudor times, as is well known to early modern scholars, the Trojan War was intimately bound up with English history.[7] The English traced their ancestry to Brutus, grandson of Aeneas of Troy, who founded Troynovant or New Troy – later rebranded as London – in the land of Albion, later rebranded as Britain.[8] It was easy, too, for Elizabethans to connect the Trojan War with their country's more immediate past. Like the Essex rebellion, it was an internecine conflict, with relatives on both sides taking arms against each other. The motive of the war, as of the rebellion, was a woman; it involved a tangled web of betrayals or acts of treason; and one of its central figures was Achilles, who had been linked with the Earl of Essex by George

Chapman in his 1598 translation of *Seaven Bookes of the Iliades of Homere, Prince of Poets*. Chapman's translation bore a prefatory epistle addressed to 'the most honored now living Instance of the Achilleian vertues eternized by divine Homere', the soldier-earl, and this sentence transforms Robert Devereux himself into an instructive example of the kind historians and historical poets seek to supply when penning their texts (sig. A3r). At the same time, Chapman argues in his prefatory epistle that poets are more reliable than historians – or indeed their living subjects – in offering exemplary nourishment for the soul, that is, for the moral and intellectual life of the mind. In the real world, Chapman contends, the soul is trapped in what he calls 'the scum of the body', that 'wormeaten Idoll'[9] which invariably fails to manifest the soul's 'excellencie' – or worse still, contrives through its influence to 'murther and burie her' (sig. A3r). Great poems, on the other hand, like those of Homer, offer the perfect bodily vehicle for the soul, communicating its qualities as no human actions can, and resurrecting past heroes with a few well-chosen syllables. As a result, 'the lyves of ... Poets' as embodied in their works can be seen as the heroes' 'earthlie Elis[i]ummes', in which the living are privileged to 'walke with survivall of all the deceased worthies we reade of: every conceipt, sentence, figure, and word being a most bewtifull lyneament of their soules infinite bodies' (sig. A3v). If this is so, then the Earl of Essex – who at the time of writing still occupied the 'wormeaten Idoll' of his living body – could never have represented Achilles as accurately as Homer's verse does; and, as if in confirmation of Chapman's words, only one year after he wrote them the Earl's 'Achilleian vertues' found themselves murdered and buried, so to speak, in the dismal failure of his 1599 campaign against the Irish and subsequent rising against the English monarch. Thus, those who remembered Chapman's dedication when they first encountered Shakespeare's play would have seen the irony in its portrayal of Achilles, whose body is verbally infested with so many diseases by the satirist Thersites. Once Achilles always Achilles – so long as Achilles is merely a verbal rather than a corporeal construct, and hence not subject to old age, lack of fitness, personal inconsistency, or infectious diseases of the body or mind.

Despite Chapman's praise of poets, Homer's account of the Trojan War was in any case viewed with distrust in early modern England. The war, in fact, was the perfect example of the untrustworthy nature of history itself, since there were so many competing versions of what happened, each weighted in favour of one of the warring sides, each accusing the other camp of inventing lies to support its cause. The versions of Homer and Dictys of Crete were said to be biased towards the Greeks, while Virgil and Dares the Phrygian sided with the Trojans. There were even suggestions from serious historians, such as Henry VII's official chronicler Polydore Vergil, that all accounts of the Trojan War had been made up, and that the concept of ancient London as new Troy was entirely fanciful. The body of evidence, like the bodies of the people who took key roles in the ten-year siege, was therefore subject to corruption, and the question of whether the exemplary function of history was damaged or enhanced by its fabricated elements was fiercely debated in the sixteenth century.

The proto-novelist Geoffrey Fenton gives one of the most detailed accounts of the uses of history in early modern England. In the Preface to his story collection *Certaine Tragicall Discourses* (1567) he states that like all arts, narratives of the past contain embedded in their particular details 'certeine speciall principles and rules for the direction of suche as searche out their disposition', and that the responsible reader's task is to extricate these general 'preceptes' from the specific examples scattered so liberally through their pages.[10] In the process the reader makes use of the past to plan for the future, on the presumption that 'the nature of man in all ages, althoughe the singler personnes bee chaunged, remeineth stil one' (6), so that consequences of the same action or political incident will be always and everywhere the same.

The point of reading history, then, is not so much to know what *happened* as to anticipate what *will* happen, in the interest of devising policies. The 'frute and chiefe gayne derived of such traveile', he writes, 'is in that wee shall see set furthe good and whoalsome lessons of all sortes, whereof wee maye take to ourselves and benefyt of our countreye, suche as we like to followe; and which presentes to us the true picture and reapport of suche enterprises as had both sinister begynnynges and much worse endes' (5). In a well-written history, 'good and whoalsome' actions must be made alluring – we need to *like to follow* them – while 'sinister' actions must be made repellent; something which, as Philip Sidney points out in his *Apology for Poetry* (c. 1580), is not always the case in authentic records, where 'the historian, being captived to the truth of a foolish world, is many times a terror from well-doing, and an encouragement to unbridled wickedness'.[11] Fenton, by contrast, seems to believe that the archives *always* show virtue rewarded and wickedness punished – that's one of the general 'rules' he has extracted from his study of history. He acknowledges that 'description figuratyve' as used by poets – in other words, fiction – has been readily accepted by many thinkers as an adequate substitute for true history (5), but asserts that we are far more inclined to emulate our ancestors than to mimic invented figures with no direct familial or national connection to ourselves. Truth is always preferable to feigning, and truth always yields instruction, because it comes from God.

The problem with the Trojan War is that it is neither wholly fictitious nor wholly factual, so that the truth of it can't easily be located. For some commentators its hybrid nature as part fact, part fiction is unproblematic. Writing in 1531, the humanist Sir Thomas Elyot defines history much as Fenton does, as a record of past events which can be used to supplement our personal experience, and he considers the question of whether or not it is authentic to be largely irrelevant to this function. 'Admytte that some histories be interlaced with leasynges [lies]', he writes,

> why shulde we therfore neglecte them? sens the affaires there reported no thynge concerneth us, we beynge therof no parteners, ne therby ... may receyve any damage. But if by redynge the sage counsayle of Nestor, the subtile

persuasions of Ulisses, the compendious gravitie of
Menelaus, the imperiall majestye of Agamemnon, the
prowesse of Achilles, and valiaunt courage of Hector, we
may apprehende any thinge wherby our wittes may be
amended and our personages be more apte to serve our
publike weale and our prince, what forceth it us [what does
it matter] though Homer write leasinges?[12]

Eliot here suggests that we need not bother about the accuracy
of Homer's account of the Trojan War because modern
Englishmen have no stake in it – they are 'therof no parteners'.
As we have seen, he is being disingenuous, since the myth of
Britain's Trojan origins meant that the Tudor regime, at least,
might be thought to have had a stake in whether or not the
story of their forebears had been made up. In 1602 an expert
in heraldry, William Segar, wrote a passage that neatly
summarizes some of the difficulties with Eliot's position:

True it is . . . that many enterprises in times past attempted
and atchieved above the expectation of men, are now
thought rather fabulous than faithfully reported: either
because we that now live did not know, or see them, or that
ignorant men cannot conceive howe they might be done, or
that want of courage doth disable them to take the like
actions in hand. . . . And who so shall well consider how
difficult a thing it is to write an history of so great trueth
and perfection, as cannot be controlled, will easily excuse
these writers that have taken in hand matter so farre from
our knowledge and understanding. For like unto all other
men, mooved with love, hate, profit, or other private
passion, they are either willing or ignorantly induced to
encrease or extenuate the actions and merits of those men,
of whom their histories have discoursed. Howsoever that
bee, I verely thinke the Acts and enterprises of Ulysses,
Aeneas, Hector, and other famous captaines . . . were indeed
of notable men, and some part of their doings such, as
writers have made mention.[13]

The opening of this passage – 'True it is' – aligns it with the heavily ironic use of the term 'truth' and its cognates in Sidney's *Apology for Poetry*, where assertions of verity invariably preface some statement about the impossibility of ascertaining the truth with any conviction.[14] Segar goes on to present us with a historical record that is always subject to the vicissitudes of 'love, hate, profit or other private passion', where historiography is always 'controlled' – a word that could mean either 'censured, criticized' or 'censored, kept in check' – and where writers are always exaggerating or excusing the behaviour of the men they favour. If some of the 'doings' of the Greek and Trojan heroes were authentic, which doings were they? It is important to know the answer if we are to use their actions and those actions' consequences as a means of planning our future enterprises.

Another way in which the Trojan War can be seen as doctrinally mixed – that is, as far from simple in the teachings it yields – is in the complicated nature of the examples it contains.[15] These are divided by early modern commentators, on the whole, along gender lines: the men involved in the conflict represent ideals to be followed, the women vices to be shunned. But surely a man's particular qualities cannot be disengaged from the larger project in the services of which he chooses to use them? It is all very well to say that Agamemnon is the perfect example of the enlightened general, or that Ulysses is the model counselor, or Achilles the ultimate warrior – but each of these men has undertaken a ten-year war to retrieve a woman who is widely cited as the ultimate example of infidelity and its consequences. And what if the judgement of women recorded by history is itself profoundly unsafe? Throughout the sixteenth century there is a tradition of defending women like Helen and Cressida – especially the latter – as having been traduced by the faithless historians mentioned by Segar. In the 1580 edition of the much-reprinted verse anthology *The Paradyse of Daintie Devises*, for instance, Troilus tells Cressida that she has become an example to all women of the effects of what he calls 'Catterwaling' (sleeping around like a lustful cat), and Cressida replies with a counter-accusation of her own:

> No gadding moode, but forced strife,
> Compelled me retyre from Troy:
> If Troylus would have vowde his wife,
> We might have dwelt in former joy.

(sigs K3V–K4R)

If Troilus had simply married Cressida, in other words, or fought to keep the woman he loved, she wouldn't have been forced to seek the protection of his Greek enemy, Diomedes; and she adds that she has been misrepresented by tradition largely thanks to Troilus's willingness to blacken her name. Troilus identifies Cressida as simply unfaithful, and as uniquely responsible for her own infidelity, but Cressida traces responsibility for her actions back to Troilus himself, in the process exposing the crudity of the humanist effort to isolate exemplary persons and episodes from their social and political contexts.

Shakespeare's own Lucrece is as conscious as Cressida of her dependence on the untrustworthy narratives of men for the example she will be deemed to have set for other women. Her urgent task after her rape by Tarquin is to pass on an accurate speaking picture of herself to future generations: she hates the idea of being fictionalized by unsympathetic male chroniclers, transformed into a distorted image which is rendered convincing by the scraps of evidence from which it is partially constructed. Her body is one such scrap of evidence, and she pleads with the Night (personified as a female deity) to keep it hidden from hostile or voyeuristic gazes:

> Make me not object to the tell-tale Day!
> The light will show, charactered in my brow,
> The story of sweet chastity's decay,
> The impious breach of holy wedlock vow.

Yea, the illiterate, that know not how
   To cipher what is read in learned books,
   Will quote my loathsome trespass in my looks.[16]

In this stanza the raped woman's body begins as a text that is read by the male god of day, Apollo, as having been 'charactered' or inscribed with 'the story of sweet chastity's decay' – a story that makes no comment on who was responsible for the decay of chastity, the rapist or the raped woman – and ends as having been subjected to endless annotations ('quoted' or 'coted') by ignorant readers who assume that all the evidence points to the woman's guilt. By the final line the 'loathsome trespass' has become definitively hers (*'my* ... trespass) rather than Tarquin's, through a process of promiscuous male tale-telling and ignorant reading, both transacted on the ambiguous non-verbal script provided by her body. The perversity of this process renders highly problematic *both* the business of communicating her version of what really happened *and* the 'learned' practice of drawing general moral and political precepts from particular historical examples.

If the process of finding or fabricating examples is problematic, their utility too is questionable, as she discovers shortly afterwards. Seeking some answer to the question of how to transmit the 'true' facts of her rape to her husband and the world in general, she finds herself examining a nearby picture of the siege of Troy, where she instantly picks out the exemplary heroes, Ulysses and Ajax, from among a crowd of Greeks, thanks to the artist's skill:

   In Ajax and Ulysses, O, what art
   Of physiognomy might one behold!
   The face of either ciphered either's heart;
   Their face their manners most expressly told:
   In Ajax' eyes blunt rage and rigour rolled;
      But the mild glance that sly Ulysses lent
      Showed deep regard and smiling government.
                                    (1394–1400)

Here the issue, from the perspective of exemplarity, is not whether the artist can represent her subjects without bias, but the perversely non-exemplary nature of the persons represented. The Ajax and Ulysses of the picture are not the idealized, simplified figures of humanist pedagogic tradition. Both are exemplary, first and foremost, of the artist's knowledge of physiognomy, the science of diagnosing the state of a person's inward being from their facial characteristics, as perfected by the Greek physician Hippocrates. Ajax's dominant quality is that of anger, much as it was in Sidney's *Apology for Poetry*, so his exemplarity is straightforward; but Ulysses is a much more complex case, flamboyantly resisting summary as the example of 'wisdom and temperance' he was for Sidney.[17] The verbal description of his portrait is troubled by the juxtaposition of conflicting adjectives: both *mild* and *sly*, both *deep* and *smiling*, his face combines charm with cunning, glib cheerfulness with profound meditation, in such a way as to render him contradictory rather than balanced, untrustworthy rather than wise. And soon after spotting him, Lucrece finds reason to question the 'art of physiognomy' his face exhibits. The most puzzling image in the picture is that of Sinon, the treacherous Greek whose pretended defection to the Trojan side helped convince Priam to bring the wooden horse within the city walls. Sinon seems to be the direct opposite of exemplary, in that his appearance completely obscures his disposition:

> But like a constant and confirmed devil
> He entertained a show so seeming just,
> And therein so ensconced his secret evil
> That jealousy itself could not mistrust
> False-creeping craft and perjury should thrust
>   Into so bright a day such black-faced storms,
>   Or blot with hell-born sin such saintlike forms.
>
> (1513–19)

Of course, Sinon is really exemplary here because the artistic representation of a traitor must embody treachery – so that his appearance must *needs* belie his actions, otherwise he would be an inaccurate image of the fatal deceiver. However, the extreme disconnect between his appearance and his treacherous behaviour elicits in Lucrece a drastic misapplication of his example. The traitor's misleading beauty recalls her encounter with the rapist Tarquin, whose appearance disastrously misled her into trusting him; and from now on, she declares, she will always assume that beautiful looks in men can only ever serve as the index of a vicious mind. At this early stage in Shakespeare's career, in other words, Troy is already associated with the problem of assigning moral or social values to a man or woman on the basis of a reading of those 'wormeaten idols' their bodies. It is also linked with the perversity often involved in extracting general 'principles and rules', in Fenton's phrase, from specific examples: even after Lucrece has identified Sinon, the general rule she derives from his appearance is scarcely a credible one. Add to this that the best-known account of Sinon's treachery occurs in a version of Troy narrated by a biased poet – Virgil, who favoured the Trojans – and the relationship between the particular and the general, the example and the precept, is plunged into crisis by the ambiguities of Trojan history.

When Shakespeare opened his Trojan history play with a Speaker of the Prologue who wears full body armour because he has no confidence in 'author's pen or actor's voice', and when that Speaker ends his speech with the couplet 'Like or find fault; do as your pleasures are; / Now good or bad, 'tis but the chance of war' – then I suggest that the Elizabethan audience would have found itself in familiar territory.[18] The competing versions of the Trojan War demonstrate exactly this: that the outcome of any particular conflict, and the factional bias of its poets, chroniclers and commentators, determine the general moral lessons it is deemed to impart, regardless of the 'true' causes and effects of its constituent episodes. And the play that follows is given over to an extended analysis of the mechanics of making examples out of men and women at a time of crisis.

In the play, examples are fabricated in different ways depending on your gender and the moral and political priorities of the faction you favour. At the centre of this version of the Trojan War are two women: Cressida, who is deemed exemplary by Troilus in particular, and Helen, who is theoretically deemed exemplary by both Greeks and Trojans but is also the topic of heated debate in Troy over the current status of her exemplarity. Both women are valued, it seems, only for their beauty, so that their exemplary function is at once limited and questionable (is bodily beauty a value or merely a trigger for erotic desire?). The limitations of their exemplarity are figured in one of the play's central scenes, Act 3 Scene 1, which sees Pandarus mistake a reference to Helen for an allusion to Cressida – in the process bringing into question men's capacity to distinguish between the women they are supposed to value most highly. The scene culminates in a song, performed by Pandarus for Helen's entertainment, which is not much more than a string of orgasmic exhalations ('"O! O!" a while, but "Ha, ha, ha!" / "O! O!" groans out for "Ha, ha, ha!" / – Heigh-ho!' [3.1.119–20]). An obscene 'O' lies at the heart of this Greek tragicomedy, conjoined with derisory laughter, and between them these empty utterances summarize the material value of the official pretext of the conflict it enacts, Helen of Troy.

The exemplarity of Helen and Cressida is in any case compromised by the fact that other Greek and Trojan women are fought over in the course of the play. Achilles withholds his support from the Greek army on the pretext of his love for Hector's sister Polyxena – a fact that compromises his exemplarity as the greatest of warriors as well as Helen's exemplarity as the most highly valued of women. And there is a fourth woman who provides a pretext for the violence between Greeks and Trojans, although it would be easy enough to overlook her presence in the play: Hector's wife Andromache. In Act 1 Scene 2, we hear that Hector has lost his temper because he was humiliated in the field by Ajax, and that his reaction to the humiliation was to lose his temper with his wife – and hence to jeopardize his own exemplary status as an embodiment of chivalry: 'He chid Andromache and struck his armourer' (1.2.6). In the following scene, however, he sends a challenge to the Trojan camp which proclaims Andromache to be the most exemplary woman of all, and urges the Greeks to fight him in single combat if they disagree. Aeneas, who brings the challenge to the Greeks, expresses it thus:

> Hector, in view of Trojans and of Greeks,
> Shall make it good, or do his best to do it,
> He hath a lady, wiser, fairer, truer,
> Than ever Greek did couple in his arms[.]
>
> (1.3.273–6)

This kind of challenge is of course familiar from chivalric romance, but in the context of the matter of Troy it is a manifest absurdity. If Andromache is so much better than any Greek lady, past or present – and if a Greek challenger is prepared to fight on the basis that his own lady, rather than Helen, is better still – what precisely is the war about? Moreover, Andromache – who was 'chid' by Hector before he issued the challenge – quickly disappears as a motive for the single combat; and when we see her again it is once more as the target for her husband's wrath. In the final act she tries to dissuade him from fighting on a day of ill omen, and he reacts with unwarranted irritability: 'Andromache, I am offended with you. / Upon the love you bear me, get you in' (5.3.77–8). Clearly, Hector's reputation as a man of war is always his first priority, and the women he fights for are always and only ever the excuse for combat, the context in which Hector's own exemplarity can best be displayed. Helen even acknowledges as much when she tells Paris in Act 3 Scene 1 that unbuckling Hector's armour (something Andromache is later unable to accomplish) will enhance her status as the loveliest of earthly women: 'Yea, what he shall receive of us in duty / Gives us more palm in beauty than we have, / Yea, overshines ourself' (3.1.150–2). For Helen, it is the actions of men, and women's actions in relation to men, that define the way a woman is read by her culture, and her association with the greatest of warriors is what affirms her as the supreme beauty – or even obliterates her from view altogether, depending on how one interprets the unfamiliar verb 'overshine'.

Troilus, by contrast with his older brother Hector, consistently identifies the woman he loves as lying at the heart of his system of values – as the centre of his world. This too, however, is problematic, since his image of her is entirely imaginary. His description of her in the first scene makes this obvious:

> O, that her hand,
> In whose comparison all whites are ink
> Writing their own reproach; to whose soft seizure
> The cygnet's down is harsh, and spirit of sense
> Hard as the palm of ploughman.
>
> (1.1.52–6)

If the whiteness of Cressida's hand makes other whites seem black as ink, the term 'white' has lost all meaning – and the argument that black is white was the classic instance of choplogic or sophistry as taught in Elizabethan schools.[19] Again, if her skin is so soft it makes a cygnet's down seem harsh, then the term 'softness' no longer has a function; while if the 'spirit of sense', which is the faculty by which we convey sense impressions to the brain, has lost its sensitivity, then we can no longer distinguish one thing from another by touch. This view of Cressida, Troilus claims, is not merely true – it *falls short* of truth; so that truth itself would seem, in his opinion, to be both imaginary and inaccessible through the senses. There is no chance at all, of course, that any woman could live up to this kind of hyperbole, and sure enough at the point when Troilus finally sleeps with Cressida – in the scene that follows Pandarus's scene with Helen, Act 3 Scene 2 – his main concern is that she won't match his expectations, that is, the masturbatory fantasies with which he has satisfied himself during their courtship. This, at least, is one interpretation of his speech before their union:

> Th'imaginary relish is so sweet
> That it enchants my sense. What will it be,
> When that the wat'ry palates taste indeed
> Love's thrice-repured nectar? Death, I fear me,
> Swooning destruction, or some joy too fine,
> Too subtle-potent, tuned too sharp in sweetness,
> For the capacity of my ruder powers.
>
> (3.2.17–23)

In other words, Troilus fears he will be unable to *feel* the delights of sex about which he has been fantasizing for so long. His private fantasies are the zenith of his sex life, and sexual action can only be a disappointment by comparison.

Cressida herself is fully aware that it is the male imagination that makes women exemplary, and that women have no agency in the process (apart from Lucrece, of course, whose technique of doing so is hardly appealing). She holds Troilus off as long as she can, as she informs the audience:

> Women are angels, wooing;
> Things won are done; joy's soul lies in the doing.
> That she beloved knows naught that knows not this:
> Men prize the thing ungained more than it is.
>
> (1.2.277–80)

Helen, too, has good reason to know that she is a construct of the male imagination. Troilus points this out, unaware that his words ironically underscore the fantastic nature of his image of Cressida: 'Helen must needs be fair,' he tells his Trojan compatriots, 'When with your blood you daily paint her thus' (1.1.86–7). The painting here is that of cosmetics, an art form that stood for deceit in Elizabethan culture; so Troilus is suggesting that Helen is not in fact what the Greeks and Trojans make her out to be – that she is, in fact, *made up* in another sense. Troilus's rival Diomedes has a similar view of her:

> For every false drop in her bawdy veins
> A Grecian's life has sunk; for every scruple
> Of her contaminated carrion weight
> A Trojan hath been slain. Since she could speak,
> She hath not given so many good words breath
> As for her Greeks and Trojans suffered death.
>
> (4.1.71–6)

Here Helen's painted body has become carrion – another 'wormeaten idol', in Chapman's phrase – hideously overwhelmed by the male corpses who have fought to uphold the myth of her exemplarity. The association of Helen with cosmetics and rotting flesh suggests that she is ageing, like the late portraits of England's queen, so that the one quality that's been ascribed to her, bodily beauty, is fading fast. The Trojan debate over her value in the play's second act therefore focuses on *time*: if she was deemed worth taking from her husband in the first place, she must of necessity be deemed worth keeping seven years later. Hector objects that her value cannot be determined by a 'particular will' (2.2.53) – presumably that of Paris – but must instead be *inherent* in her if she is to be kept, and that her inherent value is far less than the accumulated value of the lives that have been lost to keep her; he is therefore in favour of giving her back, since 'to persist / In doing wrong extenuates not wrong, / But makes it much more heavy' (2.2.186–8). Troilus and Paris, on the other hand, insist that the 'will' that imputed value to her was a *general* one, not particular – that is, that all the Trojans gave their assent to Paris's judgement of Helen's immeasurable worth. Hector continues to disagree; but the upshot of the debate is a sudden rejection on Hector's part of the philosophical principles for which he has been arguing all along. The Trojan hero chooses to dismiss what he claimed as 'truth' – that Helen is worthless – and chooses to retain her because "'tis a cause that hath no mean dependence / Upon our joint and several dignities' (2.2.192–3). A general rule – that two wrongs don't make a right – is supplanted by a different kind of generality: that the collective and individual honour of the Trojans would be impugned by any belated admission they were wrong; and thus the myth of Helen's exemplarity is prolonged for another three years. The scene makes it plain, if it wasn't already, that the Trojan War is not about women but men, and that the women who are its ostensible motive are essentially male inventions – irrelevant except insofar as they afford the occasion to test masculine 'dignities' in combat.

Men's exemplarity, meanwhile, would seem to be yet more unstable than women's. Distinguishing one man from another is a difficult matter; in the second scene, for instance, Pandarus fails to distinguish Troilus at a distance from his non-combatant brother the priestly Deiphobus (1.2.219–21) – a mistake Cressida takes great pleasure in mocking; and later Aeneas finds it hard to tell Agamemnon apart from his fellow Greeks, despite repeated heavy hints from the general himself (1.3.215–56). This difficulty explains the Greek insistence that the purpose of their continued siege of Troy is to establish the difference between heroes and ordinary men; it takes something as calamitous as a war to separate the masculine wheat from the effeminate chaff. Agamemnon's anonymity also identifies the source of the problem he faces within his camp: that of insubordination. The general is simply not sufficiently *distinguished* to take his place at the head of a military hierarchy – and this is not just the fault of Achilles, who refuses to recognize Agamemnon as his general. The same attitude is spreading through the lower ranks of the army, with the result that Agamemnon can no longer be seen as generally representative of his people. His exemplary status as the ideal *general* is therefore at risk, and he responds – on the advice of Ulysses – by hatching a plot to undermine Achilles' reputation, in turn, as the exemplary warrior. Agamemnon, then, agrees to undermine a hierarchy in a bid to restore a hierarchy, to discredit an example in a bid to restore his own exemplarity; a situation which, as Ulysses points out in his great speech on order (1.3.75–137), erases the distinction between right and wrong by erasing the basis on which such distinctions are made. The scene in which Ulysses utters his speech, Act 1 Scene 3, contains not a single mention of the woman who is the supposed pretext of the Trojan War; so in this way too the hierarchy of values has been undermined. The Greeks are clear about their real motive in fighting the war: to achieve distinction; but they are also clear about the extreme difficulty of obtaining and retaining such distinction – and contribute to this extreme difficulty by their willingness to destroy each other's reputations.

The Trojans, then, make Helen central to their cause, while exposing the fact that their real priority is the augmentation of masculine honour and dignity. The Greeks put their honour squarely at the centre of the conflict, while admitting that it is badly tarnished. The Trojans look to the past for justification of their present commitment to retaining Helen, since what they considered valuable once must be valuable still, otherwise value itself can only ever be contingent. The Greeks look to the future to justify their long campaign, and seize every opportunity to bequeath a positive image of themselves to their descendants. The Trojans pride themselves on their consistency, while the Greeks don't care about being consistent so long as they come out of the conflict smelling of roses. But the Trojans are *not* consistent, whatever they claim. Troilus swiftly loses interest in Cressida after a single night of pleasure: 'Sleep kill those pretty eyes,' he tells her next morning as he arms for battle (4.1.4), and Cressida sees at once that her prophecy has been fulfilled: 'You men will never tarry,' she complains as she tries in vain to keep him at her side (4.1.17). Hector, who has a reputation for sparing unarmed men, forgets it completely when he sees a fine suit of armour on a fleeing enemy (5.6.28–32); and we've already seen how consistent he is when it comes to women. The Greeks and the Trojans, in other words, are indistinguishable, and it is the duel between Hector and Ajax that points this up. The duel ends before it has begun because it turns out that the ox-like Greek is partly Trojan. 'Were thy commixtion Greek and Trojan so,' Hector tells him,

> That thou couldst say, 'This hand is Grecian all,
> And this is Trojan; the sinews of this leg
> All Greek, and this all Troy; my mother's blood
> Runs on the dexter cheek, and this sinister
> Bounds in my father's', by Jove multipotent,
> Thou shouldst not bear from me a Greekish member
> Wherein my sword had not impressure made
> Of our rank feud.
>
> (4.5.125–33)

But Ajax is neither one thing nor another, and neither are the warring armies between which his corporeal person is so evenly divided. Cressida, too, is neither one thing nor another, as Troilus finds; 'This is and is not Cressid,' he tells himself when he eavesdrops on her assignation with Diomedes (5.2.153). Yet even at this point he seems reluctant to let go his fantastic image of her as the touchstone by which the value of everything else is to be measured. Human beings, it seems – whether actual or fantastical – are not the best material to fashion universal principles out of. There is too much 'commixtion' in them, as Hector puts it. They are too subject to change, through time, through shifting moods, through illness, desire, the chance of war, and basic rottenness. Thersites sums it up when he verbally spreads venereal disease throughout both camps: 'Lechery, lechery, still wars and lechery ... A burning devil take them!' (5.2.201–3). The exemplary bodies Shakespeare has given us are already falling to pieces before this curse can take effect.

The process of making history from the unsatisfactory material of human flesh is best summed up in the death of Hector. When Achilles is finally goaded into fighting his Trojan rival, he finds he is too out of shape to defeat the great warrior man to man, and resorts instead to treachery. He orders his personal guard, the Myrmidons, first to isolate Hector on the battlefield, then band together to murder him; and having done so, the Myrmidons raise the cry: 'Achilles hath the mighty Hector slain' (5.9.14). In a reversal of the procedure with examples – where a particular example enables one to articulate a general precept – here a general or collective assassination is verbally translated, so to speak, into one man's particular triumph on the battlefield. As a result of this reversal of the usual procedure with history-making, two opposing versions of the Trojan War come into being: the version we've seen on stage, in which Hector is killed by treason, and the version favoured by Homer, in which he is killed by Achilles' prowess. The business of writing history could never look innocent again after Shakespeare penned this episode.

The process of deriving examples from history, meanwhile, is best summed up in another scene from the play's central act. In Act 3 Scene 2, Troilus and Cressida prepare to sleep together for the first time, and preface the longed-for moment with a formal declaration of their own exemplarity, in a warped pastiche of the marriage ceremony that never takes place between them. In his declaration, Troilus professes himself to be committed – or rather addicted – to what he calls 'truth' or loyalty, but he does so in terms that render truth itself a profoundly relativistic concept. From this time forward, he tells her, 'Troilus shall be such to Cressid as what envy can say worst shall be a mock for his truth, and what truth can speak truest not truer than Troilus' (3.2.92–4). Soon afterwards he goes a step further: 'I am as true as truth's simplicity,' he insists, 'And simpler than the infancy of truth' (3.2.164–5). By the time he has identified truth as having degrees of intensity ('truer', 'truest') and levels of maturity ('infancy' presupposes that there will inevitably be a later, more devious stage in truth's development), his climactic assertion – that all male lovers who promise to be faithful will henceforth proclaim themselves 'As true as Troilus' (3.2.177) – has been rendered meaningless as well as glibly alliterative.

More importantly, however, Troilus's declaration of his own superlative truthfulness is accompanied by an assertion that women are constitutionally incapable of equal fidelity. 'O, that I thought it could be in a woman,' he muses at one point, 'To keep her constancy in plight and youth, / Outliving beauty's outward, with a mind / That doth renew swifter than blood decays' (3.2.153–8). In other words, at the very point when Troilus declares his eternal fidelity to Cressida, he is being unfaithful to her by assuming her incapacity for similar commitment; and his assumption that she and her sex embody fickleness belies his claim to be childishly 'simple' in his attachment to her. He is making her up, in fact, in exactly the way he was at the beginning of the play when he envisaged her as unthinkably, indescribably perfect. His anticipation of her likely betrayal of his trust is an extension of his fear that she will not live up to his impossibly idealized imaginings of her; and this in its turn confirms what Cressida has always known about Troilus. Early in the play, as we have seen, she predicted that her lover would lose interest in her once he had gained access to her body ('women are angels, wooing; / Things won are done; joy's soul lies in the doing' [1.2.277–8]). What happens in this scene instead is that he starts to lose interest in her before they have even slept together, at the very point when having sex with her becomes a material possibility.

Cressida's declaration, by contrast, concerns itself with the appalling *permanence* of the image of her Troilus has just put forward, as against the transience of her perfection. Her account of how her name will be used in future – as an integral part of the clichéd aphorism 'as false as Cressid' (3.2.191) – underlines the phrase's dreadful durability, which enables it to defy the ineluctable operations of time itself as the passing minutes obliterate people, objects, buildings and kingdoms, leaving only that tritest of truisms to survive into Shakespeare's lifetime. 'If I be false,' she tells her lover,

> or swerve a hair from truth,
> When time is old and hath forgot itself,
> When waterdrops have worn the stones of Troy,
> And blind oblivion swallowed cities up,

And mighty states characterless are grated
To dusty nothing, yet let memory,
From false to false, among false maids in love,
Upbraid my falsehood!

(3.2.179–86)

The notion here of a single woman's falsehood enduring beyond the names and traces of successive civilizations, of a single identity being commemorated beyond the record of history itself – beyond her political context, beyond the system of values that governed her culture – is absurd, of course. So too is the notion that her betrayal of Troilus should be considered worse than any other betrayal – than Helen's of Menelaus, for example, which brought about the Trojan war. The absurdity of these positions is compounded by the suggestion that *all* stories of 'false maids', as handed down by the bitter male chroniclers of female fickleness, may be inaccurate: 'Let memory / From false to false' implies the falsity of the process of remembering as well as of what's remembered. And the speech as a whole transforms the humanist exercise of fabricating permanent examples out of the fickle substance of human experience into a nightmare. In this it foreshadows Shelley's celebrated vision of 'Ozymandias, king of kings' as a pair of trunkless colossal legs in an empty desert; except that the legs here are replaced by a string of syllables conveying a bit of petty slander, an unsavoury morsel of old news. It is hard to think of a bleaker epitaph for the English history play as it had been penned, performed and widely praised in the last decade of the sixteenth century.

5

New Directions

'What Art Thou, Greek?': Greeks and Greece in *Troilus and Cressida*

Miklós Péti

What are Greeks like in *Troilus and Cressida*? In the first impression, they are 'orgulous', with 'their high blood chafed', as well as 'strong and skilful to their strength, / Fierce to their skill and to their fierceness valiant'.[1] But this is not a play of first impressions: as we progress in the plot, Troilus implies the Greeks are also cunning tempters (4.4.83–90), and by the end they are referred to as 'strawy' (5.5.24) and 'cogging' (5.6.12). As the Prologue indicates, the plot skips those early stages of the conflict when 'the fresh and yet unbruised Greeks do pitch / Their brave pavilions' (14–15): there is no initial excitement, when 'expectation, tickling skittish spirits ... sets all on hazard' (20–2). No, in *Troilus and Cressida* we are right in the middle of the Trojan War, seven years into the siege (1.3.12) with no reassuring end in sight. Uniquely among his plays, Shakespeare sets the major part of the plot in the camp of an occupying army facing a disappointing stalemate, in a situation where motives, goals, personal relationships, the idea of home, or the meaning of the whole enterprise are all bound to be challenged. Homer does much the same, but while in the *Iliad* the heroes (especially Achilleus) shine all the more splendidly for their bold interrogation and active transgression of heroic values, in *Troilus and Cressida* all the martial and personal glory of Homer's godlike figures is gone. In Shakespeare's play we witness Greeks in a permanent crisis of identity: both as individuals and as members of a community they seem desperately lost – not only about who they are, but also about who they should pretend to be. This crisis is also aptly reflected in most Trojans' views: throughout the play the address 'Greek' has several different, often conflicting connotations. The 'dizzying multiplicity of views' *Troilus and Cressida* 'entertain[s]' in terms of its genre[2] is thus complemented by a bewildering array of Hellenic characteristics which include, and even boil down to, Thersites' self-definition in the fifth act:

HECTOR
> What art thou, Greek? Art thou for Hector's match? Art thou of blood and honour?

THERSITES
> No, no, I am a rascal, a scurvy railing knave, a very filthy rogue.

(5.4.25–8)

My purpose in this discussion is to show how the special representation of Greeks in *Troilus and Cressida* serves to challenge both ancient and early modern commonplaces about Hellenic characteristics. By showing us a deeply troubled Greek contingent, Shakespeare avoids casting his Greeks into romantic or demonic stereotypes, but he also steers clear of glorifying ancient heroes. As if Thersites' curse ('war and lechery confound all' [2.3.72]) had taken effect, we are confronted with bafflingly inconsistent performances of (and responses to) the once magnificent Greek characters only to be left, by the end of the play, 'on a darkling plain / Swept with confused alarms of struggle and flight / Where ignorant armies clash by night.'[3]

Troilus and Cressida has long been a field of contention for critics interested in Shakespeare's representations of Greece and Greekness. Much has been said about the influence of Chaucer, Lydgate and Caxton, and most writers and editors duly acknowledge the importance of Chapman's translation of Homer as well as contemporary popular versions of the Troy legend (e.g. those of Robert Greene, George Peele or John Ogle). A handful of studies, however, take a broader perspective to investigate the cultural significance of Greece and Greeks across a number of Shakespeare's dramas. Among these, T.J.B. Spencer's work is a pioneering assessment of the variety of Elizabethan stereotypes about Greeks. In his conclusion, Spencer insists that Shakespeare's Greeks are 'merely "Greeks"' that is, they are nothing more than reflections of contemporary commonplaces, and we had better refrain from seeing them as 'distorted' or 'debunked' versions of Homeric heroes.[4] There have been several attempts to reconsider and expand Spencer's tenets; most notably, Clifford Leech argued for a more nuanced picture of Greeks and Trojans in general (as well as Achilles and Cressida in particular), and John W. Velz called attention to Shakespeare's special take on ancient Greek political philosophy.[5] It would, of course, be foolish to underestimate the importance of such national stereotypes in Shakespeare's plays, but *Troilus and Cressida* seems to present a special case where the commonplace characteristics of Greekness are embedded in a plot problematizing one of the foundational ancient Greek experiences. It is enough to contrast Sebastian's exasperated appeal to Feste in *Twelfth Night*, 'I prithee, foolish Greek, depart from me' (4.1.17) with any address containing 'Greek' in *Troilus and Cressida* to see the difference.[6] In the former example, 'Greek' is indeed a stereotype: it is understood as 'exuberantly foolish', nothing more and nothing less, whereas in *Troilus and Cressida*, even one of the most worn expressions, 'merry Greek' (1.2.105; 4.4.55) is bound to attain larger significance against the background of the play's setting.[7] If Shakespeare's Greeks in *Troilus and Cressida* were 'merely "Greeks"', as Spencer would have it, they could be easily replaceable by stereotypical characters from any other nation (e.g. France or Italy), and the mythic background of the play would prove quite insignificant. Our experience of the play, however, suggests, that the persistent questioning of received modes of Greekness is one of its essential features, or, in other words, that Shakespeare's deployment of early modern stereotypes (presumably before a contemporary audience who could both appreciate and see through them) is only one aspect of his representation of Hellenic characters.[8]

Shakespeare's complex ideas about Greece and Greekness have been in the focus of more recent studies, too. Sara Hanna notes the 'eccentric' or 'centrifugal' tendencies of the so-called Greek plays which can become manifest on several levels from generic instability through an inclination toward fantasy to the presence of the sea which characteristically serves as 'setting, symbol, or means of trade, adventure, warfare, escape, and even suicide.'[9] In an equally important essay, A.D. Nuttall argues that the by and large Greekless Shakespeare somehow 'had a faculty for driving through the available un-Greek transmitting text to whatever lay on the other side.'[10] In the case of *Troilus and Cressida*, this also results in a distinction between traditions: the Trojans are, according to Nuttall, more chivalric and Chaucerian, while the behaviour of the Greeks resembles the brutality of the Homeric world. Due to Shakespeare's relentlessly unbiased handling of the traditional material, however, the play itself 'hovers, in wholly controlled manner, between horrified fascination and burlesque ... [and] becomes a killing field of high traditions'.[11] In the following pages I will try to muster new pieces of evidence for the latter point, but I will also try to point out those crucial aspects of Shakespeare's representation of Greeks which make these heroes of old decidedly (and ultimately) un-Homeric.

Finally, we should also take note of the most recent upsurge in scholarship concerning Shakespeare and the Greeks. Several fresh studies have demonstrated the variety of sources and ways in which Shakespeare might have encountered the cultural heritage of ancient Greece in writing *Troilus and Cressida*. Thus, Tania Demetriou and Tanya Pollard argue for a much more widespread presence, and possible influence on Shakespeare, of Homeric epics in the seventeenth century than has hitherto been conceived.[12] Similarly, Jessica Wolfe argues that Shakespeare's engagement with Chapman's Homer goes well beyond lexical borrowings or the occasional adoption of plot elements. In his translation, Chapman is especially keen on identifying and commenting on ironic or 'scoptic' features of the Homeric narrative which Shakespeare, in turn, takes to the extreme in *Troilus and Cressida*, so much so that 'it is no longer even possible to distinguish between the parody and its original'.[13] Further, in the newly-published *Shakespeare and Greece*, Alison Findlay and Vassiliki Markidou provide a comprehensive survey of the 'fluid, multifaceted mosaic' of early modern conceptions of Greekness and Greece, which is then excellently exemplified in Efterpi Mitsi's study in the same volume on how *Troilus and Cressida* 'assembles ... parallel as well as competing versions of the legend [of the Trojan War]' in service of its reflection and critique of contemporary antitheatrical stances.[14]

This cursory review of the astonishing variety of critical views and methods concerning a rather niche subject in *Troilus and Cressida* indicates that questions concerning Shakespeare's representations of Greeks will never receive completely satisfactory answers.[15] What Alexander says to Cressida about Ajax: 'There is no man hath a virtue that he hath not a glimpse of, nor any man an attaint but he carries some stain of it' (1.2.24–6) can easily be applied to any of the Hellenic heroes. The Greeks are ridden with contradictions: their individual and communal motives, actions and self-reflections are often inconsistent and are mostly in jarring contrast with the assessment of (friendly or antagonistic) outsiders. David Bevington identifies this 'dramaturgical technique ... of disillusionment' in all the Greek characters, and indeed, whereas among the Trojans Priam, and to a certain extent Hector, is comfortable in the position to check and reproach young men 'gloz[ing] superficially' and 'besotted on ... sweet delights' (2.2.165, 142–5), in the Greek camp neither Agamemnon's status, nor even Nestor's age, experience and reputation go unchallenged. Ulysses, for example, complains about Achilles' and Patroclus's crude buffoonery:

> All our abilities, gifts, natures, shapes,
> Severals and generals of grace exact,
> Achievements, plots, orders, preventions,
> Excitements to the field, or speech for truce,
> Success or loss, what is or is not, serves
> As stuff for these two to make paradoxes.
>
> (1.3.179–84)

We know (and probably Ulysses knows, too) that these rough and ready impressions are scathing exactly because the supposedly godlike heroes of the Greeks behave like parodies of themselves.[16]

The deep crisis of identity in Shakespeare's Greek host can be most clearly glimpsed in those scenes of the play where Shakespeare seems to work on the basis of some Homeric episode. The war council scene (1.3) distinctly resembles the council and assembly in Book 2 of the *Iliad*. In Chapman's *Seaven Bookes of the Iliades*, published in 1598, Shakespeare had access to Books 1, 2 and 7–11 of Homer's *Iliad*, but regardless of the similarities and the extent of actual influence, the setting and the effect of the whole scene in *Troilus and Cressida* are markedly different from what we find in Homer.[17]

In Book 2 of the *Iliad*, the council follows the violent quarrel of Achilleus and Agamemnon as a result of which Achilleus withdraws from the fight. To fulfil his promise to Thetis,

Achilleus's mother, Zeus begins to honour the incensed Achilleus by subtly thwarting the hopes of short-term Greek victory. He sends a baneful dream to Agamemnon intimating the false promise that the Greek leader might soon sack Troy.[18] Agamemnon, trusting the dream, calls together first a council of the elders, then a general assembly in which, after lengthy speeches by himself, Thersites, Odysseus and Nestor, the Achaean host is finally roused to battle (*Iliad* 2.35–483).

The situation described in *Troilus and Cressida* is in many ways similar. Both Homer and Shakespeare represent an enervated army whose leaders are scrambling to tackle the deadlock of the campaign and its consequences. The low military morale of common soldiers is also amply indicated in both works: in Homer Agamemnon's initial suggestion of the possibility to return to Greece stirs an ecstatic upheaval among common soldiers and prompts Thersites' railing (both to be repressed by Odysseus; *Iliad* 2.142–206), whereas in *Troilus and Cressida* Ulysses blames the weakness of leadership for the 'hollow tents' and 'hollow factions' in the Greek camp (1.3.80). In Shakespeare's play, even the Trojans sense the Greeks' inertia: Aeneas brings his challenge to rouse 'these lazy tents' (1.3.257) in a 'dull and long-continued truce' (1.3.262).

These apparent similarities notwithstanding, Homer and Shakespeare use their respective episodes for very different purposes. In the *Iliad*, the initial chaos and Thersites' cameo protest resulting from Agamemnon's attempt to 'test' the army (*Iliad* 2.73) serve to offset, and even to incite the ensuing 'beating of the war drums' by Odysseus, Nestor and Agamemnon himself. As the tension rises, Homer illustrates the excitement of the people with strings of similes, and, despite the apparent irony resulting from the audience's foreknowledge, the whole scene develops into a tremendous crescendo with the army ready to fight and Agamemnon elevated among the leaders. As Chapman translates:

> Mongst whome [the Greek leaders] the mightie king of men, with browes and eyes like Jove,

> Like Mars in wast, in brest like him that most doth water love,
> And as a Bull amidst the hearde most proudly far doth goe
> (For he with well-brancht Oxen fed, makes most illustrious show):
> So Jupiter made Atreus' sonne in that death-threatning day
> The bravest object of all Greeks that held supremest sway.
>
> (453–8)[19]

It is on the basis of such passages that literary critics of the Renaissance saw in the figure of Agamemnon the 'good gouernour'.[20] Indeed, from the perspective of early modern epideictic rhetoric, the Homeric episode might well serve as a dense showroom of exemplary characters with Ulysses representing good counsel and prudence, Nestor standing for the wisdom of old age, and Thersites embodying scurrility and indecorum.[21] Such interpretations of the Homeric characters were all-pervasive in early modern culture from emblem books to high poetry; what must have made the Homeric episode especially relevant and resonant for early modern readers is the focus on the nature and attributes of kingship.[22] From Agamemnon's taking his Jove-given sceptre to hand through Odysseus's insistence that there should be only 'one king whome Saturn's sonne / Hath given a scepter' (Chapman, 2.199–200), to Nestor's reminder of Zeus's promise and Agamemnon's sacrificial prayer the theme of god-derived kingship authenticates the narrative in the cosmic scheme of Zeus's will (*Iliad* 1.5) – again, even despite the obvious and bitter irony of the episode. The more general guardianship of the Olympians is reinforced by the intervention of Hera and Athene who prevent the 'glorilesse' flight of the Greeks from Troy (Chapman, 2.147) by urging Odysseus to restore order.

The council scene in *Troilus and Cressida* is certainly not informed by any such teleology; rather, it shows the Greek leaders feckless in their attempt to come to any decision. In fact, they cannot even decide on whom to blame their failure: the scene starts with Agamemnon's self-justifying speech in which he first attributes the lack of success to 'the protractive trials of great Jove' (1.3.20), but then, in the same breath, also to Fortune (1.3.23). Following him, Nestor delivers a bombastic oration about the virtues of withstanding 'the reproof of chance' (1.3.33) and 'chiding fortune' (1.3.54) only to be followed by Ulysses' long oration on degree which, as many have noted, works rather counterproductively by questioning the authority of Agamemnon and representing in offensive detail Patroclus's 'imitation' of the Greek worthies. The council is then interrupted without resolution when Aeneas enters to deliver Hector's challenge to the Greeks, and the solution of the problem is relegated to the private scheming of Nestor and Ulysses. No matter how Agamemnon insists, falsely, that 'all the Greekish lords, ... with one voice / Call Agamemnon head and general' (1.3.220–2), by the end of the scene we are reinforced in our initial impression that 'the specialty of rule hath been neglected' (1.3.78) and the 'topless deputation' (1.3.152) of the chief is severely compromised. Two episodes within the scene, Agamemnon's barking command to Menelaus (as if to his 'varlet'), and Aeneas's inability or unwillingness to recognize the supreme Greek leader are symptomatic of the state of the high command: the Greeks simply don't live up to either early modern or contemporary expectations.[23] Agamemnon is at a loss as to whether Aeneas 'scorns us, or the men of Troy / Are ceremonious courtiers' (1.3.233–4), precisely because he senses how proudly 'free ... debonair, unarmed' the Trojan's performance is (1.3.235). The whole scene leaves the impression that the Greeks are uncomfortably aware that their 'reputation is at stake' and their 'fame is shrewdly gored' (to use Achilles' own words – 3.3.229–30), still, they are not able to react as a community. 'The enterprise is sick', says Ulysses, echoed by Nestor and Agamemnon (1.3.103, 138–41). The 'plague of Greece' Thersites wishes on Ajax (2.1.11) is not the Iliadic plague that 'saw off down to Hādēs, / souls of heroes' (*Iliad* 1.3–4), but, as David Bevington also points out, the inability of the Greeks to be what they are supposed to be.[24] The development of the play shows us that this plague is highly contagious as it affects even those who come in close contact with the Greeks: Calchas, in his plea to exchange Antenor for Cressida, complains about how he has changed (3.3.1–12), and Trojans like Cressida and Hector start to behave unlike their former selves almost as soon as they set foot in the Greek camp.[25]

In the council scene, and throughout the play, two remarkable differences from Homer serve to amplify the bleak impact the Greek characters make. First, in the *Iliad*, the permanent physical presence of the Aegean and the Hellespont as well as the illustrative potential of seascapes in the similes provide a striking background and contrast to the action even in the most stifling scenes of conflict.[26] In *Troilus and Cressida*, by contrast, the few references to the sea are merely emblematic: Troilus sends Pandarus on a 'wild and wand'ring flood' to pander between himself and Cressida (1.1.96–100); Nestor uses a Senecan proverb of the stormy sea to exemplify how 'valour's worth' remains stable (1.3.34–45); and Ulysses demonstrates the lack of order with reference to the 'raging of the sea' among other things (1.3.97). The sense of adventure related to the sea which Sara Hanna ascribes to Shakespeare's Greek plays is conspicuously absent from the greatest part of *Troilus and Cressida*: the closest we get to an awareness of the story's essentially Aegean setting is in the Prologue's brief overview of the Greek's journey to Troy (1–13), and in Troilus's justification of Paris's voyage (2.2.72–5).[27] For the Greeks in the play, there is no outlook beyond the stuffy camp on the dusty plain.[28]

Another important difference from the Homeric setting concerns the classical pantheon. In Homer, gods are an integral part of the plot: they cultivate a strong relationship with mortals so much so that they often intervene in their affairs, and their general outlook on human existence provides an important alternative perspective on the conflict.[29] The council scene of the *Iliad*, as we have seen, is initiated by Zeus, throughout the debate there are several references to the gods' portents and promises (*Iliad* 2.301–2, 346–53), and it is only through the actions of Hera and Athene that the Greeks' return to Greece 'beyond destiny' is averted (*Iliad* 2.155–81). In *Troilus and Cressida*, there is no divine intervention, and the references made to Gods (Jove, Juno, Mars, Mercury) are predominantly self-serving, blasphemous, formulaic or allegoric.[30] The play stands uniquely apart from Shakespeare's other dramatic representations of war in its total lack of reference to any 'supernatural soliciting' (*Macbeth* 1.3.129): there is no further dimension, no cosmic background here to justify, or alleviate, the brutal reality of war.

The 'godlessness' of the Greeks is quite apparent in a number of scenes based on, or inspired by, the great embassy scene of the *Iliad*. In Book 9 of the *Iliad*, after repeated defeats by Hector and the Trojans, the Greek army is called to council again. Agamemnon sends Aias, Odysseus and the old Phoenix to appease Achilleus – promising sumptuous rewards if he changes his mind. The embassy is unsuccessful: the incensed hero in a powerful speech refuses to be persuaded and remains unmoved even in spite of the old Phoenix's pleas. Not only does the episode brilliantly frustrate all (including the reader's) expectations of the hero's return to battle, but by revealing Achilleus's deeply entrenched resentment of the war it also questions the heroic ideal Homer is often seen to promote. These profoundly human concerns are, however, enhanced by constant references to the significance of divine plans and divine will. The repentant Agamemnon blames his blindness on Zeus's *atê* (*Iliad* 9.17–22), the delegates of the embassy each appeal to Achilleus's piety (*Iliad* 9.502–14), and Achilleus himself reveals the prophecy given at his birth (*Iliad* 9.410–16). Although the scene delays the resolution of the conflict in focus, the characters' insistence on the divine motivation, endorsement or disapproval of human actions exposes the larger scheme in which these actions receive their significance.

In *Troilus and Cressida*, there are repeated attempts by the Greeks to approach Achilles, but none of them involve, or invoke, a metaphysical frame of reference (2.3, with earlier embassies mentioned at 2.3.76 and 3.3). These are pragmatic missions: their ulterior motive is to rouse Achilles in a roundabout manner, according to Ulysses' plan (1.3.368–87). By putting on a show to incite the 'blockish Ajax' (1.3.376) to emulate Achilles, they hope to provoke the hero to return to battle: in a kind of mock-embassy they even 'put on / A form of strangeness' and 'either greet [Achilles] not / or else disdainfully' as they 'pass along' (3.3.50–3). The strategy seems to work as Achilles realizes his 'reputation is at stake' (3.3.228). The reputation in question is not the 'imperishable renown' (*kleos aphtiton*, *Iliad* 9.413) promised to Homer's Achilles at his birth, but the 'honour' kept bright by being in 'fashion' (3.3.152–3), the 'worship' of the Greeks (3.3.183) – at least this is what finally seems to stir the hero in Ulysses' long speech (3.3.103–91). Even this rather dubious motivation is called into question, however, when, upon receiving a letter from Troy's Queen Hecuba, Achilles decides to withdraw from battle in protection of his oath to his 'fair love', Polyxena:

Fall, Greeks; fail, fame; honour, or go or stay;
My major vow lies here; this I'll obey.

(5.1.42–3)

In a fine parallel to Cressida's own dishonesty in the Greek camp, Achilles cannot deliver on his promises. His exchange of empty taunts with Hector at the feast (4.5.230–51) also serves to remind us that his mind remains 'troubled, like a fountain stirred' (3.3.309) throughout the play.

The communal troubles of the Greeks and the personal crisis of their greatest hero are also aptly reflected in Shakespeare's representation of the relationship between Achilles and Patroclus. The extraordinary comradeship of these two heroes has, since Homer's time, acquired different interpretations: already in antiquity it was considered to be one of the exemplary friendships of all time; at the same time, it was also singled out as an instance of homosexual love.[31] For early modern audiences both traditions might have made sense.[32] Shakespeare, however, seems to avoid choosing either by presenting the friendship in contradictory terms. The Greeks tend to suggest, not very subtly, a homoerotic bond between the two: Ulysses refers to the pair as lying 'upon a lazy bed the livelong day' (1.3.147), while, more explicitly, Thersites calls Patroclus Achilles' 'brach', 'male varlet', and 'masculine whore' (2.1.111, 5.1.15, 17). By contrast, as far as we can see in the plot, both Achilles and Patroclus seem to be investing their energies in heterosexual relationships: Achilles is confessedly in love with Polyxena, and among the Greeks Patroclus behaves the most flirtatiously with the newly-arrived Cressida (4.5.28–35). The words of the heroes, however, seem to tell yet another story. We get to know very little about how Achilles feels towards Patroclus: characteristically, he calls his friend 'My sweet Patroclus' only when he sends him on an errand (5.1.36): the adjective 'sweet' here, I would claim is at best a simple vocative, at worst manipulative sweet talk, very much like Troilus's solicitation to Pandarus in the first scene ('Sweet Pandarus', 1.1.80–2). Further, tellingly, when Ulysses brings news about the newly-awakened battle rage of Achilles, his 'arming, weeping, cursing, [and] vowing vengeance', his report is as much related to the Myrmidons' sorry state as Patroclus's 'wounds' (5.5.30–5).[33] Patroclus, on the other hand, does mention the 'great love' Achilles bears to him, and even urges the hero with the words 'Sweet, rouse yourself' (3.3.223–4) which, as John S. Garrison has recently pointed out 'connects martiality and love by likening Achilles' stirring towards battle to a stirring of sexual excitement'. Garrison maintains that 'in this sweetness ... we see a loving, potent, *and* heroical Achilles *and* Patroclus whose classical and medieval roots feed into Shakespeare's depiction',[34] which might be an accurate description of Patroclus's wishful thought, but is hardly borne out by the play itself. In the absence of reciprocal endearments from Achilles, Patroclus's words at best indicate that the two heroes' relationship is highly asymmetrical, but we are left in the dark as to the precise nature of their affection. Like Garrison, modern directors and commentators tend to see the 'deep and eroticized friendship' between Achilles and Patroclus as 'another response to the need for human closeness in an anarchic world'.[35] The text of *Troilus and Cressida*, I would contend, presents a less coherent, and rather bleaker picture: in the representation of the friendship between Achilles and Patroclus, Shakespeare does not simply 'select the least reputable versions of characters and events and heighten their unsavoury aspects',[36] but stages a conflict of traditional interpretations. Rather than creating a meaningful, let alone humane synthesis of received character-traits (Garrison's 'classical and medieval roots'), he leaves us with impressions just as disorientating as his general depiction of the Greeks.

More than any previous writer on the Trojan War, Shakespeare understood that this traditionally overdetermined conflict gave the best opportunity for a sustained critique of military glory and martial heroism. Accordingly, his Greeks in *Troilus and Cressida* are confused and confusing: their lethargy and moral desolation acutely represent the general mindset and behaviour of an occupying army in a prolonged campaign. The play provides Shakespeare's most radical perspective on the Trojan War, but it is a perspective that had been in the making for some years. As early as *The Rape of Lucrece* (1594), Shakespeare presented the Troy legend emphasizing the dreary realities of war rather than the glory gained by great deeds.[37] 'Here friend by friend in bloody channel lies, / And friend to friend gives unadvisèd wounds' (1487–8), observes a horrified Lucrece perusing the depiction of the siege on a 'piece / Of skilful painting' (1366–7). *Troilus and Cressida* looks beyond this panoramic view of the war and presents an uncompromising analysis of the dismal figures who are responsible for such senseless carnage.

For my conclusion, let me first turn to Marlowe. In the *Jew of Malta*, Ithamore, after Bellamira and Pilia-Borza cozen him into thinking he can cozen money out of Barabas, bursts out in a song:

> Content, but we will leave this paltry land,
> And sail from hence to Greece, to lovely Greece.

I'll be thy Jason, thou my golden fleece;
Where painted carpets o'er the meads are hurled,
And Bacchus' vineyards over-spread the world,
Where woods and forests go in goodly green,
I'll be Adonis, thou shalt be Love's Queen.
The meads, the orchards, and the primrose lanes,
Instead of sedge and reed, bear sugar-canes:
Thou in those groves, by Dis above,
Shalt live with me and be my love.

(4.2.88–98)[38]

It is customary to notice the similarity of this ditty to Marlowe's pastoral poem, 'The Passionate Shepherd to his Love'. Just like the bucolic idyll of that poem, Ithamore's song offers a powerful fantasy of an escape to an idealized world, but, together with a catalogue of natural pleasures, it also involves ancient myth, the journey of the Argonauts – with some irony in the motif of the 'golden fleece'.[39] Far from being 'pure decoration, unrelated in any way to the substance of the scene in which it occurs' – as Irving Ribner would have it – these lines offer an ironic glimpse into Ithamore's state of mind, as in an elated moment he stages his own ridiculous flight in pastoral and mythological terms.[40] We are reminded of Doctor Faustus who, in a different, but similarly exhilarated moment, also escapes to the world of Greek myth with the aid of a conjured-up Helen:

Was this the face that launched a thousand ships
And burnt the topless towers of Ilium? . . .
I will be Paris, and for love of thee
Instead of Troy shall Wittenberg be sacked,
And I will combat with weak Menelaus,
And wear thy colours on my plumèd crest.
Yea, I will wound Achilles in the heel,
And then return to Helen for a kiss.

(A-TEXT, 5.1.90–102)

Marlowe's irony is, of course, double-edged: Ithamore's projected voyage to a land of dreams and Faustus's pretensions for ancient heroism and romance might strike us as ludicrous and desperate, but they also resonate profoundly with the West's potent cultural nostalgia for idyllic situations and glorious times of old.[41] As in 'The Passionate Shepherd', Marlowe provides a sharp, but ultimately benevolent critique of our notions of idyll by creating the most exacting, but essentially exaggerated picture of the *locus amoenus*, so, also, in Ithamore's and Doctor Faustus's speeches he implies that the dreams we cherish of Greece and ancient Greece are in effect daydreams.[42]

Shakespeare was, of course, keenly aware of not only these culturally encoded nostalgic yearnings,[43] but also Marlowe's special treatment of them. In *The Merry Wives of Windsor*, 'The Passionate Shepherd' is broken into Sir Hugh Evans's strange language (3.1.10–25); in *As you like It*, the love-struck Phoebe evokes the high romance of *Hero and Leander* (3.5.882); and, more to our point, in *Troilus and Cressida*, Troilus emulates Faustus's ecstatic wonder at the beauty of Helen,

> a Grecian queen, whose youth and freshness
> Wrinkles Apollo's, and makes stale the morning.
> . . .
> Is she worth keeping? why, she is a pearl,
> Whose price hath launch'd above a thousand ships,
> And turn'd crown'd kings to merchants.
>
> (2.2.78–83)

For the young, inexperienced and still-aroused Troilus, Helen is a 'theme of honour and renown' (2.2.199), just as the Greeks are 'strong', 'skilful' and 'valiant' (1.1.7–8). As the brutal world of war inevitably overwhelms his romance with Cressida, he is bound to question the 'subtle games' of the Greeks, the 'dance' and the 'sweet talk' reminiscent of Marlowe's 'Passionate

Shepherd' (4.4.87). By the end of the play, however, his disillusionment is complete and reckless: he aims to hide his 'inward woe' with 'hope of revenge' on the 'great-sized coward', Achilles (5.11.31, 26).

Readers and audiences of Shakespeare's play are treated differently: our disenchantment is immediate rather than gradual. From their first appearance in the play, Greeks constantly fall below expectations: the conventional 'honour and renown' accorded to the original Homeric heroes are out of the question; the most these characters can hope for – as Ulysses observes – is a satirical rhyme sung by 'Greekish girls' (3.3.214–15). In *Troilus and Cressida*, we are deprived of traditional daydreams: there is no 'lovely Greece' to turn or return to, and no one, save the boorish Ajax, wants to be like Achilles. The Greeks Shakespeare represents are the proper stuff for modern nightmares: they are an 'unintelligible multitude', on 'a plain without a feature' under 'a sky like lead'.[44]

6

New Directions

'[B]its and Greasy Relics': The Politics of Relics in *Troilus and Cressida*[1]

Vassiliki Markidou

William Shakespeare's *Troilus and Cressida* showcases a highly iconoclastic dramatic appropriation of the epitomic Western war narrative (Homer's *Iliad*) so as to hold up to scrutiny late Elizabethan gender, religious and nationalist ideology. To achieve the specific goal, I would argue, this acerbically witty play paradoxically draws on the polysemous *topos* of relics. I will attempt to explore their politics in *Troilus and Cressida* and demonstrate that their irreverent use and diverse re-visions open up to critique early modern configurations of gender, religion and nation. To do so, I would like first of all to underscore some of the diverse meanings of *relic/s* as delineated by the *Oxford English Dictionary*:

(a) 'some object, such as a part of the body or clothing, an article of personal use, or the line, which remains as a memorial of a departed saint, martyr or other holy person, and as such is carefully preserved and held in esteem and veneration';

(b) 'a precious or valuable thing';

(c) 'something kept as a remembrance or souvenir of a person, thing or place; a memento';

(d) 'an old person';

(e) 'pl. that which remains or is left behind, in later use, esp. after destruction or wasting away; the remains or remaining fragments (of a thing); the remnant, residue (of a nation or people)';

(f) 'the remains of a meal or food; remnants, scraps, broken victuals';

(g) 'a surviving trace of some practice, fact, idea, quality, etc.';

(h) 'a surviving memorial of some occurrence, period, people, etc.';

(i) 'an object invested with interest by reason of its antiquity or associations with the past'.[2]

Troilus and Cressida makes use of, as well as problematizes, all these meanings as will shortly be demonstrated.

From its outset, the particular Shakespearean play both invests in the polysemy of relics and is haunted by them. The Prologue informs us that it '[b]egin[s] in the middle' (1.1.28); hence the Trojan War is still raging. Nevertheless, the late Elizabethan audience was well aware that Troy had long been ransacked and reduced to a lamentable pile of ruins. Thus, the personified Prologue's claim that he is 'armed' and 'suited / In like conditions as our argument' (1.1.243–50) fuses theatrical props with textual relics, namely those of the quintessential Western war story through the latter's re-writings by literary figures such as Virgil, Ovid, Caxton, Lydgate, Chaucer and Chapman. This familiar yet fragmentary literary landscape embedded in Shakespeare's play cuts across spatial and temporal boundaries. *Troilus and Cressida* not only memorializes the antecedent diverse appropriations of the Trojan War – while adding its own – but also underscores their fragility and contingency.[3] Unsurprisingly, therefore, the Prologue displays uneasiness as well as uncertainty about his impact on the spectators. In striking contrast to his militant appearance, a chivalric residue, he exclaims that he has appeared on stage '*not in confidence* / Of author's pen or actor's voice' but to invite them to 'Like of find fault; do as your pleasures are' (1.1.23–4, 1.1.30 – emphasis mine). Fittingly, as well as paradoxically, in a play that focuses heavily on war, till the fifth act – where 'a spectacular violation of chivalry',[4] namely Hector's anti-heroic death by Achilles' gang, takes place – far more dispute and contemplation about the Trojan War than action transpires. At the same time, the (anti-) heroic male body is dismembered repeatedly on a semiotic rather than a corporeal level. Two distinguished council scenes, one Greek (1.3), the other Trojan (2.2), rather than spectacular battlefield combats appear as touchstones of (the unstable) Trojan and Greek values, while even the two most renowned warriors, Achilles and Hector, dissect each other discursively (4.5.242–3; 4.5.254–5).

As Robin Headlam Wells points out in *Shakespeare and Masculinity*, at the end of the fifteenth century 'the old martial values' had been degraded. Indeed, chivalry turned into a relic, 'an antiquated system of values that bore increasingly little relationship to contemporary social and military reality', while by the 1520s 'that system had been superseded by an entirely different code of values'. At the end of the sixteenth century, Samuel Daniel praised the Earl of Essex in his *Civile Wars* as 'a rare example "Of ancient honor neere worne out of date"'. At the outset of the seventeenth century, when *Troilus and Cressida* was penned and staged for the first time, the fall of Essex, who had repeatedly been compared to Achilles, delivered a heavy blow to his faction's call for a revival of chivalric values. In 1605, Daniel would call himself 'the remnant of another time'.[5] Hence, the Prologue's armed appearance combined with his introduction of the Trojan War legend would have had great currency, simultaneously triggering diverse and clashing engagements in the *topos* of relics.

The link between militant appearance and relics is also foregrounded in the early *teichoskopia* scene of the play. Drawing Cressida's attention to the home-coming soldiers in order to advertise Troilus's combative superiority and bravery, her shrewd uncle stresses the prince's bloodied sword and his 'helm [that is] more hacked than Hector's' (1.2.224–5). These precious objects seem to uphold and reinforce his masculinity. Yet, the audience has already watched him unarm due to his lovelorn state (1.1.1–5), while Pandarus confuses him, even if fleetingly so, with Deiphobus –who will wed Helen after Paris dies – before extolling his martial entrance to Cressida. The Trojan lord thus challenges the very trait he is flaunting to his niece and hints at the interrelationship between Helen and her.[6] Consequently, Troilus's sword and helm are rendered mere shadows of heroic maleness. This decadence seeps through the play. Achilles, the Greek warrior *par excellence*, abstains from the battlefield and instead 'breaks scurril jests' and holds unruly 'pageants' in his tent together with his 'male varlet', Patroclus (1.3.148, 1.3.150, 5.1.15). Therefore, he unmoors himself from heroic masculinity and appears as an unmistakably idle and emasculated figure.[7] Even the greatest and most noble Trojan warrior, Hector, soils the quintessential relic of masculinity, a suit of armour, by deciding, at the spur of the moment, to kill its owner in order to possess it (5.6.28–32). Heroic manhood is exposed as a façade behind which lurk greed and shallowness.

While Troilus appears as heroic warrior *and* a mere sham, he presents Cressida as both a saintly female and a tainted woman. In Act 1 Scene 1, in his Petrarchan blazon of the Trojan maiden, Troilus extolls 'her eyes, her hair, her cheek' and claims that in comparison to 'her hand' 'all whites are ink' (51, 52, 53). This conventional praise draws on the discourse of courtly love evoking at the same time that of relic discourse since it alludes to a spate of secular, animated, mock relics that inspire their worshipper's devotion.[8] It thus alludes playfully to the Catholic veneration of relics of – or associated with – holy figures as vessels of divine grace. Yet, Shakespeare's original audiences would also be alert to the Reformist attack against such relics as illicit and dangerous artefacts associated with fraud and deceit and their concomitant removal from public worship. As Lucy Razzall points out:

> In traditional worship before the Reformation, seeing was believing, epitomised at the elevation of the transubstantiated host at the Mass. To a hostile reformer, however, the question of whether a reliquary contains the bones of St Peter or the bones of a pig is ultimately beside the point, because scripture is the only transparent source of truth, and reliquaries containing bones represent intellectual blindness to this truth.[9]

As early as the 1530s, royal injunctions attacked relics vehemently. The Royal Injunctions of 1538 called upon the faithful 'not to repose their trust of affiance in any other works devised by men's phantasies beside Scripture; as in wandering to pilgrimages, offering of money, candles or tapers to images or relics, or kissing or licking the same'.[10] As Jay Zysk notes, 'the Injunctions play on the sexual connotations of "kissing or licking" to suggest the perversion that relic worship engenders'.[11]

Shakespeare's *Troilus and Cressida* fuses relic worship and sexuality in order to bring forth a playful as well as complex re-presentation of relics in post-Reformation English writing. Cressida's aforementioned unhallowed association with the religious cult of relics is underlined by Troilus's complaint: 'I cannot come to Cressid but by Pandar' (1.1.91). While clearly centring on sexual desire and the complications that arise as regards its gratification, his complaint alludes to the practice of restricted access to sacred relics, which were thus associated with power and authority.[12] This is not the first time that a Shakespearean play pairs sexuality and religious sacrality. In *Romeo and Juliet*, for example, when Romeo lays eyes on Juliet for the first time, the following dialogue takes place:

ROMEO
> If I profane with my unworthiest hand
> This holy shrine, the gentle fine is this:
> My lips, two blushing pilgrims, ready stand
> To smooth that rough touch with a tender kiss.

JULIET
> Good pilgrim, you do wrong your hand too much,
> Which mannerly devotion shows in this;
> For saints have hands that pilgrims' hands do touch,
> And palm to palm is holy palmer's kiss.

ROMEO
> Have not saints lips, and holy palmers too?

JULIET
> Ay, pilgrim, lips that they must use in prayer.

ROMEO
> Oh, then, dear saint, let lips do what hands do.
> They pray, grant thou, lest faith turn to despair.[13]

This highly witty exchange sanctifies sexuality by conflating it with getting access to a shrine. Moreover, as Dee Dyas notes, it reflects the fact that '50 years after the dissolution of the monasteries in England and the dismantling of saints' cults by reformers, knowledge of the concept of physical intimacy with saints can be assumed and used in this playful fashion'.[14] Apart from this knowledge, the specific dialogue evokes a sharp awareness of a pilgrim's difficulty in gaining physical contact with the relics of a venerated saint. For as Romeo, the 'good pilgrim' has boldly gained direct access to his enshrined 'saint' Juliet, she underscores the transgressiveness of this act through her witty subversion of the *noli me tangere motif*: 'saints have hands that pilgrims' hands do touch'. If *Romeo and Juliet* and *Troilus and Cressida* converge at elevating the beloved female to the state of a sacralized yet secular relic, *All's Well That Ends Well* dramatizes a relevant gender reversal by having Helena state regarding her beloved Bertram: 'But now he's gone, and my idolatrous fancy / Must sanctify his relics.'[15] Helena's statement displays the Reformist attack against relics as idolatrous objects while highlighting her socially subversive act of falling in love with someone who 'is so above' her (1.1.88). Clearly, Shakespearean drama emphasizes the fact that 'the relic, as a material object which encloses both material and spiritual content, persists in English writing as a metaphor loaded with historical and religious memory, even as it appears to be de-sanctified'.[16]

To return to *Troilus and Cressida* and *Romeo and Juliet*, their paths separate in the fact that whereas Romeo gains an immediate, even if short, first access to his venerated female, Troilus has to negotiate with Pandarus in order to reach his own saintly beloved. Given that in the medieval era the only lay owners of relics were powerful rulers like kings and emperors, Pandarus's control over Troilus's contact with Cressida ironically undermines his social inferiority to the Trojan prince. The latter, like a dependent supplicant, pleads with her mediator to help him reach his object of veneration:

> ... I stalk about her door
> Like a strange soul upon the Stygian banks
> Staying for waftage. O be thou my Charon,
> Where I may wallow in the lily beds
> Propos'd for the deserver! O gentle Pandar,
> From Cupid's shoulder pluck his painted wings
> And fly with me to Cressid!
>
> (3.2.7–14)

Troilus's sexual impulses, fusing Eros and Thanatos, saturate his speech. Death imagery overlaps with love-talk; death is aestheticized and eroticized. Yet, Troilus also fashions himself as a devotee to Cressida and this devotion is charged with its Latin meaning: '"devotus" means bewitched, enchanted, cursed, consecrated, dedicated to divine service, and marked for slaughter.'[17] He thus evokes the pilgrims who would go through the pains of travelling to the revered relic and would value it to the extent of being willing to sacrifice their own lives for it.

The saucy link between Cressida and venerated relics is further reinforced in Shakespeare's play. In his effort to persuade his niece that the Trojan prince is suffering because of his feelings for her, her uncle hyperbolically 'laments that Troilus will recover his true self about as soon as Pandarus might undertake a barefoot pilgrimage to India'. (In his own words: 'Condition I had gone barefoot to India!' [1.2.53].)[18] Earlier on, in an equally hyperbolic manner, Troilus claimed that Cressida was a 'pearl' and '[h]er bed [was] India' (1.1.96); posed as a 'merchant' on a voyage to it; and presented Pandarus as his 'convoy' and 'bark' (1.1.99–100). As David Bevington points out, '[t]he image of kings behaving like merchants in quest of a pearl recalls Matthew, 13.45–6: "the kingdom of heaven is like a merchant man, that seeketh good pearls; who, having found a pearl of great price, went and sold all that he had, and bought it"'.[19] Cressida, the idealized and heavily desired Trojan maiden, is, I contend, irreverently associated by her wooer with the image of a holy relic to be reached via a pilgrimage and a heavenly 'treasure' to be 'purchased' at all costs. Moreover, she is brought veiled to Troilus by Pandarus and is unveiled at her uncle's request, in all probability by him ('Come, draw this curtain, and let's see your picture. [She is unveiled.]' – 3.2.45–6), similar to the sacred relics that were first occluded and then revealed by their custodians in their effort to manipulate them for specific ends.[20] Hence, Shakespeare's Cressida, Troilus and Pandarus are profanely associated with the religious cult of relics and may be viewed as mock relic, mock supplicant and mock-relic custodian respectively.[21] This impious tripartite configuration is invested with disturbing overtones. In his idealizing depiction of his beloved, Troilus repeatedly yokes spirituality to materialism. His aforementioned representation of Cressida as 'a pearl' (1.1.96) – an image which Helen, too, will be linked with

(2.2.81) – can also be viewed as suggesting the collapse between a hallowed relic (they were often regarded as 'treasures') and its ornamentation with precious jewels that were associated with exuberant cost and the relics trade. Indeed, Troilus appears as 'the merchant' while the mock-relic custodian, Pandarus, as a 'sailing Pandar' (1.1.99). As Bevington, following C.C. Barfoot, points out, the meaning of the word 'sailing' 'shades into "selling", attracted by "merchant"'.[22] Notwithstanding the aforementioned scriptural overtones of the image of the merchant buying a pearl, Troilus's particular speech may also be interpreted as mockingly smacking of the convention of the greedy relic custodian that would manipulate relics to turn a profit, including travelling with his wares to solicit money.[23]

The conflation of mercantile and religious discourse recurs in Troilus's argumentation in the Trojan council scene. When maintaining that Helen – who, as already mentioned, is strongly linked to Cressida – must be kept in Troy, he exclaims: 'We turn not back the silks upon the merchant / When we have soiled them' (2.2.69–70). His trade-informed metaphor centres on marriage and sexuality, yet one can discern echoes of relic discourse embedded in it. For as Martina Bagnoli notes, 'the overwhelming majority of relics [were] wrapped in silk' as the latter was associated with 'preciousness and monetary value and was used as a metaphor for the spiritual value of the relics and hence their authenticity'.[24] In addition to his allusion to tainted contact relics, Troilus may also be seen as drawing on relic theft when he asks his fellow Trojans why they 'beggar the estimation of what [they] prized / Richer than sea and land' and contends that they are 'thieves unworthy of a thing so stol'n' (2.2.94).[25] Nevertheless, he is actually referring to Helen who is later castigated as a 'whore' (just like Cressida is in 5.2.200), while the 'false drop[s] in her bawdy veins' and her 'contaminated carrion' are strikingly underscored in this puzzling play (2.3.69, 4.1.71, 4.1.73). Indeed, she will shortly be portrayed as a living corpse, a fake and rotten relic that spreads disease. *Troilus and Cressida* ironically transforms relics from hallmarks of spirituality to markers of sexuality, corruption and decay.

Along these lines, and in a stark iconoclastic mode, in the last act of the play Troilus associates his previously deified yet currently tainted paramour with false and 'greasy relics'. Following their sexual consummation and her handing over to Diomedes, Troilus reconfigures Cressida by means of a highly charged religious discourse. As he watches her dallying with the Greek warrior, he claims that 'the bonds of heaven are slipped, dissolved, and loosed' (5.2.163) and rails against 'the fractions of her faith, orts of her love, / The fragments, scraps, the bits and greasy relics / Of her o'ereaten faith' (5.2.165–7). Troilus labels what he reads as a clear indication of Cressida's infidelity as 'the remnant, residue' of faith as well as 'the remains of a meal or food; remnants, scraps, broken victuals'. He fuses repulsive carnality with false spirituality, alludes to the image of fake and sullied relics, and evokes the accusations of deception and excess that were typical of the reformist disapproval of relics.[26]

After Cressida loses her virginity to Troilus and he (unwillingly) delivers her to Diomedes, she relocates to the Greek camp with no mediator regulating access to her. In striking contrast to her uncle's earlier repeated appearances on stage, notable verbosity and intense interest in controlling access to her (despite his histrionic insistence in not wanting to act further as a liaison between his niece and the Trojan prince – 1.1.63–4, 1.1.78–9), Cressida's father says very little. Calchas appears at the beginning of Act 3 Scene 3, to ask for as well as arrange the exchange between Antenor and his daughter; and makes a fleeting reappearance in Act 5 Scene 2, following Diomedes' demand to fetch him Cressida, to which he laconically responds: 'She comes to you' (5.2.5). Following her shift to the Greek camp, Cressida evokes the image of a mock relic intimately accessed by everyone, while the kissing scene of the play derisively alludes to the desecration of a relic. In an ironic twist of the relic custodian's role, namely keeping the supplicants from unreservedly seeing or touching a relic,

Ulysses argues that there should be free access to Cressida – ''Twere better she were kissed in general' (4.5.21). The Greek generals, like mock supplicants, follow his advice one after another. In doing so, they puncture Troilus's earlier idealized representation of Cressida as an object of adoration and project a highly cynical one of a sexualized object, a 'daughter of the game' (4.5.64). Ulysses completes this 'translation' by appropriating Troilus's discourse to suit his best interests. He refers to Cressida's 'eye, her cheek, her lip ... her foot' (4.5.56, 57), reminding us of the Trojan prince's idolization of Cressida prior to their sexual gratification; however, he uses these blazonic relics to turn Cressida from a recipient of veneration to a loathed commodity. Through this relegation and the aforementioned ritualistic kissing of 'the madonna turned into the whore', Ulysses attempts to galvanize his fellow Greek men into a cohesive force; in other words, they will cement their homosocial bond by castigating a 'fallen' gendered 'other'.[27] This very process ironically highlights the arbitrariness of early modern gender norms and conventions. Within such a framework, even Cressida's attempt to cast herself into an anti-relic that refuses supplicant worship – she demands that Menelaus does not kiss her (4.5.40) – cannot fissure this highly iconoclastic process.

The iconoclasm of this scene is foreshadowed in the previous one. In Act 4 Scene 4, Troilus and Cressida exchange tokens of love prior to her enforced departure; he gives her his sleeve, she offers him her glove. These objects function as both mementos and mock-contact relics. In other words, each of these items reminds its recipient of the one who has bestowed it on him/her and derisively evokes the assumption that it functions in a metonymic manner, namely that it represents the venerated person with whom it has been in direct contact. Troilus associates Cressida's wearing his sleeve with being faithful to him and expresses his intense anxiety over this issue by exclaiming 'Be thou true' thrice in their farewell exchange of these highly charged objects (4.4.61, 64, 65). Hence, her offer of the sleeve to Diomedes is interpreted by its owner as the 'greasy relics / Of her o'ereaten faith' in him. Notwithstanding the bawdy connotations of the word 'greasy', given Troilus's intense disillusionment with Cressida who has been presented as akin to a revered relic, this striking phrase echoes wittily the decline in the faith that was once invested in relics with the advent of Reformation and their novel assessment as spurious objects that would lead one away from truth. Along similar lines, Cressida tells Diomedes that the one who offered her the sleeve 'takes my glove, / And gives memorial dainty kisses to it – / As I kiss thee' (5.2.85–6). Her glove evokes the diverse images of a mock-contact relic treated with tactile piety, a sartorial substitute for a desired body, and a deceptive and therefore highly dangerous token that functions as a symbol of falsity. Clearly, the sleeve and glove emerge as equivocal signs whose meaning depends on their owners' constructedness of their value, which in turn mirrors the continuous production of the value of each *dramatis persona* by the other.[28] In the world of *Troilus and Cressida*, both characters and key objects related to them are radically unstable signs.

This crucial instability is poignantly encapsulated in Thersites' *tour de force* performance of irreverence, iconoclasm and linguistic abuse. The deformed and illegitimate Greek deconstructs nearly all the other *dramatis personae*, excelling as a vehement and effective critic of their pervasive hollowness and falsity. Moreover, as Efterpi Mitsi notes, '[t]hrough his misanthropic invective, the legendary heroes of the Trojan War are exposed as mere physical beings, bound by the frailty and the base appetites of their bodies'.[29] Therefore, one might be highly surprised by Thersites' appropriation of religious discourse. What is the significance of this startling (ab)use which remains largely unnoticed by critics? In his first appearance on stage, after exchanging a number of verbal attacks with Ajax, Thersites exclaims: 'I shall sooner rail thee into wit and *holiness*' (2.1.15 – emphasis mine). Though responding to the Greek warrior, he may also be seen as addressing the audience and mockingly promising to 'bring [them] to a condition of intelligence and piety by abusing

[them] with jests'.[30] If this is so, he sardonically alerts them early on that his railing will be harsh yet deeply didactic in both secular and religious terms. Along these lines, he announces that he will see Achilles and Patroclus 'hanged like clotpolls ere [he] come[s] any more to [their] tents' and declares that he 'will keep where there is wit stirring and leave the faction of fools' (2.1.114–16). As Bevington points out, while assaulting the two Greek warriors as 'blockheads', Thersites 'echoes biblical passages about wise men and fools ... in a mocking tone of sanctimonious superiority'.[31] In his insult of Ajax, he also claims that 'thy horse will sooner con an oration than thou learn a prayer without book' (2.1.16–17). He thus exposes the Greek warrior's ignorance and foolishness, mirroring at the same time the Protestant denunciation of the Catholic believer's recitation of prayers as silly 'superstition' by satirically comparing the (in)capacity to engage in the specific practice to animal intelligence. Thersites even calls Achilles a 'picture of what thou seemest and idol of idiot-worshippers' (5.1.6–7). He clearly argues that the most famous Greek military figure is mere show and lacks substance, while those that idolize him are sheer fools. His sarcastic reference to idols and their idiot-worshippers, however, echoes scathingly the Protestant attack against Catholic devotional practices, such as worshipping statues and relics, undervalued by reformists as heavily idolatrous objects that would divert the believer from true union with God.

I would argue that Shakespeare's Thersites may be viewed as drawing on Protestant polemical texts like John Calvin's *Traité des reliques* (*A Treatise about Relics*), a satirical polemic that he published in 1543 against Catholic devotionalism – especially to Christ, the Virgin Mary, and the Saints – and through which he attempted to influence the common people.[32] In this text, Calvin took great pleasure in highlighting, for example, that 'in the iconoclastic riots that had taken place in Geneva in the mid-1530s what was believed to have been the arm of St Anthony proved, on closer inspection, to have been a stag's penis'.[33] As a result, he debased relics as shams linked to base sexuality. As John Jeffries Martin points out, the satirical discourse of Calvin's religiously informed text 'drew unexpectedly on allusions to what ... Mikhail Bakhtin has called "the lower body stratum," sexual organs, usually hidden from view but which proved the material for much of the laughter in medieval and Renaissance culture'.[34] Conversely, *Troilus and Cressida*'s Thersites thrives on bawdy discourse related to 'the lower body stratum' and takes the audience by surprise when he draws on religious discourse, which he splices both irreverently and mock-didactically with the former. The 'deformed and scurrilous' Greek curses all 'those that war for a placket' with the 'Neopolitan bone-ache' (2.3.18–19) and abuses Patroclus by vehemently castigating his sexuality and degradingly envisioning him as a rotten and contaminating relic. As he exclaims: 'Let thy blood be thy direction till thy death; then if she that lays thee out says thou art a fair corpse, I'll be sworn and sworn upon't she never shrouded any but lazars' (2.3.28–31). He can also relish a mock-pious exclamation: 'The heavens hear me!' (2.3.52). Undoubtedly, Thersites both appropriates religious ideology and satirically turns it on its head, unravelling its radical instability.

Once one realizes this duality, one appreciates the playwright's choice to give not only voice but also great verbosity to Thersites and grasps the complex signification of his illegitimacy. Ironically, this 'whoreson cur' (2.1.39) is the one who announces that '[a]ll the argument is a whore and a cuckold; a good quarrel to draw emulous factions and bleed to death upon' (2.3.69–71). After all, in his final speech he repeatedly moors his identity neither to misanthropic railing nor to scriptural appropriation but to bastardy, namely the offspring of adultery. As Michael Neill points out, the Latin word *adulter* was not only associated with adultery – and illegitimate offspring – but also with 'a counterfeiter or adulterator, of coin'; therefore *adultero* began to signify 'to falsify, adulterate or counterfeit'.[35] In fact, in his attack against Thersites, Nestor labels him 'a slave whose gall coins slanders like a mint' (1.3.193).[36] Furthermore, as he blends illegitimacy, deception and lowly instincts with pious discourse, Thersites disrupts the boundaries between fact and fiction, truth and falsity, high and low, spiritual practices and carnal excesses. This unsettling fusion is superbly reflected in his mockery of having 'said his prayers, and devil Envy say "Amen"' (2.3.20); the Catholic practice of reciting prayers is playfully connected with one of the seven deadly sins that were of Catholic origin yet of grave importance across confessional divisions. Thersites' bitter railing rises beyond denominational boundaries, once again underscoring their thin red lines.

Since religious ideology was inextricably linked with, and informed to a large extent, early modern national identity, it comes as no surprise that Thersites' iconoclasm is also evidenced in his relentless critique of nationalism. Matthew Greenfield argues that the specific character's 'illegitimacy liberates him from the ideological claim of the nation, whose central trope imagines citizens as brothers', inventing 'a particularly interesting alternative to national identity' in his dialogue with Margereton (5.8.5–14), 'a community defined by illegitimacy and dispossession'. Consequently, 'the genealogic trope at the heart of nationalism' is revealed as a sham relic.[37] What are the consequences of this exposure? As repeatedly noted by scholars, early modern English subjects derived their legendary descent from the Trojans and regarded London as Troynovant. In Virgil's narrative, Rome was founded by Trojans – hence medieval Europe's sympathy towards them – and Geoffrey of Monmouth adapted his story, claiming in his legendary history that 'Britain was to be a third great Trojan kingdom succeeding Rome, [as] was widely accepted in Shakespeare's day, appearing in Spenser's *Fairie Queene* and elsewhere'.[38] Troy constituted a sacrosanct relic that 'provided a magic mirror into which London looked and saw what it wanted to see;' by forging their capital as the new Troy, Elizabethans flaunted it as the latest virtuous and heroic city which towered above all the rest in the world.[39] Nevertheless, behind this lavish praise of London as the New Troy lurked a more sinister reflection, that of London as the fallen Troy, the corrupt city, which engaged in all sorts of excess that would lead to its decay and transformation to an inglorious residue. Therefore, Cassandra's sinister and highly unsettling ruinous visions ('Troy must not be, nor goodly Ilium stand; / Our firebrand brother Paris burns us all. / Cry, Trojans, cry! A Helen and a woe! / Cry, cry! Troy burns, or else let Helen go' – 2.2.109–12) would not have been missed by Shakespeare's original audiences. Indeed, Thersites' vehement attack on the sacrosanct relic of the Troynovant myth that constituted the backbone of Tudor political legitimation and his bawdy curse on it ('All the argument is a whore and a cuckold ... Now the dry serpigo on the subject, and war and lechery confound all!' – 2.3.68–72) would have amused the critics of this myth while insulting its supporters.

Shakespeare was not alone in pointing a finger at what had become by that time a cliché, namely the growing corruption of early modern London, by means of a satirical take on the Trojan legend. Thomas Nashe, for example, had written as early as in 1592: 'I warrant we have old hacksters in this great Grandmother of Corporations, Madame Troynovant, that have not backbited any of their neighbours with the tooth of envy this twenty year, in the wrinkles of whose face ye may hide false dice, and play at cherry-pit in the dint of their cheeks.'[40] Nashe wrecks the image of the English capital as a glorious New Troy by presenting it in distinctly gendered and highly sexualized terms, that is, as an old, deformed and repulsive bawd. Sexual corruption and trade are also fused in the striking image of 'this great Grandmother of Corporations, Madame Troynovant' and physical contamination becomes a mirror to moral decay.

Troilus and Cressida both voices and problematizes the same disconcerting preoccupations that converge not only on the spectre of the fallen Troy but most of all, on the 'fallen' female figure (Helen and/or Cressida following her loss of chastity) which, as has been demonstrated, is mockingly associated with false relics and around which trade, corruption and contamination are centred. Moreover, as Valerie Traub, drawing on René Girard and Linda Charnes, points out, *Troilus and Cressida* 'position[s] women as vessels but not victims of syphilitic contamination', promoting at the same time 'the image of syphilis as a threat not only to man, but ultimately to nation'.[41] Consequently, 'gender, nationalistic and erotic anxieties converg[e] in a powerful demonstration of othering: through a particular ideological slippage, the possibly diseased "woman" comes to equal the potentially invasive "foreigner"'.[42] Helen the Greek lives in the palace of Troy and Cressida the Trojan shifts to the Greek camp; both are labelled sluttish, castigated as (potential) carriers of venereal disease and most importantly, presented as shifting, and hence highly dangerous, signs.

In such a disconcertingly unreliable world, only railers and panders can have the last word. Near the closure of the play, Thersites apotheosizes his illegitimacy (5.8.8–10) while Pandarus, who delivers its epilogue, in a satiric reversal of the convention of the chaste relic custodian, bequeaths his syphilitic disease to the audience which he bawdily presents as '[b]rethen and sisters of the hold-door trade' (5.11.51). Far more crucially, as has been demonstrated, early modern religious, gender, and nationalist ideology is forcefully desecrated in *Troilus and Cressida*. Shakespeare's enigmatic, witty and highly acerbic play punctures venerated early modern myths like fake relics thrown in an iconoclastic fire and calls upon its audience to think long and hard about what is lost and gained through such an unprecedented obliteration.

7

New Directions

Scenes of Repossession: Greek Translations and Performances of *Troilus and Cressida*[1]

Paschalis Nikolaou

Towards Shakespeare's Troy

For someone who knew 'small Latin and less Greek', if we are to believe Ben Jonson's castigation, Shakespeare has travelled impressively well in other languages over the past four centuries; the very fact of an entry on 'Shakespeare translation' included in the first edition of *The Routledge Encyclopedia of Translation Studies* (1998/2001) alongside ones about biblical texts, above all suggests, for its writer Dirk Delabastita, that both have served 'unique cultural functions across centuries'.[2] *European*

Shakespeares, the milestone volume Delabastita edited with Lieven D'hulst a few years earlier in 1993, presented several reasons for Shakespeare's special place within an emerging discipline: necessary solutions to countless puns, neologisms, malapropisms, repetitions of iconic phrases, translators' attempted equivalences for those flexible iambic patterns; the range of ways in which existing material is reworded or reassigned by Shakespeare, and then how his play texts are themselves reconfigured and staged into further versions and visions, still concern intensely researchers in translation and adaptation alike.

Investigations of interlinguistic transfer often spill into studies of reception, coming across confirmations of, or challenges to, literary tradition. In this sense, traces of simultaneous impacts on literary and translation history abound: from practices of indirect translation in nineteenth-century Europe, to those of non-translation in former British colonies – the unchanging text a marker of imperialism – to post-colonial appropriations of Shakespeare. It is not without significance that a recent selection of essays, *Shakespeare and the Language of Translation*, includes an entire third part focusing on 'Postcolonial Translation, Tradaptation and Adaptation'.[3] Particularly instructive is the way in which Shakespeare's characteristic juxtaposition of high tragedy and broad farce and his disrespect for the unities of time, place and action became the reason for many eighteenth- and nineteenth-century critics and translators to use his work as a 'testing ground for literary and theatrical experimentation' in direct opposition to French neoclassical standards.[4] Leandro Fernández de Moratín's 1798 translation of *Hamlet* into Spanish is a striking exhibit of conflicted emotions, where despite the Spaniard's own neoclassical approach as playwright, he produces both a non-acculturated version of the play *and* makes his disagreements also clear in the paratexts surrounding his translation.[5]

Even within a corpus where comedy and tragedy often mingle, Shakespeare quickly establishes a dominant mode in most of his dramas. If *Troilus and Cressida* remains perhaps the most disturbing of the 'problem plays', it is because it sustains until the end a tonal and generic irresolution; this is part of the reason why this particular work invites experiment and transgressions. Moreover, across too many storylines, the failures of heroism and romance, already confounding audience expectations, are further exacerbated on the level of dialogue by what Jane Adamson calls a distinct fascination with 'self-negating forms of words'.[6] The dramatist keeps adding prefixes or suffixes that give us words such as 'distaste', 'unfamed', 'bragless', 'languageless' – words that, Adamson continues, 'take away with one hand what they give with the other'.[7] This unremitting uncertainty arguably corresponds to the text's self-consciousness. As Elizabeth Freund points out, this is a play that

> also persistently calls attention to its intertextuality, its anachronicity, its dependence upon a prodigious literary and rhetorical legacy. Within Shakespeare's dramatization of familiar legend, a vast encyclopedia of citation is embedded. The myth, the Matter of Troy, the classical topos, the set piece, the commonplace, the cliché, the name that has become a concept; references to books, texts, representations, figures of rhetoric – all these are on display as though *to insist on the text's derivative status*.[8]

A further result of this self-consciousness is a metadramatic tendency defining several scenes,[9] while tricks with time are also included in this overall logic: protagonists often appear to reach out from the past tense of history (Pandarus especially, addressing the audience at the play's end) and become aware within the performance of the significance of their names. Heather James has also looked extensively into allusions embedded in dialogue and in the characters' use of language: how Shakespeare allows his cast an intricately textual existence while they constantly question each other's morality.[10] What we experience as modernity here occurs in collisions of past and present, a demythologizing, or systematic undoing of interpretations of classical literature at the same time they are used, inflecting plot and structure, and in a language that is often debated as powerless (Pandarus to Troilus: 'Words pay no debts; give her deeds', 3.2.54). Those elements add to the challenges for the translator or perhaps incite further experiments. This is often the case when it comes to versions of *Troilus and Cressida* for the Greek stage.

A desired language within a 'Complete Works'

Modern Greek has inherited a millennia-long cultural legacy, and among the clearer points to be made when it comes to Shakespeare's plays with a classical setting is precisely the absence of certain acculturation strategies. And despite a few shifts in how (place) names are written, Greek translations encounter Shakespeare's sources in ways that inevitably tone down, even disremember the European medieval iterations embedded in, and shading, the play text. Certain re-arrivals take place that are easier to register by checking what occurs in other languages and literary traditions. In listing a range of shifts in his Czech translations, Jiří Josek acknowledges that

> Some passages were felt as neutral ('unmarked') in Shakespeare's days, as the subject matter mentioned in them was familiar to the contemporary audience, such as topical allusions, reference to ancient mythology (in which the Elizabethan audience was well read), etc. When translated literally, they become highlighted by their unfamiliarity to the present viewers and thus stylistically marked and non-equivalent. However, generalizing in translation to make the original text more comprehensible would deprive it of its flavour and richness. What the translator can do is to replace the unknown or lesser-known expression by a familiar one from the same or similar nest of references.[11]

In several places across the Greek renderings of *Troilus and Cressida*, *Pericles*, or *Timon of Athens*, translators variously recognize or subtly idealize a familiarity that may not be assumed when it comes to Czech audiences, or even contemporary English-speaking ones, experiencing the original plays. This is already the case in the first known translation of *Troilus and Cressida*, by M.N. Damiralis, appearing at the dawn of the twentieth century; it is undated but probably completed around 1908, close to Damiralis's translation of several other plays, such as *Timon of Athens* and *Richard III*.[12]

For the language that carries these references, a relatively unbroken continuation of the ancient tongue itself, Shakespeare becomes an opportunity for new designations, especially when it comes to two translators for whom the Bard's thirty-seven plays became a life's work. In Vassilis Rotas's case, this engagement lasted roughly between 1927 and 1975, from a point onwards in association with his partner, Voula Damianakou. Errikos Bellies began translating Shakespeare in the early 1980s and he completed the last translation (of *King Henry VIII*) in the summer of 2004 – before moving on to the *Sonnets*. Though we should bear in mind that theatrical translation can hardly be isolated from the context and time of performance, sometimes this is indeed the case: Bellies's *Troilus and Cressida* was published in 2001, among the last plays he worked on towards reaching the number thirty-seven. Rotas's version on the other hand was performed in Athens in 1972–3, soon after the translation was made, by Karolos Koun's pioneering Art Theatre. In this case, as Xenia Georgopoulou argues in a wide-ranging investigation of 'Shakespeare and Modern Greek Politics', Koun's choice also alluded to the nature of Greece's regime during that time. The original play's decadent image of antiquity, its anti-epic, satirical incidents combining with aspects of Koun's production of it, implied a comment on the dictators' kitsch aesthetic, the grotesque fiestas which were often organized in those years, involving men and women parading as figures from ancient Greek history, all in the service of strengthening a nationalistic discourse.

Georgopoulou further examines Marios Ploritis's introductory piece in the programme of the production, as well as several reviews that subtly encourage criticism of the political context, a little while before the fall of the seven-year dictatorship.[13] In this sense, linguistic decisions made by the translator, intensified visually in Koun's staging, and consequently picked up by theatre critics, collectively turn to an act of resistance that evades the strict attention of the censors.

Especially as they are completed towards the end of a long series, the versions of *Troilus and Cressida* by Rotas and Bellies reflect a consistent approach, both when it comes to their practice as translators of dramatic texts (Rotas also translated Aristophanes, Calderon and Hauptmann; Bellies's prodigious output includes over 300 plays, by Molière, Beckett, Strindberg, Albee, Pinter, among others) and as writers themselves. Rotas's Shakespeare is also part of a programme of *linguistic* acculturation, domesticating the plays' language into patterns and expressions as understood 'by the many'. In this way, he implements ideological callings from the Left and the Communist Party he belonged to for a language that is free from artifice encountered in the speech of the elites, more intimate with folk tradition and village songs; this is a translated literature that also transmits an empowering, *sociocultural intention* of Greece. For Rotas, it is the people, rather than literary criticism, that will be the final arbiter of the success of his project. Not only is this mind-set encountered everywhere in his work, including adaptations of classical myths for a mass audience as inserted across the publication of *Classics Illustrated* in Greece between 1951 and 1972,[14] but Rotas's decades-long work on Shakespeare also inflects his own original work: the structure of the historical plays is mirrored in *Rigas Velestinlis* (1936) and *Kolokotronis* (1955), centred on figures around the Greek War of Independence.

Yet despite a sense of moving as far away as possible from syntactical structures and lexical choices that could be associated with purist (or *katharevousa*[15]) aspects of the Greek language, Rotas's demotic is also an *intensified*, hyperbolic version; this Greek Shakespeare is very much part of a strategy. With Bellies, we find ourselves perhaps on the other side of the same coin: in published interviews,[16] the translator insisted he began almost by accident, and he progressed towards an unlikely completion through the combined encouragement of theatre companies, friends and critics. His outlook, especially when it comes to classic works, is of a translator always in service of the characters, reading criticism around the text and being led by the author's style rather than imposing an agenda. When it comes to language, however, Bellies's views are also strong, and reflect linguistic debates resolving only in the immediate past: he notes how 'growing up, we wrote in *katharevousa* and talked in demotic Greek. My generation turned everything to a colloquial language, we ensured this kind of speech entered writing ... The words I'll put in the mouths of the characters must be close to the reality around us.'[17] He further connects the language used by translators with the one of poets from his generation, figures like Kiki Dimoula and Manolis Anagnostakis, where 'what is poetic doesn't depend on lexical choices'.[18]

These complete translations of Shakespeare are parallel arguments for a wider situating and desired role for Modern Greek, even as they themselves extend a view of language, extraordinarily, over decades. Results can be uneven when it comes to the tone of different Shakespeare plays, and of course, in the case of *Troilus and Cressida*, the outcomes are miles apart: here is Rotas's introduction of Troilus in a characteristically sonorous, manufactured demotic, varying between thirteen and seventeen syllable lines:

Οι Έλληνες έχουν θάρρος, με το θάρρος γνώση,
με τη γνώση ασπλαχνιά, με την ασπλαχνιά δύναμη.
Μα 'γώ 'μαι πιο αδύνατος από γυναικείο δάκρυ,
πιο αβρός από τον ύπνο, πιο δειλός από την άγνοια,
λιγότερο αντρειωμένος από κόρη μες στη νύχτα
κι αδέξιος σαν παιδόπουλο άπραγο.[19]

> The Greeks are strong, and skillful to their strength,
> Fierce to their skill, and to their fierceness valiant;
> But I am weaker than a woman's tear,
> Tamer than sleep, fonder than ignorance,
> Less valiant than the virgin in the night,
> And skilless as unpractised infancy.

Errikos Bellies's text exists in part as a reaction to Rotas, and might stay with us longer due to its more neutral style and given how certain aspects of the original – Shakespeare's metre for instance – are largely abandoned: the translator mostly seeks rhythmical and alliterative effects within the line. It is a far more measured affair, closer indeed to the prose inclinations and colloquial patterns in Greek poetry produced from the 1960s onwards. The economies of everyday language can at several points be more understandable, resonant and relatable than previous efforts; again, from Troilus's entrance:

> Οι Έλληνες είναι ισχυροί, έμπειροι στην ισχύ τους,
> άγριοι στην πείρα τους, γενναίοι στην αγριότητά τους.
> Όμως, εγώ είμαι πιο ανίσχυρος και από γυναικείο δάκρυ,
> πιο μαλακός και από ύπνο, πιο μωρός και από την άγνοια,
> πιο δειλός και από παρθένα τα μεσάνυχτα:
> εγώ είμαι αδέξιος σαν άπραγο παιδάκι.[20]

(1.1.7–12)

Even though we may agree that Rotas's decidedly demotic Shakespeare required updating, his inclusion of introductions and prefaces, as well as often notes at the end of a translation, indicate a thorough study of critical perspectives and knowledge available at the time. In *Troilus and Cressida*,[21] a preface proceeds to relay to Greek readers how the play is apparently unfinished in places and structurally unruly; instances of formlessness and abandon result from both intertextuality as well as the Bard's intention (an awareness of disunities not necessarily reflected in the translation). Rotas also promptly cites in his notes[22] the various sources (even though he records them 'in English' as by 'Chapmann' and 'Chauser'); he connects mentions of theatre and acting in Ulysses' 'hierarchy' (or degree) speech in 1.3.75–137 to the self-referentiality of similar scenes in *Hamlet* and *Macbeth*; and he records along the way certain fragments and suspected rhythms from medieval song. This is the kind of research also admitted by later translators yet not carried into the published presentation of their work; in some cases however, this is due to restrictions not unexpected in a translation that appears within a theatre programme.

Other performances, other purposes

Across several inquiries into theatrical translation, Susan Bassnett reminds us of a process by nature collaborative, situated in an ensemble, normally removed from large-scale projects that process an oeuvre within a literary (poly)system as the ones mentioned above. Drama is translated in and for the present; the final shape of such work depends equally on who is cast to play the characters: 'Translators cannot know what an actor may find performable, they can only guess, yet once they can work with actors, revising and shaping the words in performance, the play can acquire vitality and excitement.'[23] The original itself also emerges from the dialogue between the writer and his actors. The image of Shakespeare in his desk, writing a perfect play is of course a myth: 'Shakespeare walked round on the boards handing out parts. No doubt the actors complained about some of what he had written and made him change their lines.'[24] George Steiner also offers some poignant words on an exceptionally collaborative context, shaped by different subjectivities:

> [T]he conception of workmanship, of formal production, was professional and non-egotistical to a degree we find difficult to experience ... Much of the Elizabethan theatre was nourished by multiple hands. These were at work often *ad hoc*, often cannibalizing previous material, on the same script.

Shakespeare begins as a collaborator in the *Henry VI* trilogy, most probably in *Titus Andronicus* and *Edward III*. . . . More than any other genre, the theatre always has something of the character of a laboratory, its doors wide open to society.²⁵

This was a situation that Nikos Hatzopoulos actively sought out as he worked on the most recent Greek version of *Troilus and Cressida*. The play was going to be performed in the Spring of 2012 at the National Theater in Athens, directed by Oskaras Koršunovas, a Lithuanian already known for several thought-provoking Shakespearean adaptations, including *Hamlet* at the Vilnius City Theatre in 2008 (but also for his approach to contemporary playwrights, as in Sarah Kane's *Cleansed* staged at the Stockholm Royal Drama Theatre in 2003, and again at Vilnius City Theatre in 2016). Hatzopoulos's translation was commissioned a year before the first scheduled performances which, unfortunately, never happened: for reasons connected with the director's health, the production was pulled just a few days ahead of the premiere.²⁶ The translation, which was to be included in the programme, thus remains unpublished, and all pages describing the play to prospective theatregoers were eventually taken down at the NT website. A proposed staging for the National Theatre of Northern Greece in March 2014 was similarly cancelled. In our correspondence,²⁷ Hatzopoulos revealed that initial meetings with the director did not lead to any clear conclusions on Koršunovas's desired angle for this performance; beyond contacting certain actors independently, which helped with developing characters and aspects of delivery, rehearsals were not conducive to a play text revised during this period (a first draft took nine months to complete).²⁸

Hatzopoulos's final version of *Troilus and Cressida* was in fact developed *after* the cancellations of the 2012 and the 2013 theatrical runs. These rare circumstances resulted in a peculiar two-part process, and an eventual version that pays further attention to the more literary aspects of the original as it gradually disconnects from the needs of a specific performance and audience. In some respects, there is an inverse relationship to Rotas's version, which was originally part of a long-standing project largely focused on language and was then deployed by the director, Koun, to comment on the socio-political present.

The Greek play text exists, nevertheless, as an attempt for clarity and immediacy on the stage, without a sacrifice (as for instance, in Bellies) when it comes to formal poetic effects and constructions in the original; Hatzopoulos strives to reassemble particularities of idiom and register associated with words as chosen by individual characters, and retains iambic patterns, if not syllable count. Greek words are far more polysyllabic and Hatzopoulos insists on the significance of carrying the content of individual lines and avoiding enjambments from a translation adhering also to the 10–11 syllable lines of the original.[29] In this unpublished version, Shakespeare's rhymed couplets almost always approximate traditional Greek fifteen-syllable lines. And so, Cressida's pronouncement, followed by Thersites' words in 5.2.113–20 –

> Troilus, farewell! One eye yet looks on **thee**,
> But with my heart the other eye doth **see**.
> Ah, poor our sex! This fault in us I **find**:
> The error of our eye directs our **mind**.
> What error leads must err. O, then concl**ude**:
> Minds swayed by eyes are full of turpi**tude**.   *Exit.*

THERSITES [*aside*]
> A proof of strength she could not publish **more**,
> Unless she said, 'My mind is now turned **whore**'.

– becomes in Hatzopoulos's text (syllable count follows each line):

ΧΡΥΣΗΙΔΑ
> Τρωίλε, αντίο· τα μάτια μου κοιτούν ακόμα εσ**ένα**, (18)
> όμως τα μάτια της καρδιάς τα έχω αλλού στραμμ**ένα**. (16)
> Γυναίκες μου κακόμοιρες! Να το ελάττω**μά μας**: (15)
> πως την ψυχή μας κυβερνά η σφαλερή **ματιά μας**. (15)

Ό,τι από λάθος ξεκινά, σε λάθος δρόμο βγαίνει· (16)
ψυχή σπρωγμένη απ' τη ματιά, είναι ψυχή χαμένη. (16)
Φεύγει.

ΘΕΡΣΙΤΗΣ [κατ' ιδίαν]
Εξήγηση σαφέστερη δεν χρειάστηκε τ' αυτί μου, (15)
εκτός αν έλεγε πως «πια, πουτάνα είν' η ψυχή μου». (15)

This attempt at a poetically enervated modern idiom is largely successful, despite a few lexical choices that momentarily recall older registers. Studying Hatzopoulos's translation, we observe corrections to lapses in previous attempts, especially when it comes to certain characters and their rhetoric. His Ulysses, for instance, avoids using 'dogged' in 1.3.366, a word that arrives at peculiar, if not incomprehensibly etymological renderings in Greek, both in Rotas and Bellies. (Not least as we encounter in the latter 'περίεργα σκυλάκια' ['curious little dogs'].) For Shakespeare's 'For both our honour and our shame in this / Are dogged with two strange followers' (1.3.365–6), Hatzopoulos produces in Greek: 'γιατί ό,τι φέρει αυτό για 'μάς, τιμή ή ντροπή, / θα σέρνει πίσω του δύο παράξενα επακόλουθα' ('because whatever this may bring, honour or shame, / it carries with also two strange consequences').

Especially given the pronounced difficulties in language as well as the structure of *Troilus and Cressida*, triangulations when it comes to translation are not surprising: each new Greek text alternates between iterations of the original and also results from reading existing versions. The source text itself is never a stable – or even English-speaking – Shakespeare. Indeed, how this theatre has been adjusted and re-imagined often challenges our definitions of the translating act, locating both limits and possibilities. The original plays grew even more palimpsestic through time, and in translation: many of them exist somewhere between Folio and Quarto editions (and in the case of *Troilus and Cressida* especially, some later iterations varied considerably more: the play was altered to cater to Restoration audiences when it was adapted by John Dryden in

1679 and in addressing what Dryden thought to be numerous deficiencies[30]).

There is something apt about variation resulting in what was felt to be an improved grounding of text in another language or Greek theatrical practice. Bellies admits to travelling between Quarto and Folio editions on almost every page as he produces his translation(s), and while Hatzopoulos confirms he largely uses the Arden Shakespeare (based on the Folio) he will consider occasionally Quarto variations (through the Oxford edition), because at certain points these appear to him more dependable when it comes to the flow of characters' thinking, and motivations.[31] And during the whole process, he occasionally checks previous Greek translations and also consults two of the French versions,[32] those by François Pierre Guillaume Guizot (1863) and Victor Hugo (1868). This layered surveying of articulations of *Troilus and Cressida* realizes a palimpsestic reading as part of the process and product of translating drama. (Particularly helpful and pertinent in this case, bearing in mind that embedded echoes and imitations of other texts already partake of the shape of the original.)

There is also the sense of intertextuality further invited in this potent mix, in service of a translation that may be imagined as a sort of 'analogous original': this is arguably the case with the translation by Nikolaos M. Panagiotakis performed by the National Theatre of Northern Greece in April 1983 in Thessaloniki. Here, not only the phrasing and lexical choices (notably those affecting terms of address and titles: **Prince** Troilus, **Queen** Hecuba and **lord** Ajax are translated as 'άρχοντας', 'ρήγισσα' and 'ηγεμόνας')[33] but also a quite consistent fifteen-syllable line (without use of a hemistich however), recall the romances of the Cretan Renaissance such as the *Erotokritos* (1645 or 1648; written by Cretan poet Vitzenzos Kornaros), which owed to Italian models. Panagiotakis's translation then, also draws from lifelong academic research on how Cretan literature was influenced by the period of Venetian rule (1211–1669); it doubles as a work of *philological imagination*, the Byzantine scholar (Panagiotakis) producing a more rhythmical and poetic version, closer to the Greek literary tradition despite the several linguistic anachronisms included. The metre deployed, combined with our own sense of false proximity and the intimacies of non-translation, turns Panagiotakis's *Troilus and Cressida* to an opportunity in constructing a lost Cretan original, a Shakespeare that might have been written in Greece. This subtle exercise in re-appropriation seeks possible Greek scenes for the Renaissance origins of *Troilus and Cressida*. An array of domesticating approaches colludes with intriguing – though equally often, jarring – tensions between demotic and purist strands of Greek, alongside several neologisms (in rendering curse words, for instance). Some of Pandarus's lines at the end of the play suggest what occurs on many levels:

Όσοι από εσάς εδώ γύρω συντρόφια του Πανδάρου **είστε**, (19)
Ώσπου να βγουν τα μάτια σας, την πτώση του θρηνή**στε·** (15)
Κι αν θρήνος δεν σας βγαίνει από μέσα, βόγγοι ας βγού**νε**, (15)
Όχι για μένα, για τα κόκκαλά σας που πονού**νε**.[34] (15)

As many as be here of Panders' **hall**,
Your eyes, half out, weep out at Pandar's **fall**;
Or if you cannot weep, yet give some **groans**,
Though not for me, yet for your aching **bones**. [5.11.47–50]

As directed by Nikos Charalambous, however, reviews perceived a disconnect; the text was used in a modernizing approach which overwhelmed viewers and lacked the subtleties demanded by Shakespeare. And some reviewers indeed anticipated the predicament with the play's reception: that it can be especially hard for Greek audiences to bypass preconceptions about these characters and to comprehend the extent of Shakespeare's appropriation of them, how they reflect more on Elizabethan England rather than classical Greece.[35]

Besides the renderings by Panagiotakis and Hatzopoulos, another translation of the play by Elli Avloniti was used in the

1991 production of *Troilus and Cressida* by the Municipal and Regional Theatre of the City of Kalamata, directed by Yannis Kakleas. Published in the programme, the 29-page text has a freer approach to conventions and formal features, recalling in a few places Rotas's demoticism but lacking interest in replicating intertextual dynamics. This was, at the time, on par with the avant-garde scenic proposal of its young director, an insistently modern version in terms of lexis, conversational tendencies and in abandoning metre in the service of immediacy. The rhymes Hatzopoulos achieved above become in Avloniti's translation blocks of unbroken text; the same happens to Pandarus's speech at the end of the play. A back translation also confirms how little the following resembles the Panagiotakis version cited earlier:

> Καλοί μου σωματέμποροι, γράψτε αυτό στο λάβαρό σας. Όσοι από σας είναι στο σωματείο του Πανδάρου, με μάτια τσιμπλιασμένα κλάψτε τον χαμό του. Μα αν δεν μπορείτε δάκρυα, τότε στενάξτε για μένα, κι αν όχι για μένα, τότε για τα κόκαλά σας τα πονεμένα.

[My dear pimps, put these words on your banner. Those of you who are members in Pandarus's guild, with your crusty eyes, do cry for his demise. If you can't manage the tears, well then groan for me, and if not for me, for your own aching bones.][36]

Reviews published at the time praised the directness of scenes including the two lovers. They also pointed out how Shakespeare's subversive gaze towards ancient myth was captured while transporting audiences to the present through decisions in lighting and costume design. Nonetheless, for some reviewers, dressing Achaean leaders with German Nazi uniforms might have been a step too far.[37] In the context of this overall approach, we should perhaps not be surprised by the fact that certain parts of the play are compressed, or even entirely missing, in the translation.

Compounds of theme and method

A more adventurous, and personal engagement with Shakespeare's play extends for nearly a decade in two adaptations (2003 and 2011) directed by Raia Mouzenidou for 'Dipylon', an Athens theatre she herself set up. 'When translating for the theatre,' Mouzenidou insists in our communication, 'several things must be decided taking into account the way speech will sound. Everything I write, I also speak it aloud, and many times over in some cases, before I reach a decision; following that, I will still reconsider choices when hearing those lines from an actor's mouth, and as I observe them moving on the stage'.[38] Such pronouncements resemble many others coming from practitioners. Researchers in drama translation will often examine inclinations of philological precision in the more conservative translations primarily for the page *vis à vis* the creativity demanded by versions for the stage[39] (alongside definitions of speakability or performabilty,[40] entangled in discussions of a theatrical translation as always completed beyond the written text).

There are further complications in Mouzenidou's case, not least initial points of contact with Shakespeare's play; she reads *Troilus and Cressida* firstly in the Victor Hugo translation during her theatre studies in Sorbonne; then, in the Greek translation by Rotas.[41] When she finally arrives at the English text (like others, she mostly uses the Folio edition with occasional references to the Quarto), we may naturally expect an original that is inflected by its later echoes in two other languages. While translating,[42] Mouzenidou consults with the other Greek versions and is also significantly influenced by René Girard's 1990 study, *Shakespeare: les feux de l'envie*, where he defends the coherence of plays like *Troilus and Cressida* through their logic of an all-permeating envy, or 'mimetic desire'.[43] What takes place beyond this point is more fascinating still: three play texts have been published by Mouzenidou, all through an imprint based at her theatre; the third one is her actual translation of *Troilus and Cressida*, an effort defined by a language more decidedly contemporary than Avloniti's, and with frequent recourses to slang and idiomatic use in bringing characters and their interactions to life. The translator admits her focus is on carrying across, and distilling 'rhythm, musicality, the sheer madness of the text'.[44] What is even more interesting is that this is yet another translation that remains unperformed: the productions staged in 2003 and 2011 are variously extracted, and abstracting, from this 'translation proper' towards smaller-scale, experimental recastings. They exist as collages of material transmuting or exaggerating intertextual relationships, unpicking the essential juxtaposition of distinct plots at the heart of Shakespeare's original. The Greek play texts coincide with a visible examination of his themes in ways poignantly engendering processes in-between, and associations of, translation and adaptation.

In 2003, a provisional 'First Shot' becomes part of the title: it follows a staging of *Romeo and Juliet* in 'Dipylon' the year before, and turns to a composite of that play and *Troilus and Cressida*. In fact, we largely follow the action of the latter – with relatively few deviations from the then unpublished translation – to which seven (parts of) scenes from *Romeo and Juliet* are interjected. For instance, brief, key exchanges from the balcony scene and the wedding scene frame the one between Cressida and Troilus in 3.2.38–203. The new arrangement becomes also a comment on thematic similarities,[45] and in this combining of Shakespeare with Shakespeare, Verona – and its sense of internecine conflict – quoted within Troy's war, we become more conscious of the play as *text* within literary history. Reviewers note how these comparisons take place, including decisions to separate the parts selected from the two plays on the stage. What is more, lines from *The Monogram* (1971) by Greek poet Odysseus Elytis were heard by the audience: eight at the beginning and seven at the end. This perhaps reflects Mouzenidou's understanding of Shakespeare's play itself as a long poem; the lovers are thus bookended by a well-known, Modern Greek poem on love. Beyond such radical grafts, we keep to the action and events of the original. Yet the approach here is thoroughly modern, appropriate for a relatively small space and cast, and a performance also including contemporary costumes, set design and, at points, video art.[46] Shakespeare's text is compressed, losing most metrical features in favour of everyday speech that might be called urban, streetwise. The setting remains Troy until, like the original play, Pandarus addresses the audience at the end; but this time, we hear about 'women of the northern suburbs',[47] as he points to today's Athens.

Mouzenidou's return to the play eight years later loses the fragments from *Romeo and Juliet* and Elytis, and stays with *Troilus and Cressida* alone, only to relegate it to a subtitle, after Όλα είναι πόλεμος (War is Everything). The change signifies instantly the pivot to the other main plot, as well as its radical treatment. The connection to what has occurred before is also present by indicating 'Second Shot' at the end; indeed, in the programme, after a list of previous performances we read that 'this time around, the main theme is a politics of war and its range of consequences. We thus come to a dark satire that seeks to demolish everything: politicians, generals, heroes, friendships, familial relationships and the works of love. It holds to account the powerful decision-makers of this world and brings their true motivations out in the open.'[48] There is an increase of intervisuality in the fabric of what becomes an original based on themes that were at an earlier point digested in Elizabethan theatre: not least in terms of several scenes updated to suggest the prevalence of warfare across history. A method of juxtaposition gives its place to an abundance of anachronism. For instance, the new play begins with soldiers discussing use of mobile phones in the army; and Achilles plays golf while staying away from the battlefield. The very fact of *returning* to the play holds interest. While anachronism is nothing new when it comes to revisionist treatments of Shakespeare which, quite often, include *Troilus and Cressida*,[49] here we find a 'war plot' essentially expanded to encompass also the classical texts first channelling and verbalizing the nature of human conflict. The audience also dwells in that timeless battlefield, with Shakespeare's play removed from its original setting only for us to properly realize we never much left the Iliadic world.

Mouzenidou does not consider her work so much an appropriation of Shakespeare – certainly where language is concerned. Rather, she seeks equivalences, trying to somehow imagine the choices Shakespeare himself would have made if he were living today. She confesses that she strives to be faithful to his perceived modernity when it comes to both vocabulary and psychological insight. When Mouzenidou argues that, she essentially proposes a clear set of priorities: textual accuracy is less important than a similar effect in terms of reception. What really matters is a consistent effort to recreate that socio-cultural impact for a contemporary Greek audience. There is yet a further reason that her text now becomes even more elliptical: she notes that Shakespeare is 'putting too many words in characters' mouths and that is the one thing out of step with our time. This day and age, we communicate with half words and sentences.'[50]

An adaptation that excessively updates the original in attempting to speak to us in the cultural present is not rare in theatre (and can be said to occur even more in translating it[51]); yet these are connected sightings of *Troilus and Cressida*, seemingly *enacting* drafts instead of final texts. From their very titles, they dramatize a gradual discovery or disassembling of a 'problem play'; its nets of relations and possible emphases. Mouzenidou is treating her own translation of *Troilus and Cressida* as an original, alongside Shakespeare's; or as a 'literal' one that can precisely be used towards a serialization of readings. If she succeeds in her desire to also stage her actual translation of the play, would this third performance, of what was in fact the earlier play text composed, not inevitably embed the memory of the ones that succeeded it?

Conclusion: Scenes of translation

Formal and thematic recombinations taking place in experimental stagings like the ones described above serve to remind us of Shakespeare's original genius; how he himself fuses the love plot and the war plot, themes and narrative elements encountered both in the *Iliad* initially and the later romances, in ways that become anti-epic, non-romantic. Complications in the text devised by Shakespeare appropriately reflect a constant questioning of absolutes, of heroic code and all-powerful, idealistic love alike.

The play may return us to the classical past, but the dialogue between the two points in time is problematic. The morality aspired to or conveyed in Chapman and others is essentially misunderstood, and if *Troilus and Cressida* tries one thing consistently, it is suggesting blind spots in Elizabethan imaginations of classical Greece as part of what comprised a humanist education. Shakespeare manages to illuminate constants of human behaviour as well as immense distances in engaging and reflecting on them since the oral epic tradition. This is already a modern tragedy that can achieve this.

In discussing later acts of translating or appropriating Shakespeare, we can hardly lose sight of the fact that so many senses of translation are encountered in his dramatic works, often coinciding with fragments of previous texts arranged within new wholes – *Troilus and Cressida* no less, in its remarkable intertextual imports. So much so that it becomes, rather, an entire process: Willis Barnstone reminds us that even though the poetic dramas of Shakespeare are very often imitations or translations of earlier narratives, indeed, the word 'translation' is

> seldom used to describe the transportation and transformation of sources into Shakespeare's plays, since *translation* suggests a closeness to the form, genre, and length of the original text. Even the words *adaptation* or *imitation*, the freest forms of translation 'proper', are rarely applied to Shakespeare's

translation process – though some might, without recourse to translation theory, call his plays adaptations.[52]

The result in such cases like Shakespeare's are often stretches of translation that assume the status of masterly re-creations, something we more readily recognize in terms of a version of the Bible, or in approaches to narrative epics like the *Iliad*. And in these 'good translations', Barnstone continues, 'there is no division of art and originality. They exist in both the source and the target text. There is Troilus, a character in various classical tales, and Troilus the lover of Cressida, in a tripartite communion of Shakespeare, Chaucer and Boccaccio.'[53]

And to Shakespeare, of course, we owe one of the most famous literary utterances of the word, when Quince, in *A Midsummer Night's Dream* addresses his friend Bottom – whose head has changed for that of an ass: 'Bless thee, Bottom, bless thee. / Thou art translated'.[54] Matthew Reynolds reminds us that '[t]his uncertain image of translation reflects searchingly upon translation between languages, for the play within a play that Bottom goes on to act in derives from a translation, *The XV Bookes of P. Ovidius Naso, Entytled Metamorphoses*, done by Arthur Golding'[55] in 1569. The emphasis is also on 'uncertain': the transformation seemingly is partial and its extent depends on individual productions of the play. This recalls aspects of textual instability which define writing for the stage. Any play text is already fluid, always open to live changes by the specific actors cast or adjustments and rewritings by directors during rehearsals. In Shakespeare's case, the versions and revisions at the hands of different editors, reviewers and publishers across centuries are emblematic of this essential condition – one that also perhaps adds to the tonal indecision and metadramatic tendencies of a 'problem play' such as *Troilus and Cressida*.

Interlinguistic transfer, in cases like this, complicates matters even further, and offers possibilities for comment, both literary and sociocultural. This chapter has surveyed versions of *Troilus and Cressida* for Greek audiences done over nearly four decades, considering along the way a range of positions for theatrical translators, from the responsibility of initial encounters to radical reconfigurations of the Shakespearean text that intensify its themes. Translators are notably assisted in creating Greek versions by multiple sources of, and paratextual material on, *Troilus and Cressida*. Previous commentary and the needs of the cultural moment can suggest crucial inflections, especially when it comes to a Greek-themed play that simultaneously reproduces and problematizes Elizabethan representations of ancient Greece.

Certain approaches more clearly turn to become acts of repossession, re-appropriation: in terms of the language spoken in the case of Rotas; as search for equivalences in Greek literary tradition for a 'love plot' that was not there in Homer, in Panagiotakis; a highlighting of constants of human behaviour in the work of Mouzenidou, as she also combines the Shakespearean text with Greek literary and cultural references. Layers of allusion and the welding of ancient setting and fourteenth- to sixteenth-century literary invention are thus reset as well – and in the work of perhaps the two best-known Greek translators of Shakespeare, Vassilis Rotas and Errikos Bellies, (literary) language itself is part of the agenda: perspectives on aspired status and use of Greek are superimposed on the particularities of *Troilus and Cressida* and link it unmistakably with their overall strategies in translations done before and after. In other cases, play texts are commissioned and, thus, respond to a variety of creative intentions, cultural moments and collaborative settings. Again, a common thread is a sense of linguistic inhabitation – paradoxical, when we remind ourselves that so many structures and characters did not exist in Homer – even as different proximities are encountered between 1973, 1991 and 2012. Greek manifestations of *Troilus and Cressida* often resemble curious 'negative films' of a complexly devised original, as translators variously attempt to reacquire its composite material. It is arguably the collisions of past and present defining the original, its explorations of intertextuality that render the work of translation, especially into Greek, a more experimental, as well as linguistically poignant space. The opportunity to witness how a different sociocultural milieu imagined Greece progressed towards performances such as those at the Art Theatre or Dipylon (separated by nearly forty years) commenting on the political present and those who exert influence on it. At the same time, through Shakespeare, audiences were offered ways to establish blind spots that exist also with respect to how Greeks understand their own relationship with antiquity.

Interviewing translators and studying paratextual material and critical pieces on these performances and translations yield further insights into individual methods and relationships with the text that sometimes can double as a creative deployment of philological interests (Panagiotakis), an intense retuning towards the immediacies of everyday language (Avloniti), a conscious effort to correct past imbalances (Hatzopoulos) or a long-standing investigation (Mouzenidou), where a director-translator produces a sequence of play texts (the first a translation, the second a collation of translations of *two* Shakespeare plays, the third a rather forceful adaptation), which are *collectively instructive* for the knowing theatre-goer as they imply modes and analogies of reception. Of course, such re-compositions and metabolisms quicken an understanding of Shakespeare's essential dramatic imperatives and are certainly apt when it comes to a play that already ranks among his most experimental designs.

8

'Degrees in Schools'

Learning and Teaching Strategies

Richard Stacey

Troilus and Cressida famously has two states, or front-pieces, in its first Quarto run of 1609. One informs the reader that it was 'acted by the *Kings Maiesties* / seruants at the Globe', the other that it was never 'stal'd with the Stage'.[1] Which of these is true? The former presents the play as a text for performance, the latter for reading and literary scrutiny; one is a blueprint, the other is a studied work of art.[2] For the teacher, this can be a rich opportunity to engage with the twin fields of literature and theatre in order to bring the play to life. As a classical love tragedy inspired by Homer, Boccacio and Chaucer, *Troilus and Cressida* has some of the most complex and demanding language in the mid-Shakespearean canon, melding hard philosophical debate with seedy and often prurient satire. Yet this tonal discrepancy has often found favour with directors and theatre practitioners, particularly in a contemporary culture more comfortable with the spiky pleasures of aesthetic dissonance. Taking its cue from the indeterminate two states of the Quarto, this chapter will offer a range of pedagogical techniques which are able to bring the play to life for undergraduates. The first section will focus on text-based approaches, analysing the function of words, images and tropes; the second will offer a number of strategies centred on dramaturgy and performance. Hopefully, the ideas discussed will help to illuminate some of the more obscure elements of *Troilus and Cressida*, and demonstrate how its dark energies and technical intricacies are perfect for galvanizing discussion of Shakespeare's dramatic achievement in the classroom.

Words, images and tropes

When Troilus is handed a letter from Cressida moments after he has witnessed her apparent betrayal, he tears it up in a fit of pique and throws the fragments in the air: 'Go, wind, to wind! There turn and change together!' (5.3.109). Troilus imagines that Cressida's language is overly mimetic and cannot be trusted; like her assignation with Diomedes, it is predicated on mutability and 'change' rather than constancy, and is therefore unable to denote the truth. However, the righteousness of Troilus's assertion is belied by the use of the rhetorical trope antanaclasis, in which a word or phrase is repeated throughout a sentence with subtle grammatical differences each time it is applied.[3] The homonym 'wind' is first used as a noun to personify the air, then is quickly converted to a verb which mimics the twisting movement of the scraps of paper as they drift to the ground. Not only is the import of the metaphor literalized through the tearing of the letter, unifying the word with the movement it signifies, the antanaclasis converts an abstraction into action, making 'wind' both fixed and syntactically mobile. Yet is not Troilus also guilty of the rhetorical artfulness which he castigates Cressida for practising? In order to convey his heightened feeling, he appears to enact what he berates, using a trope to condemn the ease with which language can be rendered deceptive through figuration. It seems that Troilus is caught in a troubling dynamic where he can only articulate the depth of his pain by utilizing the resources which have caused his pain in the first place.

Troilus's struggle with rhetoric is a recurring feature of a play in which the scope of linguistic efficacy is relentlessly questioned. The Greeks debate the best way to breach the impasse of the siege and are swayed by Ulysses' passionate evocation of 'degree' and strong leadership (1.3.75–137); the Trojans weigh the possibility of returning Helen and are persuaded by Hector's warning of its impact on their 'joint and several dignities' (2.2.193); and both Troilus and Cressida attempt to reinforce their mutual commitment across battle lines by transforming their names into metonymic icons of fidelity and betrayal, 'as true as Troilus' (3.2.177), 'as false as Cressid' (3.2.191). The first section of this chapter will engage with the interpretative possibilities opened up by Shakespeare's use of language. As most of the thematic topics in the play have a linguistic basis, the cultivation of close and careful reading will help students to situate their arguments in a syntactic register which is innovative, obscure and often demanding. Shakespeare's grammar school education provided him with a thorough grounding in the skills needed to master the challenges of textual composition, emphasizing the value of quite precise and minute linguistic choices alongside disciplines such as translation and disputation. In particular, the focus on the work of classical authors such as Virgil, Ovid and Horace, alongside the oratorical manuals of Cicero and Quintilian, would have emphasized the social and aesthetic value of translating ancient narratives into a contemporary English idiom.

Troilus and Cressida is a dense play with an unusual number of coinages. There are four different ways in which the exploration and analysis of individual words can be pursued: new words to the English language which first appear in the play; words for which Shakespeare appears to have produced a brand new meaning; words which appear only once in the Shakespeare corpus; and the creation of compounds. In order to gain a sense of the critical opportunities opened up by lexical analysis, it would be useful to introduce students to two excellent resources, the *Oxford English Dictionary* (*OED*) and the *Shakespeare Concordance*. The *OED* is the most respected dictionary in the Anglophone world and can be accessed by many universities: http://www.oed.com/. It is an extensive database which enables the user to research almost every aspect of a word, from its class, etymology and first appearance to the full range of meanings which it is able to accommodate. The section on 'Sources' may be the most useful as a teaching aid, as it enables a word to be traced back to its originator and the text in which it first appeared. The *Shakespeare Concordance* is an online repository of every word ever used by Shakespeare in his corpus and can be accessed at: http://www.opensourceshakespeare.org/concordance. The database functions as a dictionary with a search bar allowing the user to research how many times an individual word is applied and which play or text it is featured in. It is excellent for tracing the frequency of words and their cognates, and often reveals interesting clusters in particular genres, or at certain points in Shakespeare's career; it also enables the researcher to analyse the creation of unique meanings which are often missed by the *OED*.[4]

Troilus and Cressida contains a significant number of words which make their first appearance in the English language; it is therefore reasonable to assume that these are able to convey a signification for which there is no existing word available. In order to research Shakespeare's coinages, direct the student to the 'Source' section on the *OED*, choose William Shakespeare under 'Top 1,000 sources', and click on the 'First In Entry' tab; a list of words comes up with the corresponding play in which they appear. There are a range of words which extend the lexicon of the play in unusual and startling directions, but the following four might be an interesting place to start: **'tortive'** (1.3.9); **'deracinate'** (1.3.99); **'abruption'** (3.2.63); and **'imminence'** (5.11.13). These words do not come out of nowhere, so it would be good to research their etymological roots and see if they are related to any existing cognates. For instance, 'tortive' is the principal stem of the Latin word 'tortīvus', meaning to squeeze; Shakespeare couples it with the adjective-forming suffix 'ive' to create a kind of semantic contortion, demonstrating, at the level of language, Ulysses' wider point about plans which have gone 'errant' (1.3.9). Alongside coinages, *Troilus and Cressida* also contains a number of examples where a word is stretched to encompass a brand new meaning in the English language. In order to locate where these occur in the text, click the 'First in Sense' tab under William Shakespeare and look for any examples which seem pertinent or interesting; initial suggestions are '**villain**' (3.2.31); '**quality**' (4.1.46); '**grasp**' (4.2.14); and '**savage**' (5.3.49). From the example above, we can see that both 'villain' and 'savage' are ontological categories of being which insist upon the pejorative depiction of a rival; perhaps in the pressured context of war, both sides are using increasingly inventive – and tenuous – ways of conceptualizing the enemy they are fighting against. In order to assess why a new inference has been created, it might be wise to research the standard range of meanings before Shakespeare used the word to see exactly what semantic terrain is being mapped out; the student could also use the *Shakespeare Concordance* to track its complementary use in other plays across the canon.

The *Shakespeare Concordance* is invaluable in enabling the reader to trace the frequency or scarcity of Shakespeare's use of words. *Troilus and Cressida* contains a number of examples of single usage, where the effect of a phrase is grammatically dependent on a word which is so crucial to the meaning it is only deployed once; the rarer the word in the corpus, the more likely it is to be carrying a heightened load of interpretative weight. In order to research these units, and consider what critical work they might be capable of performing, direct the student to the *Shakespeare Concordance* and type in any unusual words in the 'Search Text' box; a list will come up of appearances by play with reference to the character who uses them and a short extract to place them in context. It can be trickier to identify single usage as there is no explicit search option for this task, but here are some interesting examples to start with: **'mastic'** (1.3.73); **'maculation'** (4.4.63); **'untraded'** (4.5.179); and **'orifex'** (5.2.158). 'Mastic' is defined by the *OED* as an 'An aromatic gum or resin which exudes from the bark of the lentisk or mastic tree', so its single use in Shakespeare could exploit its linguistic rareness to extenuate the cultural gap between the Trojans and the Greeks at the level of verbal expression.[5] Another way to explore Shakespeare's inventiveness is to research any compound words he has created. If we access the *OED* list titled 'First in Sense', we can immediately see an odd interest in animal imagery throughout the play: **'cob-loaf'** (2.1.36); **'lion-sick'** (2.3.84); **'bull-bearing'** (2.3.241); and **'dog-fox'** (5.4.10). The recourse to animal referents to generate new coinages may be a way of comically associating rhetorical ingenuity with less elevated forms of breeding or gestation, as well as anthropomorphizing the personal qualities of the character who uses them. Exploring Shakespeare's linguistic experimentation and invention is therefore a good way of providing an entry-point into the wider thematic key-notes of the text, as well as considering how they intersect with other elements of dramatic construction, such as characterization, world-building and mimetic discourse.

If the student is interested in exploring the scope of individual words in more analytical depth, it might be profitable to engage with the area of morphology. The use of established prefixes and suffixes can particularize words by activating the small units of grammar which are added to either end of a base-word or stem. Take, for example, the word **'rejoindure'** (4.4.35) which is defined by the *OED* as 'The act or process of rejoining or being rejoined; reunion'. The word is a Shakespearean coinage which is used by Troilus moments before Cressida is to be exchanged for Antenor; in his distress at her parting, he bemoans how the impervious force of time 'rudely beguiles our lips / Of all rejoindure' (4.4.34–5), preventing the repeated action of kissing which the two lovers have hitherto enjoyed without interruption. Shakespeare creates this word to encapsulate the discrepancy between action and language, as the longed-for kiss, unifying two bodily elements into one, is displaced onto a hybrid word which substitutes for the erotic contact which has been indefinitely postponed. In order to achieve this effect, and usher in a new grammatical register where language is increasingly divorced from its signification, Shakespeare adds the prefix 're' to the base word 'join' and completes it with the suffix 'ure'.[6] None of these morphological units are Shakespearean inventions, and each is replete with its own embedded meaning; according to the *OED*, 're' has the 'general sense of "back" or again' and 'ure' denotes 'action or process'. Therefore, 'rejoindure' encapsulates the impossibility of satiating human desire in perpetuity by inventing a word to perform, almost tauntingly, what the two lovers are unable themselves to enact in the flesh. More crucially, though, it activates a structural irony whereby the only repeated joining of lips will occur between Cressida and Diomedes in the Greek camp when the trade is completed. Tracking the preponderance of individual prefixes and suffixes is thus a good way of assessing the wider frames of thematic meaning which are modulated by Shakespeare's morphological choices. The word 'rejoindure' is actually part of a cluster of words which end in 'ure' throughout the play, most of which are either new coinages or very rare occurrences in the Shakespearean corpus; examples include '**insisture**' (1.3.87); '**mixture**' (1.3.95); '**flexure**' (2.2.104); '**rapture**' (2.2.122; 3.2.126); '**composure**' (2.3.97, 234); '**repure**' (3.2.20); '**soilure**' (4.1.58); '**embrasure**' (4.4.36); '**mature**' (4.5.98); and '**impressure**' (4.5.132). Evidently the suffix is crucial in establishing a lexical mood in which the ability to initiate action is articulated without necessarily being activated, defining the unsatisfactory experience of the central lovers as commensurate with other types of impasse, such as the central military deadlock.

The *Shakespeare Concordance* is also invaluable for showing how individual words and their components are used to build larger clusters of imagery. An investigation of this technique is useful because images are often able to cultivate meanings which take on an interpretative agency their own.

The image used by a character is sometimes offset by a cumulative resonance of which they may not be aware, placing their perspective in a schema whereby its deeper meaning is dependent on the cultural recognition of the reader or spectator. Certain images are used by Shakespeare at particular points in the narrative, working across the text to evoke past moments or lay the groundwork for future or imminent ironies; they are also used to triangulate relationships, add a covert social or political dimension to exchanges which may seem sedate on first reading, and summon deeper intertextual affiliations with classical or biblical antecedents. A particularly interesting example in *Troilus and Cressida* is Shakespeare's use of the word 'pearl'. The *Shakespeare Concordance* tells us that it is used twice in the play, both times by Troilus:

> Tell me, Apollo, for thy Daphne's love,
> What Cressid is, what Pandar, and what we?
> Her bed is India; there she lies a pearl.
>
> (1.1.94–6)

Troilus stabilizes his new, shifting identity as lover by depicting Cressida as a 'pearl', evidently reaching for a metaphor which correlates his beloved with high value in order to convey her prestige. However, it also figures her as an object which can be culturally appropriated due to its perceived exoticism and high market value, and introduces a subtle fissure, at the level of imagery, between Cressida's opaque identity and the linguistic strategies used to make that identity legible, that which 'is and is not Cressid' (5.2.153).[7] Troilus later recourses to the same metaphor under very different circumstances in a debate about the political value of Helen with the Trojan war-council:

> Is she worth keeping? Why, she is a pearl
> Whose price hath launched above a thousand ships
> And turned crowned kings to merchants.
>
> (2.2.89–91)

Here the 'pearl' image is associated with the arbitrariness with which both sides have esteemed the woman over whom they are fighting for possession. Troilus's intensification of its mercantile implications not only reduces the Greek warships to a trade convoy but also implies that Helen's value is subject to barter and exchange, rather than something which is absolute. As this second iteration is pejorative and dismissive of intrinsic female worth, Shakespeare encourages the reader or audience member to re-trace the image back to its original use; what they will find is the activation of an irony that hinges on Troilus's deployment of a metaphor to articulate a desire he later castigates without question. Although he is later horrified by Cressida's transference of her affections to Diomedes, perhaps the attitude is subtly embedded in a verbal pre-condition which assumes the likelihood of female inconstancy even before it occurs. The currency of the 'pearl' image is amplified due to its intersection with an allusion to the most well-known quotation in the Marlovian canon, when Faustus glorifies Helen as the 'face that launched a thousand ships' (5.91) in the play *Doctor Faustus*.[8] The pearl image is part of a nexus which is acquired, almost object-like, from the linguistic space of another text and passed around without any kind of privileged ownership. Further recourse to the *Shakespeare Concordance* stresses these implications by revealing that Shakespeare tends to couple 'pearl' with the word 'orient', creating an adjectival-modifier which stresses its alien qualities and cultural unfamiliarity. Taken together, the image is indicative of ownership, common currency and the substitution of female agency for an object which is wholly reliant on fluctuating markers of value; no wonder it is unable to function as a satisfactory index of Cressida's poetic and cultural identity in Trojan society.

Shakespeare was educated in a pedagogical culture which prioritized rhetorical learning over other aspects of language acquisition; as such, his plays are replete with the ingenious use of schemes and tropes.[9] It is useful practice to encourage students to familiarize themselves with the oratorical strategies used by the characters to give form to their language. The two most effective resources to engage with rhetorical methodology are *Silva Rhetoricae* and *Early English Books Online*. *Silva Rhetoricae* (http://rhetoric.byu.edu/) is a comprehensive guide to a vast range of figures, complete with definitions, examples and sources. It also has a search bar in which tropes are grouped based on their topic or function, and is excellent for easy browsing to aid familiarization with the more complex elements of rhetorical technique. *Early English Books Online*, or *EEBO* (http://eebo.chadwyck.com/home), is a comprehensive collection of printed documents covering almost every genre of the early modern period, from plays and poems to sermons and historical tracts. It is invaluable for exploring the various texts which were circulating alongside literary works, and provides unique access to the source material which directly shaped the composition of Shakespeare's plays. *EEBO* is not open access, but many institutions of higher education will have a subscription.

A complex trope which recurs at key moments throughout *Troilus and Cressida* is anadiplosis, in which the last word of a clause is repeated at the start of a new one. Anadiplosis is an effect which exploits phonetic and syntactic repetition to enhance a cumulative sense of order and cohesion throughout a sentence. It is defined by Henry Peacham, a rhetorician who wrote an influential guide to oratory named *The Garden of Eloquence* in 1577, in the following way:

> Anadiplosis, when the laste worde of the fyrst clause is the fyrst word of the second ... this fygure is very pleasaunte, for that it doth as it were, stryke a double stroake, or rehearseth the last word agayn, lyke a resounding Eccoe.[10]

Anadiplosis is able to facilitate an 'Eccoe' through a type of repetition which insists on the reverberation of a word across grammar. Yet each word is placed in a slightly different grammatical position depending on where it functions within a clause, opening up the possibility that the meaning of the word can be reinscribed with each iteration. Anadiplosis is therefore able to evoke a sense of order and progression whilst subtly encouraging the listener to scrutinize the modulations upon which that order rests. Shakespeare is fully attuned to the complexities of this particular trope, and uses it when Ulysses is attempting to promote an ideological agenda of 'degree' centred on social and political conservatism:

> Then everything includes itself in power,
> Power into will, will into appetite;
> And appetite, an universal wolf,
> So doubly seconded with will and power,
> Must make perforce an universal prey
> And last eat up himself.
>
> (1.3.119–24)

At a crucial juncture, Ulysses makes a highly shrewd plea for the reinforcement of strong leadership to mobilize the Greeks and push for a resolution to the conflict. The use of anadiplosis is a replication of order in miniature, placing each word in a schema which insists on connectivity and 'degree' (1.3.86). Yet this is not really what the trope is doing. If the logic of the syntax is followed, then Ulysses is demonstrating how an approximation of order can be swallowed up and absorbed by a rogue element – in this case the 'wolf' – which reflexively turns the trope on its head. Anadiplosis is used by Ulysses as a decoy rather than a genuine iteration of order, exposing the ease with which it can be discarded when its effects have been skilfully deployed by a clever, ambitious orator. Troilus appears to be aware of Ulysses' scepticism regarding the efficacy of anadiplosis when he uses it to articulate his anger at Cressida's apparent betrayal:

> If souls guide vows, if vows be sanctimonies,
> If sanctimony be the gods' delight,
> If there be rule in unity itself,
> This is not she. O, madness of discourse,
> That cause sets up with and against itself!
>
> (5.2.146–50)

Troilus attempts to justify Cressida's behaviour by using anadiplosis to construct a model of order which can account for the perceived absence of her true self; as Cressida has already articulated that she has 'a kind of self that resides with you, / But an unkind self that itself will leave' (3.2.143–4), her lack of fidelity is attributed to the loosely governed part of her identity which is absent from Troilus. As this is evidently a rhetorical supposition rather than a detached assessment of Cressida's behaviour, anadiplosis is used by Troilus to denote the collapse of order rather than its instantiation, as its supposedly logical culmination – Cressida as the apex of a system predicated on vowing, sanctimony and divine unity – is unfulfilled with no hope of completion. Not only this, the absence of the expected outcome seems to split apart language itself, reducing 'discourse' to a 'madness' which is able to undo its own stability as the most effective method of self-articulation in Trojan (and early modern) culture. Exploring the effects generated by a trope such as anadiplosis, then, is a useful way for the student to engage with the oratorical structures which shape the construction of identity or character, alongside the slipperiness that often compromises the apparent security and poise of figurative language.

Performance, playing and directorial interpretation

Troilus and Cressida is quite rare in the Shakespearean canon as it opens with an allegorical Prologue, dressed in armour. As an entry point into the text, it embodies some of the topics that the audience will encounter – an epic focus on the military exploits of war; the initiation of action *in medias res*, in the middle rather than at the start; and the transformation of human beings into culturally recognizable archetypes.[11] These topics are crucial to the literate tenor of the play, but it is interesting to note that they are physicalized through the body of the actor on stage; we might say that the Prologue is a site where the text is made legible through the resources of dramatic performance. This next section will offer some ways in which the dramaturgical properties of *Troilus and Cressida* can be used to provoke critical enquiry. Although the study of rhetoric is crucial for providing access to some of the more abstract cultural ideas at work centred on language, politics and classical reception, there are limits as to how far an exclusive study of the play on the page can take us. Unlocking the potentiality of performance provides a complementary methodology to text-based lines of investigation which can probe into areas of interpretative enquiry not exhaustively focused on linguistic effects. If we turn to the gaps between the words – the moments which rely on the extension of meaning through staging, performance strategy and directorial choice – the scope for discussion will be infinitely enhanced.

There are elements of the play which actively depend on theatricalization in order to tease out the full range of inferences embedded within certain textual features. An interesting example is Troilus's 'sleeve' (4.4.69), which he offers to Cressida as a guarantee of his constancy, only for it to be transferred to Diomedes in the Greek camp and later worn to taunt Troilus in battle. Although Troilus swears an oath to retrieve the sleeve, the text on the page does not tell us whether this is accomplished or not; there is merely a frustrating gap where a stage direction or a verbal confirmation should be. Shakespeare goes to a lot of trouble to emphasize the significance of the sleeve as a quasi-sacred object which is tasked with guaranteeing the vows of fidelity of the two lovers;[12] when Troilus encounters Diomedes on the battlefield he personifies the sleeve alongside his rival as coterminous entities – 'Soft! Now comes sleeve and t'other' (5.4.17) – and the two exit fighting to a chanting chorus of 'Now the sleeve, now the sleeve!' (5.4.24) by Thersites. It seems unambiguous that the ultimate success of the conflict will be defined to some extent by what happens to the sleeve, but when Diomedes enters in the next scene he puzzlingly says that he has taken Troilus's 'horse' (5.5.1) as a gift for Cressida. Troilus and Diomedes fight again (5.6.7–12) without any mention of the sleeve, and when Troilus enters for the last time it is to inform the Trojans that Hector has been killed, again without informing us of who finally claims the prize (5.11.3–34).

The object being fought over so strenuously is constructed by Shakespeare as a barometer of sexual and military success. If Diomedes keeps the sleeve, Troilus's humiliation as a lover is compounded by a lack of skill on the battlefield and, along with the murder of Hector, the Greeks are ultimately presented as sneering and immoral. If Troilus wins it back, however, it provides a small degree of respite in the face of overwhelming loss, and may even offer an expanded view of Trojan autonomy which gestures to the hopeful outcome of Virgil's poem *The Aeneid*. There are two very different interpretations at work here, but the text on the page refrains from prioritizing one over the other. It might therefore be appropriate to suggest that the sleeve is a locus of indeterminacy in a source-text which is largely pre-ordained, escaping the strictures of a plot which is fundamentally unchangeable. However, this reading does not strictly work in a production of the play on stage, as the audience can see the sleeve and is able to track its circulation, making the final destination a crucial factor in determining where to place their sympathy. Tantalizingly, it is up to the director and the creative team to provide an answer and to offer a critical response where the text falls short; in other words, it is their task to *stage* what happens to the sleeve through dramaturgical interpretation. There are a number of outcomes which can be deployed here which the student could explore. What happens if the sleeve is claimed by either Diomedes or Troilus? What if it is taken by another character, or is lost, or discarded on the battlefield, or turned to another use such as a bandage? All of these directorial choices perform critical work in that they provide an individual reading for an ambiguous prompt embedded in the text. Exploring other elements of the play which not only exploit dramatic interpretation but actually rely on it would be a suggestive way of presenting such features as intrinsic agents of critical enquiry.

Troilus and Cressida has a complex editorial history. As briefly touched on at the start of this chapter, there are two 'states' of the 1609 Quarto edition which construct the play as either a reading edition or a performance document, alongside a third version in the Folio of 1623.[13] There are some discrepancies between the two variant forms, which have prompted editors to form various theories regarding the nature of the base-text upon which the printed plays were composed. Although it is slightly beyond the scope of this section to engage with the differences between foul papers, fair copies and prompt books, it is necessary to point out that *Troilus and Cressida* has been subject to various stages of modulation and revision, both in the theatre and the printing house, which has resulted in a far more hybridized text than older scholarship has sometimes been willing to acknowledge. The modern editor is therefore tasked with tidying up the variants and cruxes in order to produce a version of the play which is a reasonable approximation of the best elements of all the existing copies. This is problematic for a number of reasons, but it is particularly acute in relation to performance cues such as stage directions, exits and entrances, and character names. It may not seem obvious, but something as innocuous as a stage direction is able to perform critical work at the level of meaning. Most editors are not theatre practitioners, however, and while their efforts are invaluable for clarifying a reading edition of the play, some of their choices can slightly obscure inferences which are able to be powerfully ignited on stage.

In Act 4, Scene 5 of David Bevington's *Troilus and Cressida* (The Arden Shakespeare, Third Series), revised in 2015, there are a number of stage directions for the Greeks and Trojans to embrace. None of these appear in either the Quarto or Folio texts and have been included by Bevington to clarify performance cues embedded in the speech of various characters. This is a crucial moment in which the two sides engage in a mock-tournament to alleviate the boredom of a long drawn-out war. In Bevington's edition, the maternal cousins Hector and Ajax embrace the most: 'Let me embrace thee, Ajax';

[*They embrace.*] (4.5.136, 139); 'The issue is embracement' [*They embrace again.*] (148, 149). These stage directions are included to create an image of reconciliation across battle-lines and provide a small degree of hope that a diplomatic negotiation might be reached; it is also a skilful way of emphasizing the futility of the war in physical terms before the betrayal of Hector by Achilles and the Myrmidons, and is also directly responsive to a textual cue. However, there are other moments where a similar stage direction is included even though the dialogue does not appear to indicate that an embrace is specifically required. When Menelaus meets the Trojan delegates, for instance, he states 'You brace of warlike brothers, welcome hither' (4.5.176) with the accompanying direction [*He embraces Troilus and Hector.*] (177). However, Hector does not appear to recognize Menelaus on sight, and immediately scorns him as a cuckold. Not only is there no explicit suggestion of embracement in the original line, Bevington's choice minimizes some of the friction inherent in Hector's satire and could even betray a slight pro-Trojan bias through associating the delegation with repeated acts of reconciliation.

Bevington's edition also refrains from including the stage direction when the supporting textual evidence is equally as suggestive as the line quoted above, if not more so. When Hector later engages Achilles in mock-combat he states 'Thy hand upon that match' (4.5.270) with a decisive rejection of the offer. Achilles' rebuff is a further extension of sympathy for the Trojans by implying that the disregard for courtly protocol prefigures in some sense the eventual murder of Hector when he is unarmed. Although Bevington's choice is useful in foreshadowing the outcome of the plot, it precludes other possible interpretations held in play in the original source text, such as the idea that Achilles could waver, or that his duplicitousness could be finely calibrated even at this early stage through reciprocation. Paying attention to performance cues in a reading edition of the play, therefore, is not only useful for measuring how particular interpretations are shaped and fostered at the level of editorial choice, but sharpens awareness of the expanded range of playing strategies that can be initiated through the withdrawal – or inclusion – of explicit performance topoi. It might be a useful seminar exercise to compare examples such as this from different editions, with an attendant focus on the diverging meanings which each staging interpolation is able to foster. Taking this further, the elements under investigation could then be directly measured against the directorial choices of individual productions on stage via archival recordings, in order to tease out the different inflections which performance and text-based methodologies are able to invoke.

Researching the different staging choices of productions of *Troilus and Cressida* is an excellent way to consider how dramaturgy is able to facilitate critical debate. The play has been staged extensively since the 1960s and is arguably one of the most prominent works in the current Shakespeare repertoire; the despondent tone and fascination with sexual pragmatism may strike a chord in a post-war culture more attuned to cynical behaviour than previous ages. There are a number of different ways in which archival reviews of plays can be accessed. The easiest point of reference is the journal *Theatre Review*, which collates every single review of major London and regional productions and places them alongside each other on the page for ease of access. If there is a particular reviewer whom the student wishes to focus on, then almost all individual newspapers have archival material available in online repositories, including the *Guardian*, the *Independent*, *The Times* and the *Telegraph*; in the US, resources include the *New York Times*, *Chicago Tribune* and *Playbill*. Reviews of prominent productions also appear in scholarly journals, although they are primarily academic in focus; these include *Shakespeare Survey*, *Shakespeare* and *Cahiers Élisabéthains*.

One of the most problematic elements of the plot is the death of Hector at the hands of Achilles and the Myrmidons. Not only does this provide a betrayal of military protocol to offset Cressida's rejection of Troilus, it facilitates a shift from formal codes of warfare to the prioritization of individual survival in battle. However, its appearance in the play is quite stark; after Hector pleads for mercy – 'I am unarmed. Forgo this vantage, Greek' (5.9.9) – the Myrmidons attack on Achilles' orders: 'Strike, fellows, strike!' (5.9.10). Although we know that this is a group massacre and that Hector does not have a weapon to hand, the actual method of ambush is not directly outlined by the text. The choices made to depict this moment on stage can therefore be used to focalize certain embedded or ambiguous readings, particularly the extent to which Hector's murder is regarded as unethical. Ian Judge's production, performed in 1996 at the RSC, cultivated a 'camp aesthetic', to quote Dominic Cavendish, in which Achilles' provocative behaviour is directly connected to the murder; Benedict Nightingale noted that 'when Philip Quast's Achilles wants to menace Louis Hilyer's hefty, sweating Hector, he does so by slipping out of his gown and flashing his naked body at him'.[14] Hector's communal butchering by the leather-clad Myrmidons, in which he is 'raised aloft on a body of spears', associates his death with sadomasochism and presents a slightly outmoded view of homoerotic culture as threatening, particularly when counterpoised against a model of heteronormative masculine conduct which is associated with honour.

In contrast, Michael Boyd's 1998 production, also for the RSC, used the death of Hector to accentuate the culture clash between the Greeks and the Trojans. Charles Spencer observed that 'The Greeks shoot their own man, Patroclus', resulting in a lone execution in which 'Hector's heart is pulled out by an Achilles who is into voodoo'; interestingly 'there are no Myrmidons', creating a version of the scene which is based on single combat and is therefore vastly different from the thuggish group massacre of other productions.[15] Boyd's interpretation emphasizes the isolation of Achilles from his Greek compatriots due to his interest in magic, and slightly compromises his supposed physical prowess through a reliance on supernatural forces; he is also oblivious to the realpolitik of his Greek contemporaries when they assassinate Patroclus to goad him into action. In contrast, Trevor Nunn's 1999 production for the National Theatre is deeply responsive to the cultural dimension of the murder of Hector, which is accentuated through the decision to cast predominantly black actors for the Trojan characters and white actors for the Greeks. For Jonathan Gibbs, the communal butchering of Hector by the Myrmidons by its 'racially split' ensemble evoked 'disturbing memories of contemporary racism'; that Hector was 'unarmed and ambushed' associated the attitude of the Greeks with imperialist entitlement which also recalled the aggressive intervention by Western states in the conflicts of smaller nations.[16] Each production of *Troilus and Cressida*, then, is able to adopt a sparse textual cue such as '[*They fall upon Hector and kill him.*]' (5.11.11) and use it to reinforce a particular view of the deeper currents which run through the play. In all of these examples, we can see that the readings offered by theatre critics are analogous to the interpretative work of literary scholars. Both disciplines are critical endeavours which are tasked with investigating the opaque and often riddling meanings inherent in the text, offering accounts which stress the resonance of the play in relation to theoretical discourses as diverse as homoeroticism and postcolonial theory.

As a final pedagogical approach based on performance strategies, the student might be directed to consider the self-reflexive models of theatricality which are often used by Shakespeare to shape particular scenes. When Troilus and Cressida are together on stage, they are almost never alone. During their first assignation in Act 3, Scene 2, they are viewed, by Pandarus, and when Cressida meets Diomedes she is spied on by Troilus and Ulysses, and also Thersites. At these two crucial moments, Shakespeare places the gestation and destruction of the love affair in frames of observation, whose development is subject to scrutiny by proxy audience members. In 3.2.166–91, Troilus's fateful decision to transform the names 'Troilus' and 'Cressida' into a miniature moral exemplar is bolstered by the performative context in which it is first articulated; its didactic function as a sexual policing agent, promoting fidelity at the expense of gratification for the early modern audience, is ironized through the heightened emphasis on the scrutiny upon which it depends for its efficacy. Pandarus's observation – and that of the audience in the theatre – is therefore analogous to the cultural process by which the public condemnation of perceived sexual immorality entails a paradoxical fascination with its finer, more prurient details, even at the point where the condemnatory judgement is asserted.

Shakespeare's second use of the frame of observation in 5.2.6–112 is distinguished by a subtle doubling effect in which Thersites effectively observes the observers. Interestingly, some of Cressida's dialogue is couched in an inaudible whisper which is inaccessible either to the audience in the theatre or the reader of the material text. The effect of this occlusive strategy is to prioritize the *interpretation* of her behaviour by the male cabal on stage, subtly encouraging the spectator to reflect upon their own observation of Cressida, and possibly condemn the lingering obsession with female sexual conduct which her transformation into an exemplar entails. Shakespeare exploits the performative dynamic inherent in this grouping of characters to reflect upon the potential of excessive surveillance to stymy the agency of a young, sexually alert female. Paying attention to the exploitation of theatrical resources in the construction of key moments from the play is not only useful for emphasizing the blurred line between text and performance, it also reinforces how crucial a theatrically rich device such as audience participation is to the larger, more culturally dense questions the play is interested in probing at any given time.

Bibliography

Below is a brief, non-comprehensive guide to a range of critical works which are best suited to clarify and expand upon some of the central pedagogical strategies outlined in this chapter.

Editions

Shakespeare, William, *Troilus and Cressida*, The Arden Shakespeare, ed. David Bevington (London: Bloomsbury, 1998; revised 2015).

Shakespeare, William, *Troilus and Cressida*, ed. Anthony B. Dawson (Cambridge: Cambridge University Press, 2003; revised 2008).

Shakespeare, William, *Troilus and Cressida*, ed. Kenneth Muir (Oxford: Oxford University Press, 1982).

There are a number of collected editions in which the play appears, although the editorial apparatus is not as detailed, and the introductions are general rather than specific to the text. If a collected edition is required for teaching purposes then the following three are recommended:

Kastan, David Scott, Richard Proudfoot and Ann Thompson, eds, *The Arden Shakespeare (Complete Works)*, The Arden Shakespeare, rev. edn (London: Bloomsbury, 2001).

Bate, Jonathan and Eric Rasmussen, eds, *The RSC Shakespeare: The Complete Works of William Shakespeare* (Basingstoke: Palgrave Macmillan, 2007).

Wells, Stanley and Gary Taylor, general eds, *William Shakespeare: The Complete Works (Oxford Shakespeare)* (Oxford: Oxford University Press, rev. edn, 2005).

Words, images and tropes

Crystal, David and Ben Crystal, *Shakespeare's Words: A Glossary and Language Companion* (London: Penguin, 2002).

Erne, Lukas, *Shakespeare as Literary Dramatist* (Cambridge: Cambridge University Press, 2003).

Franziska Fahey, Maria, *Metaphor and Shakespearean Drama: Unchaste Signification* (London: Palgrave, 2011).

Hope, Jonathan, *Shakespeare and Language: Reason, Eloquence and Artifice in the Renaissance*, The Arden Shakespeare (London: Bloomsbury, 2010).

Keller, Stefan Daniel, *The Development of Shakespeare's Rhetoric: A Study of Nine Plays* (Tübingen: Franke-Verlang, 2009).

Lyne, Raphael, *Shakespeare, Rhetoric and Cognition* (Cambridge: Cambridge University Press, 2011).

Mack, Peter, *Elizabethan Rhetoric: Theory and Practice* (Cambridge: Cambridge University Press, 2002).

McDonald, Russ, *Shakespeare and the Arts of Language*, Oxford: Oxford University Press, 2001.

Palfrey, Simon, *Doing Shakespeare*, The Arden Shakespeare, 2nd edn (London: Bloomsbury, 2011).

Vickers, Brian, 'Shakespeare's Use of Rhetoric', in *A New Companion to Shakespeare Studies*, ed. Kenneth Muir and S. Schoenbaum (Cambridge: Cambridge University Press, 1971).

Performance, playing and directorial interpretation

Apfelbaum, Roger, *Shakespeare's Troilus and Cressida: Textual Problems and Performance Solutions* (Newark, DE: University of Delaware Press, 2004).

Dessen, Alan C., *Recovering Shakespeare's Theatrical Vocabulary* (Cambridge: Cambridge University Press, 1995).

Gil Harris, Jonathan and Natasha Korda, eds, *Staged Properties in Early Modern English Drama* (Cambridge: Cambridge University Press, 2002).

Gurr, Andrew, *The Shakespearean Stage, 1574–1642*, 3rd edn (Cambridge: Cambridge University Press, 1992).

Gurr, Andrew and Mariko Ichikawa, *Staging in Shakespeare's Theatres* (Oxford: Oxford University Press, 2000).

Karim-Cooper, Farah and Tiffany Stern, eds, *Shakespeare's Theatre and the Effects of Performance*, The Arden Shakespeare (London: Bloomsbury, 2013.

Shirley, Frances A., *Troilus and Cressida: Shakespeare in Production* (Cambridge: Cambridge University Press, 2005).

Stern, Tiffany, *Making Shakespeare: From Stage to Page* (London: Routledge, 2004).

Tribble, Evelyn, *Early Modern Actors and Shakespeare's Theatre: Thinking with the Body*, The Arden Shakespeare (London: Bloomsbury, 2017).

Weimann, Robert and Douglas Bruster, *Shakespeare and the Power of Performance: Stage and Page in Elizabethan Theatre* (Cambridge: Cambridge University Press, 2008).

APPENDIX: THEATRE RESOURCES

Below is a list of the main performance resources held in the archives of the major theatrical companies in the UK and the USA. If the student is interested in researching the conditions of a particular performance in depth, then it is possible to contact the archivist and arrange a special visit. These resources are invaluable for charting the creative and practical choices made by the director of each individual production.

The British Universities Film and Video Council contains archival footage of most plays, although the quality is uneven, particularly in performances staged when video technology was less developed. Again, it is possible to access archival material for many institutions of higher education.

RSC

http://collections.shakespeare.org.uk/ (prompt books; production records; stage manager's scripts; photography stills; costume and set designs; sound cues; historical research, e.g. duels):

   1985, dir. Howard Davies
   1990, dir. Sam Mendes
   1996, dir. Ian Judge
   1998, dir. Michael Boyd
   2006, dir. Peter Stein.

National Theatre

http://catalogue.nationaltheatre.org.uk/CalmView/Default.aspx (prompt book; production materials; photograph stills; costume records):

   1999, dir. Trevor Nunn.

The Globe

https://archive.shakespearesglobe.com/calmview/ (prompt books; production materials; wardrobe bibles; music; stage management notes; audience notes):

2005, dir. Giles Block
2009, dir. Matthew Dunster
2012, dir. Rachel House.

Cheek by Jowl

http://www.cheekbyjowl.com/troilus_and_cressida.php (prompt book; rehearsal notes; online programme):

2008, dir. Declan Donnelly.

Tobacco Factory

SATTF Archive, University of Bristol (Theatre Collection):

2003, dir. Andrew Hilton.

BBC

DVD (The Shakespeare Collection):

1981, dir. Jonathan Miller.

Shakespeare in the Park

https://www.publictheater.org/troilusandcressida/ (production clips; general information on the company):

2016, dir. Daniel Sullivan.

Wooster Group (with the RSC)

https://thewoostergroup.org/blog (numerous video diaries on the production of the play, including interviews with the cast):

2012, dir. Elizabeth LeCompte and Mark Ravenhill.

Oregon Shakespeare Festival

https://www.osfashland.org/productions/plays/troilus-and-cressida.aspx (Videos on directorial interpretation; list of reviews):

2012, dir. Rob Melrose.

NOTES

Introduction

1 All quotations are from William Shakespeare, *Troilus and Cressida*, ed. David Bevington, The Arden Shakespeare, Third Series, rev. edn (London: Bloomsbury, 2015) (4.5.162–74); hereafter cited parenthetically in the text.

2 See Sonnet 15: 'Where wasteful Time debateth with decay', *Shakespeare's Sonnets*, ed. Katherine Duncan-Jones, The Arden Shakespeare, Third Series, rev. edn (London and New York: Bloomsbury, 2010).

3 David Bevington, 'Introduction', in *Troilus and Cressida*, 90. On time and oblivion in the play, see also John Bayley, 'Time and the Trojans', *Essays in Criticism* XXV, no. 1 (1975): 55–73.

4 Agamemnon's reference to the ruins of time is especially striking in the context of his public greeting of Hector, which according to Andrew Hiscock is a 'tactical performance of hospitality', asserting his power and authority as a leader. See Andrew Hiscock, '"Will You Walk in, My Lord?" Shakespeare's *Troilus and Cressida* and the Anxiety of *Oikos*', in *Shakespeare and Hospitality: Ethics Politics, and Exchange*, ed. David B. Goldstein and Julia Reinhard Lupton (Abingdon: Routledge, 2016), 29.

5 For a discussion of the textual history of the play, see Bevington, 233–464; *Troilus and Cressida*, ed. Anthony B. Dawson (Cambridge: Cambridge University Press, 2003), 234–52; and William Godschalk, 'The Texts of *Troilus and Cressida*', *Early Modern Literary Studies* 1 (1995): 1–54.

6 See Bevington, 'Introduction', in *Troilus and Cressida*, 1–3, 11–19, 88–9. On the likelihood of theatrical performance, see also Anthony Dawson, 'Introduction', in *Troilus and Cressida*, 7–9.

7 The theory was first suggested by Peter Alexander, '*Troilus and Cressida*, 1609', *The Library* s4–IX, no. 3 (1928): 267–86. See Chapter 2 ('The Performance History') and Chapter 3 ('The State of the Art') on the play's original audience and theatrical context.

8 See Chapter 2 on John Barton's three productions of *Troilus and Cressida*.

9 Boas also added *Hamlet* in this group of plays, arguing that: 'The last-named play [*Hamlet*] is, of course, distinguished from the others by its tragic ending, but it is akin to them in its general temper and atmosphere.' See Frederick S. Boas, *Shakspere and his Predecessors* (London: John Murray, 1910), 345; see also Chapter 1 in this book on Boas's classification of the play.

10 The fifteenth-century Scottish poet departs from Chaucer's version of the love story not only by introducing Cresseid's leprosy but also by focusing on Cresseid as a character who after being abandoned by Diomede and punished by the gods realizes her errors and possibly finds redemption. See Robert L. Kindrick, 'Introduction', *The Testament of Cresseid*, ed. Robert L. Kindrick (Kalamazoo, MI: Medieval Institute Publications, 1997). Seamus Heaney has done a modern translation of *The Testament of Cresseid and Seven Fables* (London: Faber and Faber Ltd, 2009).

11 On the sources of *Troilus and Cressida*, see Bevington, '"Instructed by the Antiquary Times": Shakespeare's Sources', in *Troilus and Cressida*, 409–31.

12 Frances Yates, *Astrea: The Imperial Theme in the Sixteenth Century* (1975) (London: Routledge, 2013), 50.

13 Heather James, *Shakespeare and Troy: Drama, Politics, and the Translation of Empire* (Cambridge: Cambridge University Press, 1997), 97.

14 See Bevington, 'Introduction', in *Troilus and Cressida*, 11–18.

15 George Chapman, *Seauen Bookes of the Iliades* (London: Printed by John Windet, 1598), sig. A3r.

16 See Paul E.J. Hammer, *The Polarisation of Elizabethan Politics: The Political Career of Robert Devereux, 2nd Earl of Essex, 1585–1597* (Cambridge Studies in Early Modern British History) (Cambridge: Cambridge University Press, 1999), 379–80, 386–7.

17 *The Rape of Lucrece*, lines 1366–7, in *Shakespeare's Poems*, ed. Katherine Duncan-Jones and Henry Woudhuysen, The Arden Shakespeare, Third Series (London and New York: Bloomsbury, 2007). All further references will be cited parenthetically in the text.

18 For a discussion of the ekphrasis in *The Rape of Lucrece*, see S. Clark Hulse, '"A Piece of Skilful Painting" in Shakespeare's *Lucrece*', *Shakespeare Survey* 31 (1978): 13–22; James Heffernan, *Museum of Words: The Poetics of Ekphrasis from Homer to Ashberry* (Chicago, IL: University of Chicago Press), 75–88; Leonard Barkan, 'Making Pictures Speak: Renaissance Art, Elizabethan Literature, Modern Scholarship', *Renaissance Quarterly* 48, no. 2 (1995): 326–51; Marion A. Wells, '"To Find a Face Where All Distress is Stell'd": *Enargeia*, *Ekphrasis* and Mourning in *The Rape of Lucrece* and the *Aeneid*', *Comparative Literature* 54, no. 2 (2002): 97–126, and Richard Meek, *Narrating the Visual in Shakespeare* (London: Routledge, 2009).

19 On metatheatre and specular imagery in the play, see Bevington, 'Introduction', in *Troilus and Cressida*, 78–9, and Chapter 3 in this book.

20 On detachment in *Troilus and Cressida* producing *Verfremdungseffekt* (detachment, alienation), see R.S. White, '*Troilus and Cressida* as Brechtian Theatre', in *Shakespearean Continuities: Essays in Honour of E. A. J. Honigmann*, ed. John Batchelor, Tom Cain and Claire Lamont (Basingstoke: Palgrave Macmillan, 1997), 221–37.

21 Jan Kott, *Shakespeare our Contemporary*, trans. Boleslaw Taboriki (London: Methuen, 1964), 62.

Chapter 1

1 *The Complete Works of Samuel Taylor Coleridge. With an Introductory Essay upon His Philosophical and Theological Opinions*, ed. Professor Shedd, vol. IV, *Lectures upon Shakespeare and Other Dramatists* (New York: Harper, 1858), 98.

2 William Hazlitt, *Characters of Shakespeare's Plays* (London: R. Hunter and C. and J. Oliver, 1817), 83.

3   Algernon Charles Swinburne, *A Study of Shakespeare* (London: Chatto & Windus, 1880), 200.
4   Mark Van Doren, *Shakespeare* (New York: Holt & Co., 1939), 203.
5   David Bevington, 'Preface', in *Troilus and Cressida*, by William Shakespeare, The Arden Shakespeare, Third Series, rev. edn, ed. David Bevington (London and New York: Bloomsbury, 2015), xxi.
6   Nicholas Marsh, *Shakespeare: Three Problem Plays* (Basingstoke: Palgrave Macmillan, 2003), 1.
7   David Bevington, 'Additions and Reconsiderations', in *Troilus and Cressida*, ed. David Bevington, 125.
8   David Bevington, 'Introduction' in *Troilus and Cressida*, ed. David Bevington, 5.
9   W.L. Godshalk, 'The Texts of *Troilus and Cressida*', *Early Modern Literary Studies* 1, no. 2 (1995): 2.1–54, par. 2.
10 Ibid.
11 Ibid. (Original italics.)
12 See facsimiles of both states in William Shakespeare, *Troilus and Cressida*, ed. David Bevington, 148–49.
13 Bevington, 'Introduction', in *Troilus and Cressida*, 1.
14 Godshalk, 'The Texts of *Troilus and Cressida*', par. 2.
15 All parenthetical citations refer to the following edition: William Shakespeare, *Troilus and Cressida*, ed. David Bevington.
16 Peter Alexander, '*Troilus and Cressida*, 1609', *The Library* s4–IX, no. 3 (1928): 267–86. See also Chapter 2 ('The Performance History') and Chapter 3 ('The State of the Art') on the play's original audience and theatrical context.
17 Lewis F. Mott, '*Troilus and Cressida* – Epilogue', *Shakespeare Association Bulletin* 9, no. 4 (October 1934): 185.
18 Godshalk, 'The Texts of *Troilus and Cressida*', par. 2.
19 Ibid.; see also Marsh, *Three Problem Plays*, 226.
20 Folger Shakespeare Library, 'Troilus and Cressida', *Folger Shakespeare Library*. n.d. Available at: http://www.folger.edu/troilus-and-cressida. (accessed 4 August 2018).

21 Bevington, 'Preface', xvii.
22 Ibid., xviii.
23 B.D.R. Higgins, 'Printing the First Folio', in *The Cambridge Companion to Shakespeare's First Folio*, ed. Emma Smith (Cambridge: Cambridge University Press, 2016), 42.
24 Roger Apfelbaum, '"What verse for it? What instance for it?": Authority, Closure, and the Endings of *Troilus and Cressida* in Text and Performance', *Critical Survey* 9, no. 3 (1 January 1997), 91.
25 *The Works of John Dryden*, vol. XIII, ed. Maximillian E. Novak et al. (Berkeley, CA, and London: University of California Press, 1984), 499.
26 Ibid., 497.
27 Ibid., 218.
28 Bevington, 'Introduction', 94.
29 J.W.E. [Joseph Woodfall Ebsworth], 'Duke, Richard', *Dictionary of National Biography*, ed. Leslie Stephen, vol. 16 (London: Smith, Elder & Co., 1888), 144–5.
30 Emma Smith, ed., *Shakespeare's Tragedies* (Oxford: Wiley-Blackwell, 2003), 13.
31 Michèle Willems, 'Voltaire', in *Voltaire, Goethe, Schlegel, Coleridge: Great Shakespeareans Vol. III*, ed. Roger Paulin (London and New York: Bloomsbury, 2010), 21.
32 'Some Account of the Life, etc. of Mr. William Shakespear', in *The Works of Mr. William Shakespear*, vol. I., ed. Nicholas Rowe (London: Jacob Tonson, 1709), xix.
33 *The Works of Shakespear in Six Volumes*, ed. Alexander Pope (London: Jacob Tonson, 1725), xi.
34 Ibid., xiv.
35 *The Works of Mr. William Shakespear*, vol. IV, ed. Nicholas Rowe (London: Jacob Tonson, 1709), 1841.
36 Lewis Theobald, 'Preface' in *The Works of Shakespeare: in Seven Volumes*, ed. Lewis Theobald (London: A. Bettesworth et al., 1733), xlix.
37 *The Works of Shakespeare: in Seven Volumes*, ed. Lewis Theobald, vol. VII (London: A. Bettesworth et al., 1733), 43.

38 *The Works of Mr. William Shakespear*, ed. Sir Thomas Hanmer, vol. VI (Oxford: at the Theatre, 1744), 7.

39 Edward Tomarken, *Samuel Johnson on Shakespeare: The Discipline of Criticism* (Athens: University of Georgia Press, 1991), 35.

40 Ibid.

41 *The Plays of William Shakespeare in Eight Volumes*, ed. Samuel Johnson, vol. VII (London: J. and R. Tonson et al., 1765), 547.

42 Ibid.

43 Tomarken, *Samuel Johnson on Shakespeare*, 37.

44 Ibid., 50.

45 Andrew Murphy, 'The Birth of the Editor', in *A Concise Companion to Shakespeare and the Text*, ed. Andrew Murphy (Malden, MA: Blackwell, 2007), 105.

46 Emma Smith, *Shakespeare's First Folio: Four Centuries of an Iconic Book* (Oxford: Oxford University Press, 2016), 199.

47 Ibid., 196.

48 D. Nichol Smith, 'Introduction. Shakespearian Criticism in the Eighteenth Century', in *Eighteenth-Century Essays on Shakespeare*, ed. D. Nichol Smith (Glasgow: MacLehose, 1903), 4.

49 Christine Roger and Roger Paulin, 'August Wilhelm Schlegel', in *Voltaire, Goethe, Schlegel, Coleridge: Great Shakespeareans Vol. III*, edited by Roger Paulin (London and New York: Bloomsbury, 2010), 124.

50 Augustus William Schlegel, *A Course of Lectures on Dramatic Art and Literature*, trans. John Black (London: Baldwin, Cradock & Joy; Edinburgh: William Blackwood; and Dublin: John Cumming, 1815), vol. 2, 213.

51 Ibid., 215.

52 Ibid., 217.

53 Hazlitt, *Characters of Shakespeare's Plays*, xvi.

54 Ibid., xvi.

55 Ibid., 83.

56 Ibid.

57 Ibid., ix.
58 Ibid., 86.
59 Ibid., 83.
60 Ibid., 88.
61 Ibid.
62 Ibid., 89–90.
63 Ibid., 90.
64 Ibid., 92.
65 *Goethe's Literary Essays*, ed. J.E. Springarn (London: Humphrey Milford, Oxford University Press, 1921), 195.
66 Ibid.
67 *Goethe's Werke*, vol. 46 (Stuttgart and Tübingen: J.G. Cotta'schen Buchhandlung, 1833), 9.
68 Coleridge, *The Complete Works*, 98.
69 Ibid., 91 (italics in original).
70 Charles Lamb, 'Those Big Boobies', in *Shakespeare Troilus and Cressida: A Casebook*, ed. Priscilla Martin (London and Basingstoke: Macmillan, 1976), 43 (italics in original).
71 Gerhard Höhn, *Heine-Handbuch. Zeit, Person, Werk* (Stuttgart and Weimar: Verlag J.B. Metzler, 2004), 395.
72 Ibid., 396 (my translation).
73 *Heine on Shakespeare. A Translation of His Notes on Shakespeare Heroines*, trans. Ida Benecke (Westminster: Archibald Constable and Co., 1895), 43.
74 Ibid., 48.
75 Ibid., 45.
76 Ibid., 26.
77 Hermann Ulrici, *Shakespeare's Dramatic Art: And His Relation to Calderon and Goethe*, trans. A.J.W. Morrison (London: Chapman Brothers, 1846), 334.
78 G.G. Gervinus, *Shakespeare Commentaries*, trans. F.E. Bunnett (London: Smith, Elder &. Co, 1875), 693.
79 Ibid., 694.
80 Ibid.

81 *Heine on Shakespeare*, 45 (italics in original).

82 Gervinus, *Shakespeare Commentaries*, 684.

83 Ibid., 685.

84 Ibid., 695.

85 Ibid., 697.

86 Swinburne, *A Study of Shakespeare*, 193.

87 Ibid., 194.

88 Ibid., 196

89 Ibid.

90 Ibid., 203.

91 Ibid., 199.

92 Ibid., 198–9.

93 Robert Sawyer, *Victorian Appropriations of Shakespeare: George Eliot, A.C. Swinburne, Robert Browning, and Charles Dickens* (Madison and Teaneck: Fairleigh Dickinson University Press, and London: Associated University Presses, 2003), 63.

94 Swinburne, *A Study of Shakespeare*, 214.

95 George [*sic*] Brandes, *William Shakespeare* (London: William Heinemann, 1898), 515.

96 Coleridge, *The Complete Works*, 98.

97 *Heine on Shakespeare*, 41.

98 Gervinus, *Shakespeare Commentaries*, 683.

99 Swinburne, *A Study of Shakespeare*, 202.

100 G.B. Shaw, 'Shakespear's First Real Woman', in *Shakespeare Troilus and Cressida: A Casebook*, ed. Priscilla Martin (London and Basingstoke: Macmillan, 1976), 57.

101 Brandes, *William Shakespeare*, 501.

102 Ibid.

103 Ibid., 503.

104 Ibid., 502.

105 Ibid.

106 Ibid., 507.

107 Ibid., 514.

108 Ibid., 528.
109 Ibid., 525.
110 Ibid., 518.
111 Ibid., 521.
112 Priscilla Martin, 'Introduction', in *Shakespeare Troilus and Cressida: A Casebook*, ed. Priscilla Martin (London and Basingstoke: Macmillan, 1976), 11.
113 William B. Toole, *Shakespeare's Problem Plays. Studies in Form and Meaning* (London, The Hague and Paris: Mouton, 1966), 10.
114 Edward Dowden, *Shakespeare: A Critical Study of His Mind and Art* (Cambridge: Cambridge University Press, 2009), 94.
115 Frederick S. Boas, *Shakspere and his Predecessors* (London: John Murray, 1910), 345.
116 Ernest Schanzer, *The Problem Plays of Shakespeare. A Study of Julius Caesar, Measure for Measure, Antony and Cleopatra* (New York: Schocken Books, 1963), 2.
117 Boas, *Shakspere and his Predecessors*, 345.
118 G.B. Shaw, 'Preface Mainly About Myself', in *Plays Pleasant and Unpleasant, The First Volume, Containing the Three Unpleasant Plays* (Chicago, IL, and New York: Herbert S. Stone and Co, 1898), xxvi.
119 A.C. Bradley, *Shakespearean Tragedy. Lectures on Hamlet, Othello, King Lear, Macbeth* (London: Macmillan, 1963), 226.
120 Ibid., 227, n.3.
121 Ibid., 150.
122 Arthur Symons, '*Troilus and Cressida*', *Harper's Monthly Magazine* CXV (October 1907): 664.
123 Ibid.
124 Ibid., 660.
125 Brandes, *William Shakespeare*, 523.
126 Symons, '*Troilus and Cressida*', 660.
127 Ibid., 664.
128 Michael Jamieson, 'The Problem Plays, 1920–1970: A Retrospect', *Shakespeare Survey* 25 (1972): 1.

129 Ibid., 2.
130 G. Wilson Knight, *The Wheel of Fire: Interpretations of Shakespearean Tragedy* (London and New York: Routledge, 2001), x.
131 Ibid., 50–1.
132 Ibid., 70.
133 Ibid., 74.
134 Ibid., 78.
135 Ibid., 76.
136 Ibid., 51.
137 William Witherle Lawrence, *Shakespeare's Problem Comedies* (New York: Frederick Ungar Publishing Co., 1960), viii.
138 Ibid., 17.
139 Charles J. Sisson, '*Shakespeare's Problem Comedies*. By W.W. Lawrence. New York: The Macmillan Company; London: Macmillan. 1931', *The Modern Language Review* 27, no. 2 (April 1932): 217.
140 Caroline Spurgeon, *Shakespeare's Imagery and What it Tells Us* (Cambridge: Cambridge University Press, 1935), 320.
141 Oscar James Campbell, *Comicall Satyre and Shakespeare's 'Troilus and Cressida'* (San Marino, CA: C.F. Braun & Co, 1959), 212.
142 Gary A. Schmidt, *Renaissance Hybrids: Culture and Genre in Early Modern England* (London and New York: Routledge, 2016), 172.
143 Una Ellis-Fermor, *The Frontiers of Drama* (London: Methuen, 1946), v.
144 Ibid., 56.
145 Ibid., 62.
146 Ibid., 58.
147 Ibid., 57.
148 G.B. Harrison, *Shakespeare's Tragedies* (London and New York: Routledge, 1951, repr. Abingdon: Routledge, 2005), 114.
149 Ibid., 115.

150 Ibid., 116.
151 Toole, *Shakespeare's Problem Plays*, 10.
152 E.M.W. Tillyard, *Shakespeare's Problem Plays* (London: Chatto & Windus, 1951), 1.
153 Schanzer, *The Problem Plays of Shakespeare*, ix.
154 Northrop Frye, *A Natural Perspective. The Development of Shakespearean Comedy and Romance* (New York and London: Columbia University Press, 1965).
155 Northrop Frye, *Fools of Time. Studies in Shakespearean Tragedy* (Toronto: University of Toronto Press, 1967).
156 Northrop Frye, *The Myth of Deliverance: Reflections on Shakespeare's Problem Comedies* (Toronto: University of Toronto Press, 1983), 62.
157 Ibid., 85.
158 Toole, *Shakespeare's Problem Plays*, 9.
159 Kenneth Muir, 'Troilus and Cressida', *Shakespeare Survey* 8, The Comedies (1955): 28.
160 M.C. Bradbrook, 'What Shakespeare Did to Chaucer's *Troilus and Criseyde*', *Shakespeare Quarterly* 9, no. 3 (Summer 1958): 311–12.
161 Jan Kott, *Shakespeare Our Contemporary*, trans. Boleslaw Taborski (London: Methuen, 1964), 65.
162 Ibid.
163 Ibid., 66.
164 Joyce Carol Oates (J. Oates Smith), 'Essence and Existence in Shakespeare's *Troilus and Cressida*', *Philological Quarterly* 46, (April 1967): 167–85.
165 Muir, 'Troilus and Cressida', 35.
166 Ibid., 38.
167 Jamieson, 'The Problem Plays, 1920–1970: A Retrospect', 1.
168 A.P. Rossiter, 'Troilus as "Inquisition" (1961)', in *Shakespeare Troilus and Cressida: A Casebook*, ed. Priscilla Martin (London and Basingstoke: Macmillan, 1976), 118.
169 Willard Farnham, 'Troilus in Shapes of Infinite Desire', *Shakespeare Quarterly* 15, no. 2. (Spring 1964): 258.

170 Norman Sanders, 'The Year's Contributions to Shakespearian Study. (1) Critical Studies', *Shakespeare Survey* 20 (1967): 154.

171 R.A. Foakes, '*Troilus and Cressida* Reconsidered', *University of Toronto Quarterly* XXXII (January 1963): 142–54.

172 Nevill Coghill, *Shakespeare's Professional Skills* (Cambridge: Cambridge University Press, 1964).

173 Norman Rabkin, '*Troilus and Cressida*: The Uses of the Double Plot', *Shakespeare Studies* 1 (1965): 264–82.

174 David Kaula, 'Will and Reason in *Troilus and Cressida*', *Shakespeare Quarterly* 12, no. 3 (1961): 274.

175 R.J. Kaufman, 'Ceremonies for Chaos: The Status of *Troilus and Cressida*', *ELH* 32, no. 2 (1965): 140.

176 R.J. Kaufman, 'Ceremonies for Chaos', 146.

177 Anne Barton (Anne Righter), *Shakespeare and the Idea of the Play* (New York: Barnes & Noble, 1962), 173.

178 Ibid., 181.

179 T. McAlindon, 'Language, Style, and Meaning in *Troilus and Cressida*', *PMLA* 84, no. 1 (1969): 30.

180 Mark Sacharoff and T. McAlindon, 'Critical Comment in Response to T. McAlindon's "Language, Style, and Meaning in *Troilus and Cressida*"', *PMLA* 87, no. 1 (1972): 93.

181 R.A. Yoder, '"Sons and Daughters of the Game"': An Essay on Shakespeare's *Troilus and Cressida*', *Shakespeare Survey* 25: The Problem Plays (1972): 11.

182 Ibid.

183 John Bayley, 'Time and the Trojans', *Essays in Criticism* XXV, no. 1 (1975): 58.

Chapter 2

1 William Shakespeare, *Troilus and Cressida*, ed. David Bevington (London: Bloomsbury, 2015), rev. edn, 145. All references from the play are to this edition.

2 Ibid., 146.

3 David Bevington, 'Introduction', in *Troilus and Cressida*, rev. edn (London: Bloomsbury, 2015), 92.

4 Peter Alexander ('*Troilus and Cressida*, 1609', *The Library* 4th ser., 9 (1928–29): 267–86) first proposed the idea of performance at the Inns of Court and this continues to be an influential view. However, Nevill Coghill, in *Shakespeare's Professional Skills* (Cambridge: Cambridge University Press, 1964), has suggested that the play was originally acted at the Globe and only later taken to the Inns of Court. See also Chapter 1.

5 Such a performance by the Lord Chamberlain's Men would probably have seen Thersites played by Robert Armin, who replaced Will Kempe as the company's Fool in 1599. Small, with a twisted physique, there would have been an obvious physical resemblance between Armin and the deformed Thersites. Moreover, Thersites' cynical comments on other characters in the play are similar to the speeches of other world-weary Fools played by Armin such as Feste in *Twelfth Night* or Lear's Fool, although more sarcastic in tone. The roles of Cressida and Helen would have been played by boy actors, although the differences between these two characters also suggest a range of skills and physical attributes among these boy actors. See Robert H. Bell, *Shakespeare's Great Stage of Fools* (New York: Palgrave Macmillan, 2011), 92–100, for a useful analysis of the role of Thersites in the play.

6 See Adrian Poole, 'Relic, Pageant, Sunken Wreck: Shakespeare in 1816,' in *Celebrating Shakespeare: Commemoration and Cultural Memory*, ed. Clara Calvo and Coppélia Kahn (Cambridge: Cambridge University Press, 2015), 69.

7 In Act 2 Scene 2, the Trojans debate whether to keep Helen or hand her back to the Greeks. While Hector argues that 'she is not worth what she doth cost / The holding' (2.2.51–2), Troilus counters 'What's aught but as 'tis valued?' (2.2.52), suggesting that while Helen is intrinsically not worth the loss of Trojan lives, to hand her back would involve a loss of honour on the part of the Trojans. Hector reluctantly comes round to Troilus's view and the war continues.

8 John Dryden, Preface to *Troilus and Cressida, or Truth Found Too Late: A Tragedy* . . . First edn, first issue. (Printed for Jacob Tonson at the Judges-Head in Chancery-lane near Fleet-street, and Abel Swall, at the Unicorn at the West-end of S. Pauls, 1679). Reprinted edition at Early English Books Online: http://quod.lib.

umich.edu/cgi/t/text/text-idx?c=eebo;idno=A36704.0001.001 (accessed 10 January 2017)

9 Ibid., 'Prologue'.
10 Ibid., 'Prologue'.
11 Ibid., 'Preface'.
12 Ibid., 'Prologue'.
13 Jeanne T. Newlin, 'The Darkened Stage. J.P. Kemble and *Troilus and Cressida*', in *The Triple Bond: Plays, Mainly Shakespearean in Performance*, ed. J.G. Price (University Park and London: Pennsylvania University Press, 1975), 190–202.
14 For a discussion of twentieth-century performances of the play, see Roger Apfelbaum, *Shakespeare's Troilus and Cressida: Textual Problems and Performances Solutions* (Newark, DE: University of Delaware Press, 2003).
15 In his director's notes on the play, Guthrie observed:

> One of its important premises is that war is sport, a gallant and delightful employment, indeed the only suitable employment for young men of the Upper Class. This is a premise to which no one nowadays can possibly subscribe. Therefore we have set the play back to a date when such a view was still widely held but as near as possible to our own times: namely just before 1914.

16 See Samuel L. Leiter, *Shakespeare around the Globe: A Guide to Notable Postwar Revivals* (New York: Greenwood Press, 1986), 755.
17 Stephen Orgel, 'Afterword', in *Shakespeare, Memory and Performance*, ed. Peter Holland (Cambridge: Cambridge University Press, 2006), 349.
18 Carol Rutter, *Enter the Body: Women and Representation on Shakespeare's Stage* (London: Routledge, 2001), 126.
19 Paul Prescott, 'Review of *Troilus and Cressida* (directed by Peter Stein) at the Royal Shakespeare Theatre September 2006', *Shakespeare* 3, no. 2 (2007): 238.
20 Jan Kott, *Shakespeare our Contemporary*, trans. Boleslaw Taboriki (London: Methuen, 1964), 62.
21 Ibid., 66–7.

22 Avraham Oz, 'Shakespeare in Israel', *Shakespeare Quarterly* 31, no. 3 (1980): 404.
23 Wolfgang Riehle, 'Shakespeare in Austria', *Shakespeare Quarterly* 31, no. 3 (1980): 424–7.
24 Ibid., 425.
25 Andrej Zurovski, 'Cressida's Children: *Troilus and Cressida* in Gdansk', *Shakespeare Quarterly* 42, no. 3 (1991): 359.
26 Ibid., 363.
27 Rutter, *Enter the Body*, 130. Rutter's stimulating chapter on costume design illustrates the significance of costume in performance conceptions of Helen and Cressida. While Helen is invariably costumed in a way that points to the difference between her actual and symbolic value, Cressida's costumes tend to stress her sexual availability.
28 See Dennis Kennedy, *Looking at Shakespeare: A Visual History of Twentieth-century Performance,* 2nd edn (Cambridge: Cambridge University Press, 2001), 336.
29 See the representation of Helen as 'the face that launched a thousand ships / And burnt the topless towers of Ilium', in Christopher Marlowe, *Doctor Faustus*, 5.2.97–8.
30 Bevington. 'Introduction', 125.
31 Matt Trueman, 'Wooster Group and the RSC: Strange bedfellows . . .', *Independent*, 1 August 2012. Available at: http://www.independent.co.uk/arts-entertainment/theatre-dance/features/wooster-group-and-the-rsc-strange-bedfellows-7994784.html (accessed 10 January 2017).
32 Dennis Kennedy, *Foreign Shakespeare: Contemporary Performance* (Cambridge: Cambridge University Press, 1993), 240.
33 Ibid., 241.
34 Ibid., 242.
35 Kennedy, *Looking at Shakespeare*, 350. On this production, see also Sylvia Zyszet, 'Apocalyptic Beginnings at the End of the New Millennium: Stefan Bachmann's *Troilus and Cressida*', in *Four Hundred Years of Shakespeare in Europe,* ed. A. Luis Pujante and Ton Hoenselaars (Newark, DE: University of Delaware Press, 2003), 196–210.

36 Veronica Schandl has dealt with Purcarete's production in an unpublished paper '"Of nature and of nations speak aloud": Silviu Purcarete's *Troilus and Cressida* in Budapest, 2005'.

37 Paul Taylor, '*Troilus and Cressida*, Riverside Studios, London', *Independent*, 31 August 2012. Available at: http://www.independent.co.uk/arts-entertainment/theatre-dance/reviews/troilus-and-cressida-riverside-studios-london-8099436.html (accessed 10 March 2017).

38 Kara Reilly, '*Troilus and Cressida* (Wooster/RSC)', *Theatre Journal* 65, no. 2 (2013): 278.

39 Benjamin Fowler, 'Culture Clash: What the Wooster Group Revealed about the RSC (and British Theater Hegemony) in *Troilus and Cressida*', *Shakespeare Bulletin* 32, no. 2 (Summer 2014): 209.

40 Thomas Cartelli, 'The Killing Stops Here: Unmaking the Myths of Troy in Wooster Group/RSC *Troilus and Cressida*', *Shakespeare Quarterly* 64, no. 2 (Summer 2013): 233.

41 See Elizabeth LeCompte, Kate Valk and Maria Shevtsova, 'A Conversation on the Wooster Group's *Troilus and Cressida* with the RSC', *New Theatre Quarterly* 29, no. 3 (August 2013): 233–66.

42 Cartelli, 'The Killing Stops Here', 234.

43 Stephen Purcell, 'Shakespeare, Spectatorship and the "Olympic Spirit"', in *Shakespeare and the Global Stage: Performance and Festivity in the Olympic Year*, ed. Paul Prescott and Erin Sullivan (London: Bloomsbury, 2015), 211.

44 Catherine Silverstone, 'Festival Showcasing and Cultural Regeneration: Aotearoa New Zealand, Shakespeare's Globe and Ngakau's *A Toroihi rāua ko Kahira* (*Troilus and Cressida*) in te reo Maori', in *Shakespeare Beyond English: A Global Experiment*, ed. Susan Bennett and Christie Carson (Cambridge: Cambridge University Press, 2013), 41.

45 See Claire M. Tylee, 'The Text of Cressida and Every Ticklish Reader: *Troilus and Cressida*, The Greek Camp Scene', *Shakespeare Survey* 41 (1989): 63–76, for a discussion of this controversy, where the perspective of Lesser, Miller and series consultant John Wilders prevailed over Burden's view of the main characters.

Chapter 3

1. As well as these resources, it is worth consulting the Penguin, Folger, New Cambridge, and earlier Arden single editions of the play, as well as the Norton and New Oxford complete works.
2. On the imagined audiences of Shakespeare's plays, see Bettina Boecker, *Imagining Shakespeare's Original Audience, 1660–2000: Groundlings, Gallants, Grocers* (Basingstoke: Palgrave, 2015).
3. Much ink has been spilled by critics on readings of this preface, see, for example, Johann Gregory, 'Shakespeare's "Sugred Sonnets", *Troilus and Cressida* and the *Odcombian Banquet*: An Exploration of Promising Paratexts, Expectations and Matters of Taste', *Shakespeare*, 6, no. 2 (2010): 185–208, and John Jowett, 'The Material Book', in *Shakespeare and Text: Oxford Shakespeare Topics* (Oxford and New York: Oxford University Press, 2007), 46–68. The notes to Pervez Rizi's recent essay contain further references to bibliographical scholarship on the play: 'The Bibliographical Relationship between the Texts of *Troilus and Cressida*', *The Library* 14, no. 3 (2013): 271–312.
4. Peter Alexander, '*Troilus and Cressida*, 1609', *The Library*, 4th ser., no. 9 (1928–29): 279.
5. Alexander, '*Troilus and Cressida*, 1609', 278.
6. W.R. Elton, *Shakespeare's 'Troilus and Cressida' and the Inns of Court Revels* (Aldershot and Brookfield, VT: Ashgate, 2000), 168.
7. Ibid., 168.
8. Anthony B. Dawson, 'Book Review: *Shakespeare's "Troilus and Cressida" and the Inns of Court Revels*', *Modern Language Review* 97, no. 2 (2002): 391.
9. See Paul Yachnin, '"The Perfection of Ten": Populuxe Art and Artisanal Value in *Troilus and Cressida*', *Shakespeare Quarterly* 56, no. 3 (2005): 306–27.
10. Bridget Escolme, *Talking to the Audience: Shakespeare, Performance, Self* (London and New York: Routledge, 2005), 46.
11. Henk Gras, 'Review: *Shakespeare & the Poets' War* by James P. Bednarz', *Modern Language Review* 98, no. 4 (2003): 960.

12 See James P. Bednarz, 'Shakespeare's Purge of Jonson: The Theatrical Context of *Troilus and Cressida*' in his book *Shakespeare & the Poets' War* (New York and Chichester: Columbia University Press, 2001), 32.

13 Matthew Steggle, 'Review of James Bednarz, *Shakespeare & the Poets' War*', *Early Modern Literary Studies* 7, no. 3 (2002): 6 (par. 5). Available at: http://purl.oclc.org/emls/07-3/steg1rev.htm (accessed 13 February 2017).

14 Ibid., par. 5.

15 Ken Jackson, 'Review: *Shakespeare and the Poets' War*', *The Sixteenth Century Journal* 33, no. 2 (2002): 503.

16 For this relationship, see Johann Gregory, 'The "author's drift" in Shakespeare's *Troilus and Cressida*: A Poetics of Reflection', *Medieval and Early Modern Authorship: SPELL: Swiss Papers in English Language and Literature 25*, ed. Guillemette Bolens and Lukas Erne (Tübingen: Gunter Narr Verlag, 2011), 93–106.

17 Edward Gieskes, '"Honest and Vulgar Praise": The Poets' War and the Literary Field', *Medieval and Renaissance Drama in England* 18 (2005): 77.

18 See Jan Kott, '*Troilus and Cressida* – Amazing and Modern', in *Shakespeare Our Contemporary*, trans. Boleslaw Taborski (1964; New York and London: Norton, 1974), 75–83.

19 E.A.J. Honigmann, 'Shakespeare Suppressed: The Unfortunate History of *Troilus and Cressida*' (1985), in *Myriad-minded Shakespeare: Essays, Chiefly on the Tragedies and Problem Comedies* (Basingstoke: Macmillan, 1989), 118 and 125.

20 Eric S. Mallin, 'Emulous Factions and the Collapse of Chivalry: *Troilus and Cressida*', in *Inscribing the Time: Shakespeare and the End of Elizabethan England* (Berkeley, CA, and London: University of California Press, 1995), 29 (first publ. in *Representations* 29, no. 4 (1990): 145–79). For a broadly new historicist analysis of the play in relation to the 'violent propaganda commissioned by the Tudor bishops throughout the 1590s', see Joseph Navitsky, 'Scurrilous Jests and Retaliatory Abuse in Shakespeare's *Troilus and Cressida*', *English Literary Renaissance* 42, no. 1 (2012): 4.

21 Mallin, *Inscribing the Time*, 38.

22 Ibid., 39 and 60.

23 Heather James, *Shakespeare's Troy: Drama, Politics, and the Translation of Empire* (Cambridge and New York: Cambridge University Press, 1997), 91. Andrew Griffin also reads the historicity of the play in 'The Banality of History in *Troilus and Cressida*', *Early Modern Literary Studies*, 12, no. 2 (2007): n.p. Available at: http://purl.oclc.org/emls/12-2/grifbana.htm (accessed 10 March 2017).
24 James, *Shakespeare's Troy*, 90.
25 Ibid., 118.
26 A.G. Harmon, 'Perfection in Reversion: The Mock Contract in *Troilus and Cressida*', in *Eternal Bonds, True Contracts: Law and Nature in Shakespeare's Problem Plays* (Albany, NY: SUNY Press, 2004), 55–80.
27 Emily Ross, '"Words, Vows, Gifts, Tears and Love's Full Sacrifice": An Assessment of the Status of Troilus and Cressida's Relationship According to Customary Elizabethan Marriage Procedure', *Shakespeare* 4, no. 4 (2008): 413–37; John Kerrigan, 'Shakespeare, Oaths and Vows', *Proceedings of the British Academy: 2009 Lectures* 167 (2011): 61–89, and the chapter 'Troilus, Cressida and Constancy' in his book *Shakespeare's Binding Language* (Oxford: Oxford University Press, 2016), 256–89.
28 William Shakespeare, *Troilus and Cressida*, ed. David Bevington rev. edn (London: Bloomsbury Arden Shakespeare, 2015), 409–31.
29 See Andrew James Johnston, Russell West-Pavlov and Elisabeth Kempf (eds), *Love, History and Emotion in Chaucer and Shakespeare: 'Troilus and Criseyde' and 'Troilus and Cressida'* (Manchester: Manchester University Press, 2016).
30 Raymond Southall, '*Troilus and Cressida* and the Spirit of Capitalism', in *Shakespeare in a Changing World*, ed. Arnold Kettle (London: Lawrence & Wishart, 1964), 231.
31 C.C. Barfoot, '*Troilus and Cressida*: "Praise us as we are tasted"', *Shakespeare Quarterly* 39, no. 1 (1988): 56.
32 Joseph Lenz, 'Base Trade: Theater as Prostitution', *English Literary History* 60, no. 4 (1993): 833.
33 Ibid., 852.
34 Douglas Bruster, '"The alteration of men": *Troilus and Cressida*, Troynovant, and Trade', in *Drama and the Market in the Age*

of *Shakespeare* (Cambridge and New York: Cambridge
University Press, 1992), 97–117; Lars Engle, 'Always Already in
the Market: the Politics of Evaluation in *Troilus and Cressida*',
in *Shakespearean Pragmatism: Market of His Time* (Chicago, IL,
and London: University of Chicago Press, 1993), 147–63;
and Hugh Grady, '"Mad Idolatry": Commodification and
Reification in *Troilus and Cressida*', in *Shakespeare's Universal
Wolf: Studies in Early Modern Reification* (Oxford and
New York: Oxford University Press, 1996), 58–94. See also
Edward Wilson-Lee, 'Shakespeare by Numbers: Mathematical
Crisis in *Troilus and Cressida*', *Shakespeare Quarterly* 64,
no. 4 (2013): 449–72.

35 Jonathan Dollimore, 'Emergence: Marston's Antonio Plays
(*c.* 1599–1601) and Shakespeare's *Troilus and Cressida*', in
*Radical Tragedy: Religion, Ideology and Power in the Drama
of Shakespeare and his Contemporaries*, 2nd edn (London and
New York: Harvester, 1989), 29–50.

36 Gayle Greene, 'Language and Value in Shakespeare's *Troilus and
Cressida*', *Studies in English Literature 1500–1900* 21, no. 2
(1981): 272.

37 Ibid.

38 Roberta Kwan, '"You Are in the State of Grace?": The Absence
of Grace and Semantic Embranglement in Shakespeare's *Troilus
and Cressida*', *English Studies* 97, no. 4 (2016): 362–82.

39 David Hillman, 'The Gastric Epic: *Troilus and Cressida*',
Shakespeare Quarterly 48, no. 3 (1997): 313. See also Elizabeth
Freund, '"Ariachne's Broken Woof": The Rhetoric of Citation in
Troilus and Cressida', in *Shakespeare and the Question of
Theory*, ed. Patricia Parker and Geoffrey Hartman (London:
Methuen, 1985), 19–36.

40 Patricia Parker, 'Dilation and Inflation: *All's Well That Ends
Well, Troilus and Cressida*, and Shakespearean Increase', in
Shakespeare from the Margins: Language, Culture, Context
(Chicago, IL, and London: Chicago University Press, 1996), 224.
Jonathan Gil Harris provides a reading of the play's language of
the humours and disease in 'Canker/Serpigo and Value: Gerard
Malynes, *Troilus and Cressida*', in his book *Sick Economies:
Drama, Mercantilism, and Disease in Shakespeare's England*
(Philadelphia, PA: University of Pennsylvania Press, 2004),

82–107. Hester Lees-Jeffries discusses the materiality of wordplay in the play in 'A Subtle Point: Sleeves, Tents and "Ariachne's Broken Woof" (Again)', *Shakespeare Survey* 62 (2009): 92–103.

41 Lars Engle, *Shakespearean Pragmatism*, 148.

42 A.D. Nuttall, 'Stoics and Sceptics', in *Shakespeare the Thinker* (New Haven, CT, and London: Yale University Press, 2007), 207.

43 David Hillman, 'The Worst Case of Knowing the Other? Stanley Cavell and *Troilus and Cressida*', *Philosophy and Literature* 32, no. 1 (2008): 13.

44 Andrew Hiscock, '"Will You Walk in, My Lord?" Shakespeare's *Troilus and Cressida* and the Anxiety of Oikos', in *Shakespeare and Hospitality: Ethics, Politics, and Exchange*, ed. David B. Goldstein and Julia Reinhard Lupton (Abingdon: Routledge, 2016), 19; and Alex Schulman, 'The Birth of Tragicomedy (In Defeat of Hector by Ulysses)', in *Rethinking Shakespeare's Political Philosophy* (Edinburgh: Edinburgh University Press, 2014).

45 Neil Powell, 'Hero and Human: The Problem of Achilles', *Critical Quarterly* 21, no. 2 (1979): 27.

46 Jean-Pierre Maquerlot, 'When Playing is Foiling: *Troilus and Cressida*', in *Shakespeare and the Mannerist Tradition: Five Problem Plays* (Cambridge and New York: Cambridge University Press, 1995), 145.

47 Rolf P. Lessenich, 'Shakespeare's *Troilus and Cressida*: The Vision of Decadence', *Studia Neophilological* 49, no. 2 (1977): 227.

48 Linda Charnes, '"So Unsecret to Ourselves": Notorious Identity and the Material Subject in Shakespeare's *Troilus and Cressida*', *Shakespeare Quarterly* 40, no. 4 (1989): 440.

49 Eric Byville, 'Aesthetic Uncommon Sense: Early Modern Taste and the Satirical Sublime', *Criticism* 54, no. 4 (2012): 602. See also Johann Gregory, 'Shakespeare's *Troilus and Cressida*: Visualising Expectations as a Matter of Taste', in *Shakespeare et les arts de la table: Actes du Congrès organisé par la Société Française Shakespeare*, ed. Pierre Kapitaniak, Christophe Hausermann and Dominique Goy-Blanquet (Paris: Société

Française Shakespeare, 2012), 47–66. Available at: http://www.societefrancaiseshakespeare.org/document.php?id=1705 (accessed 1 March 2017).

50 Patrick Cheney, 'The Epic Spear of Achilles: Self-Concealing Authorship in *The Rape of Lucrece*, *Troilus and Cressida*, and *Hamlet*', in *Shakespeare's Literary Authorship* (Cambridge and New York: Cambridge University Press, 2008), 60; Gretchen E. Minton, '"Discharging less than the Tenth Part of One": Performance Anxiety and/in *Troilus and Cressida*', in *Shakespeare and the Cultures of Performance*, ed. Paul Yachnin and Patricia Badir (Aldershot and Burlington, VT: Ashgate, 2008), 118.

51 Efterpi Mitsi, 'Greece "Digested in a Play": Consuming Greek Heroism in *The School of Abuse* and *Troilus and Cressida*', in *Shakespeare and Greece*, ed. Alison Findlay and Vassiliki Markidou (London: Bloomsbury Arden Shakespeare, 2017), 93–114.

52 Escolme, *Talking to the Audience*, 51. For another useful gender-conscious performance studies reading, see Carol Chillington Rutter, 'Designs on Shakespeare: Troilus's Sleeve, Cressida's Glove, Helen's Placket', in *Enter The Body: Women and Representation on Shakespeare's Stage* (London and New York: Routledge, 2001), 104–41.

53 Arlin J. Hiken, 'Texture in *Troilus and Cressida*', *Educational Theatre Journal* 19, no. 3 (1967): 367.

54 Gayle Greene, 'Shakespeare's Cressida: "A kind of self"', in *The Woman's Part: Feminist Criticism of Shakespeare*, ed. Carolyn Ruth Swift Lenz, Gayle Greene and Carol Thomas Neely (Urbana, IL, and London: University of Illinois Press, 1983), 133.

55 Alice Walker, 'Introduction', *Troilus and Cressida*, ed. Alice Walker and John Dover Wilson (Cambridge: Cambridge University Press, 1957), xii.

56 Arnold Stein, '*Troilus and Cressida*: The Disjunctive Imagination', *English Literary History* 36, no. 1 (1969): 149.

57 Carolyn Asp, 'In Defense of Cressida', *Studies in Philology* 74, no. 4 (1977): 407; Asp also provides examples of uncomplimentary critical opinion towards Cressida, 406, n.1.

58 For other feminist or gender-concerned writing focussed on Cressida, see, for example: Laurie E. Maguire, 'Performing Anger: The Anatomy of Abuse(s) in *Troilus and Cressida*', *Renaissance Drama* n.s., 31 (2002): 153–83; Simon Palfrey, *Doing Shakespeare* (London: Thomson Learning, 2005), 248–68; and Alexander Leggatt, '*Troilus and Cressida*: This is and is not Cressid', in *Shakespeare's Tragedies: Violation and Identity* (Cambridge and New York: Cambridge University Press, 2005), 84–113.

59 Barbara E. Bowen, *Gender in the Theater of War: Shakespeare's 'Troilus and Cressida'* (New York and London: Garland, 1993).

60 Gary Spear, 'Shakespeare's "Manly" Parts: Masculinity and Effeminacy in *Troilus and Cressida*', *Shakespeare Quarterly* 44, no. 4 (1993): 409–22; Daniel Juan Gil, 'At the Limits of the Social World: Fear and Pride in *Troilus and Cressida*', *Shakespeare Quarterly* 52, no. 3 (2001): 336–59; and Robin Headlam Wells, 'The Chivalric Revival: *Henry V* and *Troilus and Cressida*', in *Shakespeare on Masculinity* (Cambridge and New York: Cambridge University Press, 2000), 31–60.

61 Alan Sinfield, 'The Leather Men and the Lovely Boy: Reading Positions in *Troilus and Cressida*', in *Shakesqueer: A Queer Companion to the Complete Works of Shakespeare*, ed. Madhavi Menon (Durham, NC, and London: Duke University Press, 2011), 380.

62 See, for example, Janet Adelman, '"Is Thy Union Here?": Union and Its Discontents in *Troilus and Cressida* and *Othello*', in *Suffocating Mothers: Fantasies of Maternal Origin in Shakespeare's Plays, 'Hamlet' to 'The Tempest'* (London and New York: Routledge, 1992), 38–75; Philip Armstrong, '*Troilus and Cressida*: Space Wars', in *Shakespeare's Visual Regime: Tragedy, Psychoanalysis and the Gaze* (Basingstoke and New York: Palgrave, 2000), 91–134.

63 Barbara Hodgdon, 'He Do Cressida in Different Voices', *English Literary Renaissance* 20, no. 2 (1990): 258. See also Johann Gregory and Alice Leonard, 'Assuming Gender in *Hamlet* and *Troilus and Cressida*: "Are We to Assume that there were Women in the Audience?"', *Assuming Gender* 1, no. 2 (2010): 44–61. Virginia Mason Vaughan provides a newer historicist reading in, 'Daughters of the Game: *Troilus and Cressida* and

the Sexual Discourse of 16th-Century England', *Women's Studies International Forum* 13, no. 3 (1990): 209–20.

64 Gayle Greene, 'Shakespeare's Cressida', 145.

65 René Girard, *A Theatre of Envy: William Shakespeare* (Oxford: Oxford University Press, 1991), 123.

66 Ibid., 123.

67 Ibid., 121.

68 Hugh Grady and Terence Hawkes, 'Introduction: Presenting Presentism', in *Presentist Shakespeares*, ed. Hugh Grady and Terence Hawkes (London and New York: Routledge, 2007), 1.

69 Ibid., 1–2.

70 Ibid., 4.

71 Kiernan Ryan, '*Troilus and Cressida*: The Perils of Presentism', in *Presentist Shakespeares*, ed. Hugh Grady and Terence Hawkes (London and New York: Routledge, 2007), 183. For a reading of the play from a broadly presentist perspective, see also Linda Charnes, 'The Two Party System in *Troilus and Cressida*', in *A Companion to Shakespeare's Works, Volume IV: The Poems, Problem Comedies, Late Plays*, ed. Richard Dutton and Jean E. Howard (Oxford and Malden, MA: Blackwell, 2003), 302–15.

72 Ibid., 182.

73 Ibid., 165.

74 Rebecca Bushnell, 'Shakespeare and Nature', in *Shakespeare in Our Time: A Shakespeare Association of America Collection*, ed. Dympna Callaghan and Suzanne Gossett (London and New York: Bloomsbury Arden Shakespeare, 2016), 331.

75 Steve Mentz, 'Shakespeare without Nature', in *Shakespeare in Our Time*, 335.

76 Karen Raber, 'The Chicken and the Egg', in *Shakespeare in Our Time*, 341.

77 A.P. Rossiter, '*Troilus and Cressida*', in *Angels with Horns; Fifteen Lectures on Shakespeare*, ed. Graham Storey (London and New York: Longman, 1989), 131.

78 Anne Barton 'Introduction to *Troilus and Cressida*', in *The Riverside Shakespeare*, ed. G. Blakemore Evans with J.J.M. Tobin, 2nd edn (Boston, MA, and New York: Mifflin, 1997), 479.

79 Michel de Montaigne, *The Essayes or Morall, Politike and Millitarie Discourses of Lo: Michaell de Montaigne*, trans. John Florio (London, 1603), Z4v (260).
80 Slavoj Žižek, '"Wicked meaning in a lawful deed": Shakespeare on the Obscenity of Power', in *Shakespeare After 9/11: How a Social Trauma Reshapes Interpretation*, ed. Matthew Biberman and Julia Reinhard Lupton (Lewiston, NY, Queenston and Lampeter: Mellen, 2011), 87.

Chapter 4

1 For the reasoning behind this date for the play, see *Troilus and Cressida*, The Arden Shakespeare, Third Series, rev. edn, ed. David Bevington (London: Bloomsbury, 2015), 'Introduction', 6–19.
2 Southampton was imprisoned and sentenced to death for his role in the insurrection, though he was released on the accession of James I.
3 It is widely assumed that this play was Shakespeare's. For a summary of the arguments for and against this likelihood, and of the various possible links between Shakespeare's *Richard II* and the Earl of Essex, see Margaret Shewring, *King Richard II*, Shakespeare in Performance (Manchester and New York: Manchester University Press, 1996), 24–8.
4 *King Henry V*, ed. T.W. Craik, The Arden Shakespeare, Third Series (London: Bloomsbury, 1995), 335. It has sometimes been argued that the reference is not to Essex but to his successor as Lord Deputy of Ireland, Charles Blount (see W.D. Smith, 'The Henry V Choruses in the First Folio', *Journal of English and Germanic Philology* 53 (1954): 38–57; a response to Smith's theory was given in R.A Law, 'The Choruses in *Henry the Fifth*', *University of Texas Studies in English* 31 (1956): 11–21).
5 On humanism in England in Shakespeare's lifetime, see Mike Pincombe, *Elizabethan Humanism: Literature and Learning in the later Sixteenth Century* (Harlow: Longman, 2001). The phrase 'indirect, crooked ways' comes from *King Henry IV, Part 2*, 4.3.313, ed. James C. Bulman, The Arden Shakespeare, Third Series (London and New York: Bloomsbury, 2016), 382.

6 The most significant work on early modern exemplarity is Timothy Hampton, *Writing from History: The Rhetoric of Exemplarity in Renaissance Literature* (Ithaca, NY: Cornell University Press, 1990). See also Alexander Gelley (ed.), *Unruly Examples: On the Rhetoric of Exemplarity* (Stanford, CA: Stanford University Press, 1995).

7 On the historical interpretations of the play, see Chapter 3.

8 For a full account of England and Britain's Trojan history, see Heather James, *Shakespeare's Troy: Drama, Politics, and the Translation of Empire* (Cambridge: Cambridge University Press, 1997), 'Introduction', Chapter 1, and especially the first part of Chapter 3, '"Tricks We Play on the Dead": Making History in *Troilus and Cressida*', 85–9. For an analysis of Troy's wider significance in Europe, see *Fantasies of Troy: Classical Tales and the Social Imaginary in Medieval and Early Modern Europe*, ed. Alan Shepard and Stephen D. Powell (Toronto: Centre for Reformation and Renaissance Studies, 2004). See also Chapter 6 in this volume on London as the new Troy.

9 In *Troilus and Cressida*, the word idol appears in 5.1.6–7, when Thersites calls Achilles 'idol of idiot-worshippers' (5.1.6–7).

10 Fenton, *Certaine Tragicall Discourses*, ed. Robert Langdon Douglas (London: David Nutt, 1898), 2 vols., vol. 1, 4–5.

11 Sidney, *An Apology for Poetry*, ed. Geoffrey Shepherd, revised R.W. Maslen (Manchester and New York: Manchester University Press, 2002), 93. line 44; 94, line 2.

12 Sir Thomas Eliot, *The Boke Named The Governour* (1531), sig. H4v.

13 William Segar, *Honor Military, and Civill* (1602), Book 2, Chapter 6, 58.

14 See Sidney, *Apology for Poetry*, ed. Shepherd, revised Maslen, 'Introduction', 4.

15 For the notion of 'simplicity' in the sixteenth century see my *Elizabethan Fictions: Espionage, Counter-espionage and the Duplicity of Fiction in Early Elizabethan Prose Narratives*, Oxford English Monographs (Oxford: Clarendon Press, 1997), Chapter 1.

16 *The Rape of Lucrece*, lines 806–12, in *Shakespeare's Poems*, ed. Katherine Duncan-Jones and Henry Woudhuysen, The Arden Shakespeare, Third Series (London: Bloomsbury, 2007), 304–5.

17 Sidney, *Apology for Poetry*, ed. Shepherd, revised Maslen, 91, lines 3–8.

18 'Prologue', 24–31. All references are to *Troilus and Cressida*, Arden Shakespeare Third Series, rev. edn, ed. David Bevington (London: Bloomsbury, 2015).

19 One of the best examples of turning black into white as an example of sophistry or false logic comes in Marlowe's *Edward II*, when Lancaster protests against Mortimer's plan to repeal Gaveston's banishment: 'Can this be true, 'twas good to banish him, / And is this true, to call him home again? / Such reasons make white black and dark night day . . . In no respect can contraries be true' (*Edward II*, 1.4.245–9). Christopher Marlowe, *Doctor Faustus and Other Plays*, ed. David Bevington and Eric Rasmussen, Oxford World's Classics (Oxford and New York: Oxford University Press, 1995), 340.

Chapter 5

1 All references to *Troilus and Cressida* are to The Arden Shakespeare, Third Series, rev. edn, ed. David Bevington (London: Bloomsbury, 2015), 'Prologue' 2, 1.1.7–8; hereafter cited parenthetically in the text.

2 Walter Cohen, 'Introduction to Troilus and Cressida', in *The Norton Shakespeare*, ed. Stephen Greenblatt et al. (New York: Norton, 1997), 1823–32, 1827.

3 Matthew Arnold, 'Dover Beach', in Matthew Arnold, *Dover Beach and Other Poems*, ed. Candace Ward (New York: Dover Publications, 1994), 87.

4 T.J.B. Spencer, '"Greeks" and "Merrygreeks": A Background to *Timon of Athens* and *Troilus and Cressida*', in *Essays on Shakespeare and Elizabethan Drama in Honor of Hardin Craig*, ed. Richard Hosley (Columbia, MI: University of Missouri Press, 1962), 223–33, 233.

5   Clifford Leech, 'Shakespeare's Greeks', in *Stratford Papers on Shakespeare*, ed. B.W. Jackson (Toronto: W.J. Gage, 1963), 1–20; John W. Velz, 'The Ancient World in Shakespeare: Authenticity or Anachronism? A Retrospect', *Shakespeare Survey* 31 (1978): 1–12, 6–7.

6   *Twelfth Night*, The Arden Shakespeare, Third Series, ed. Keir Elam (London: Bloomsbury, 2008).

7   Cf. *OED* s.v. 'Greek, n.' I.5. OED Online, Oxford University Press, June 2017. Available at: www.oed.com/view/Entry/81156 (accessed 27 September 2017).

8   Cf. W.R. Elton's proposition that the play was intended for an Inns of Court audience: *Shakespeare's* Troilus and Cressida *and the Inns of Court Revels* (Aldershot: Ashgate, 2000). Importantly, the chief paratext to the play, the publisher's preface of the 1609 Qb, insists on Shakespeare's refined Hellenic wit and thus the play's 'Greek' origins: 'So much and such savoured salt of wit is in his comedies that they seem, for their height of pleasure, to be born in that sea that brought forth Venus' (19–21).

9   Sara Hanna, 'Shakespeare's Greek World: The Temptations of the Sea', in *Playing the Globe: Genre and Geography in English Renaissance Drama*, ed. John Gillies and Virginia Mason Vaughan (Madison, NJ: Fairleigh Dickinson University Press, 1998), 107–28.

10 A.D. Nuttall, 'Action at a Distance: Shakespeare and the Greeks', in *Shakespeare and the Classics*, ed. Charles Martindale and A.B. Taylor (Cambridge: Cambridge University Press, 2004), 209–24, 214.

11 Ibid., 216.

12 Tania Demetriou and Tanya Pollard, 'Homer and Greek Tragedy in Early Modern England's Theatres: An Introduction', *Classical Receptions Journal* 9, no. 1 (2017): 1–35.

13 Jessica Wolfe, *Homer and the Question of Strife from Erasmus to Hobbes* (Toronto: University of Toronto Press, 2015), 304.

14 Alison Findlay and Vassiliki Markidou, 'Introduction', in *Shakespeare and Greece,* ed. Alison Findlay and Vassiliki Markidou (London: Bloomsbury, 2017), 1–44, 33; Efterpi Mitsi, 'Greece "Digested in a Play"': Consuming Greek Heroism in *The*

School of Abuse and *Troilus and Cressida*', in ibid., 93–114, 102.

15 Similarly to, e.g., questions of law and order in the play, cf. György Endre Szőnyi, 'Indecorum and Subversion of Equity in Shakespeare's *Troilus and* Cressida', in *The Concept of Equity: An Interdisciplinary Assessment*, ed. Daniela Carpi (Heidelberg: Winter, 2007), 209–22, 209.

16 Cf. Thersites' address to Achilles, 'Why, thou picture of what thou seemest and idol of idiot-worshippers' (5.1.6–7). Cf. also Linda Charnes's observation that 'Rather than trying to make these figures "new" to his audience, Shakespeare's strategy is to portray their desire, and their inability, to be new *even to themselves*' (emphasis in original). '"So Unsecret to Ourselves": Notorious Identity and the Material Subject in Shakespeare's *Troilus and Cressida*', *Shakespeare Quarterly* 40, no. 4 (1989): 413–40, 418.

17 Arthur Hall's 1581 translation from the French, the *Ten books of Homers Iliades*, might also have been available to Shakespeare.

18 *Iliad*, 2.1–34. All references to the *Iliad* are to Homer, *The Iliad: A New Translation by Peter Green* (Oakland, CA: University of California Press, 2015), henceforth cited parenthetically in the text.

19 *Chapman's Homer: The Iliad*, ed. Allardyce Nicoll (Princeton, NJ: Princeton University Press, 1998). All further references to Chapman's translation are to this volume cited as 'Chapman' parenthetically in the text.

20 Spenser, 'A Letter of the Authors', in *The Poetical Works of Edmund Spenser*, ed. J.C. Smith and E. de Selincourt (Oxford: Oxford University Press, 1932), 407.

21 For a brief overview of the ethical-rhetorical literary 'theory' of the Renaissance, see the 'Introduction' to Brian Vickers's *English Renaissance Literary Criticism* (Oxford: Clarendon, 1999), 1–57.

22 On the play's treatment of historical exemplarity, see also Chapter 4 in this volume.

23 Agamemnon's raw instruction 'What trumpet? Look, Menelaus' (1.3.213) as well as the kissing scene (4.5) might indeed reflect

Chapman's influence on *Troilus and Cressida*. In his translation, Chapman spared no occasion to ridicule Menelaus: the traditional epithet *boen agathos* ('great at the war cry') was rendered as 'sweet-voic't' in the *Seaven Bookes* (2.393), while in later editions the translator opted for the even less flattering 'at-a-martiall-crie good Menelaus' (2.355–6) with elaborate commentary on the character of this notorious cuckold.

24 See 2.1.11n.

25 Cf. also Troilus's protest: 'This is and is not Cressid' (5.2.153).

26 For just one example of many, cf. Achilleus's expostulation to Agamemnon in the first book (*Iliad* 1.152–7).

27 Sara Hanna, 'Shakespeare's Greek World'.

28 See also Clifford Leech, 'Ephesus, Troy, Athens: Shakespeare's Use of Locality', in *Stratford Papers on Shakespeare*, ed. B. W. Jackson (Toronto: W.J. Gage, 1963), 151–69, esp. 161–5.

29 See Jasper Griffin, *Homer on Life and Death* (Oxford: Oxford University Press, 1983), 144–204.

30 Cf., e.g., 1.3.20: Agamemnon blaming the Greeks' failure on Jove; 2.1.52: Thersites calling Ajax 'Mars his idiot'; 2.3.9–13: Thersites' mock-prayer to Jove and Mercury; 4.5.199: Nestor swearing by Mars. Ulysses' reference to the conflict Achilles' deeds stirred among the gods (3.3.191) has distinct *Iliadic* overtones (see Bevington's longer note *ad loc.*), but it is just a conventional exaggeration, especially since Achilles seems completely untouched by it.

31 See David Konstan, *Friendship in the Classical World* (Cambridge: Cambridge University Press, 1997), 24; K.J. Dover, *Greek Homosexuality* (Cambridge, MA: Harvard University Press, 1989), 197.

32 John S. Garrison, *Friendship and Queer Theory in the Renaissance: Gender and Sexuality in Early Modern England* (London: Routledge, 2014), 36–7.

33 Ulysses' mentioning of Ajax's 'wrath' in the speech carries further irony as it offsets Achilles' traditionally unique grief for Patroclus (5.5.35–7).

34 Garrison, *Friendship and Queer Theory*, 38 (emphases in the original).

35 Bevington, ed., *Troilus and Cressida*, 27–9; Cohen, 'Introduction', 1832.

36 Heather James, *Shakespeare's Troy: Drama, Politics, and the Translation of Empire* (Cambridge: Cambridge University Press, 2007), 93.

37 We could also mention Hamlet's famous evocation of the 'malicious sport' Pyrrhus made at the sack of Troy (*Hamlet*, 2.2), a description which is informed by Virgil's anti-Greek attitude.

38 Christopher Marlowe, *Doctor Faustus and Other Plays*, ed. David Bevington and Eric Rasmussen (Oxford: Oxford University Press, 1995). All further references to Marlowe are to this edition and are cited parenthetically in the text.

39 Ibid., 468n.

40 Irving Ribner, 'Marlowe and Shakespeare', *Shakespeare Quarterly* 15, no. 2 (1964): 41–53, 52.

41 Marlowe might well have been inspired by the ancients themselves in such scenes; cf. the famous 'escape ode' of Euripides's *Hippolytus* (732–75).

42 We might add that the first two Sestiads of *Hero and Leander* work similarly in relation to our conceptions of sexual love. It is interesting that Marlowe's contemporaries felt these ironies have to be explained: witness Ralegh's 'The Nymph's Reply' and the several attempts to finish *Hero and Leander*.

43 Cf., e.g., King Lear's reverse 'escape ode' to Cordelia: 'Come, let's away to prison', etc., *King Lear*, The Arden Shakespeare, Third Series, 3rd rev. edn, ed. R.A. Foakes (London: Bloomsbury, 1997), 5.3.8–19.

44 W.H. Auden, 'The Shield of Achilles' (lines 8, 9, 13). In *The Shield of Achilles* (London: Faber and Faber, 1995), 35.

Chapter 6

1 A small part of this chapter draws on the following source: Vassiliki Markidou, 'Shakespeare's Greek Plays', PhD diss., Lancaster University, 1998. Available at ETHOS (British Library

e-theses online service): http://ethos.bl.uk/OrderDetails. do?uin=uk.bl.ethos.533059 (accessed 3 August 2018). All quotations are from William Shakespeare, *Troilus and Cressida*, ed. David Bevington, The Arden Shakespeare, Third Series, rev. edn (London: Bloomsbury, 2015) (5.2.166); hereafter cited parenthetically in the text. I would like to thank The Special Account for Research Grants, National and Kapodistrian University of Athens, for funding the research for this chapter.

2 J.A. Simpson and E.S.C. Weiner (eds), *The Oxford English Dictionary*, 2nd edn, vol. XIII (Oxford: Clarendon Press, 1989), 562–3.

3 Heather James notes that *Troilus and Cressida* 'entertains the spectral appearances of all *auctores* in the tradition – classical, medieval, and contemporary; epic, chronicle, romance, ballad, and satire. . . . As a result of the nationalist and literary battles waged on its ground, however, it is fragmentary and inconsistent – a totality menaced by its various parts.' See Heather James, *Shakespeare's Troy: Drama, Politics, and the Translation of Empire* (Cambridge: Cambridge University Press, 1997), 89.

4 Daniel Juan Gil, 'At the Limits of the Social World: Fear and Pride in *Troilus and Cressida*', *Shakespeare Quarterly* 52, no. 3 (Fall 2001): 336–59, 357, n.33.

5 Robin Headlam Wells, *Shakespeare and Masculinity* (Cambridge: Cambridge University Press, 2000), 12, 13, 17, 18. For *Troilus and Cressida* and the Earl of Essex, see Bevington, 'Introduction', *Troilus and Cressida*, 11–18. On the play's possible references to Essex, see also Chapter 3 ('The State of the Art') and Chapter 4 ('The Decay of Exemplarity in *Troilus and Cressida*').

6 Cressida is compared to Helen by both Troilus (1.1.96; 2.2.81–3) and Pandarus (1.1.71–3); the interchangeability of the two female *dramatis personae* is also reflected in the dialogue conducted between Pandarus and a Servant (3.1.29–33).

7 On militancy and masculinity in *Troilus and Cressida*, see, for example, Susan Harlan, 'Militant Prologues, Memory, and Models of Masculinity in Shakespeare's *Henry V* and *Troilus and Cressida*', in *Violent Masculinities: Male Aggression in Early Modern Texts and Culture*, ed. Jennifer Feather and Catherine E. Thomas (New York: Palgrave Macmillan, 2013), 23–6; and

Katherine Heavey, '"Properer Men": Myth, Manhood and the Trojan War in Greene, Shakespeare and Heywood', *Journal of the Northern Renaissance* 7 (2015): 2–18. Available at: http://www.northernrenaissance.org/properer-men-myth-manhood-and-the-trojan-war-in-greene-shakespeare-and-heywood/ (accessed 22 February 2017).

8   Roberta Kwan focuses as well on religious discourse in *Troilus and Cressida*, yet her argument differs from mine; she unravels the interrelationship between language and the doctrine of divine grace in Shakespeare's puzzling drama. See Roberta Kwan, '"You are in the state of grace?": The Absence of Grace and Semantic Embranglement in Shakespeare's *Troilus and Cressida*', *English Studies* 97, no. 4 (2016): 363–82. My own argument is indebted to Robyn Malo (see note 21) and Jay Zysk, 'Relics and Unreliable Bodies in *The Changeling*', *English Literary Renaissance* 45, no. 3 (2015): 400–24. Zysk astutely argues that Thomas Middleton and William Rowley's play 'shows how relics were re-imagined on the English stage in the wake of the Protestant Reformation' (400), while his article includes a useful delineation of the function of relics in Catholic devotion and their rejection by Protestant reformists.

9   Lucy Razzall, '"A good Booke is the pretious life-blood of a master-spirit": Recollecting Relics in Post-Reformation English Writing', *Journal of the Northern Renaissance* 2 (2010): 1–27, 15. Available at: http://www.northernrenaissance.org/a-good-booke-is-the-pretious-life-blood-of-a-master-spirit-recollecting-relics-in-post-reformation-english-writing/ (accessed 5 October 2017).

10 The Royal Injunctions, 1536, 1538, in *Medieval and Early Modern Devotional Objects in Global Perspective: Translations of the Sacred*, ed. Elizabeth Robertson and Jennifer Jahner (New York: Palgrave MacMillan, 2010), 246–8. Cited in Zysk, 'Relics and Unreliable Bodies in *The Changeling*', 412–13.

11 Zysk, 'Relics and Unreliable Bodies in *The Changeling*', 413.

12 As Robyn Malo points out, the relics' 'political operation . . . depended in part upon the regulation of when and by whom a relic could be accessed'. See Robyn Malo, 'The Pardoner's Relics (And Why They Matter the Most)', *The Chaucer Review* 43, no. 1 (2008): 82–102, 88.

13 William Shakespeare, *Romeo and Juliet*, ed. René Weis, The Arden Shakespeare, Third Series (London: Bloomsbury, 2012) (1.5.93–104). Interestingly, in the same scene, Romeo presents Juliet as 'a rich jewel in an Ethiop's ear – / Beauty too rich for use, for earth too dear' (1.5.46–7). Shakespeare's play thus fuses the profane with the sacred, the mercantile with the religious. For *Troilus and Cressida*'s similar conflation and its significance, see pp. 153–4 in this chapter.

14 Dee Dyas, 'To be a Pilgrim: Tactile Piety, Virtual Pilgrimage and the Experience of Place in Christian Pilgrimage', in *Matter of Faith: An Interdisciplinary Study of Relics and Relic Veneration in the Medieval Period*, ed. James Robinson and Lloyd de Beer with Anna Harnden (London: The British Museum, 2014), 1–7, 1.

15 William Shakespeare, *All's Well That Ends Well*, ed. G.K. Hunter, The Arden Shakespeare, Second Series (London: Bloomsbury, 1967; repr. 2006) (1.1.98–9). The second reference is to this edition as well.

16 Razzall, 'A good Booke is the pretious life-blood of a masterspirit', 26. I cite this sentence out of context as Razzall does not refer to Shakespeare's works.

17 Camille Paglia, *Sexual Personae: Art and Decadence from Nefertiti to Emily Dickinson* (London: Penguin Books, 1990), 527.

18 Bevington, *Troilus and Cressida*, 166, n.72.

19 Bevington, *Troilus and Cressida*, 389, longer note on 2.2.81–3.

20 Malo notes that 'a relic custodian's special job was to care for the remains of the saints: he guarded, regulated and controlled relics, and the access to them'. See Malo, 'The Pardoner's Relics', 84. Bevington argues that '[a]lthough editors [of *Troilus and Cressida*] generally assume that Pandarus unveils his niece, she may do so herself'. See Bevington, *Troilus and Cressida*, 255, nn.45–6. I concur with the majority of editors as regards the specific issue.

21 My argument builds on Malo's insightful reading of Criseyde as relic and shrine, Troilus as supplicant, and Pandarus as a relic custodian in Chaucer's *Troilus and Criseyde*. See Robyn Malo, *Relics and Writing in Late Medieval England* (Toronto: University of Toronto Press, 2013), especially Chapter 4: 'Relic

Discourse in the Pardoner's Prologue and Tale and *Troilus and Criseyde*'. In this light, one may read in Shakespeare's *Troilus and Cressida* a self-conscious parody of the imagery that Chaucer employs in *Troilus and Creseyde*.

22 Bevington, *Troilus and Cressida*, 161, n.99; C.C. Barfoot, '*Troilus and Cressida*: "Praise us as we are tasted"', *Shakespeare Quarterly* 39 (1988): 45–57, 47.

23 For this convention, see, for example, Geoffrey Chaucer, 'The Pardoner's Tale', in *The Canterbury Tales*, The Riverside Chaucer, ed. Larry D. Benson (New York: Houghton Mifflin, 1987); and John Heywood, 'The Pardoner and the Frere', in *The Plays of John Heywood*, ed. Richard Axton and Peter Happe (Cambridge: D.S. Brewer, 1991). On the politics of mobile relics, see Kate Craig, 'The Saint at the Gate: Giving Relics a "Royal Entry" in Eleventh-to-Twelfth-Century France', in *Authority and Spectacle in Medieval and Early Modern Europe: Essays in Honor of Teofilo F. Ruiz*, ed. Yuen-Gen Liang and Jarbel Rodriguez (New York: Routledge, 2017), 121–33. Troilus's reference to 'India' (1.1.96) also draws on early modern England's unprecedented mercantile expansion to remote geographical spaces, reinforcing the element of materialism in the play.

24 Martina Bagnoli, 'Dressing the Relics: Some Thoughts on the Custom of Relic Wrapping in Medieval Christianity', in *Matter of Faith: An Interdisciplinary Study of Relics and Relic Veneration in the Medieval Period*, ed. James Robinson and Lloyd de Beer with Anna Harnden (London: The British Museum, 2014), 100–9, 105, 106.

25 As Julia M.H. Smith points out, in 1958 the clerical scholar Bernard Kötting coined the term 'contact relics', which is commonly used in definitions of relics to refer to objects that 'took their efficacy and spiritual meaning from having touched the saint's body'. He subdivided them into three categories: first, 'objects which had come into contact with a saint during the person's lifetime'; second, 'instruments of martyrdom' among which primary was the Cross, and third, 'substances sanctified by their contact with a saint's tomb but not the body itself, notably oil, water, or cloth'. See Julia M.H. Smith, 'An Evolving Tradition in Latin Christianity', in *Saints and Sacred Matter: The*

Cult of Relics in Byzantium and Beyond, ed. Cynthia Hahn and Holger A. Klein (Washington, DC: Dumbarton Oaks Research Library and Collection, 2015), 41–60, 44. For relic thefts, see Patrick J. Geary, *Furta Sacra: Thefts of Relics in the Central Middle Ages*, rev. edn (Princeton, NJ: Princeton University Press, 2011).

26 For reformist objections to relics, see, for example, Alexandra Walsham, 'Skeletons in the Cupboard: Relics after the English Reformation', *Past and Present*, Literary Supplement 5 (2010): 121–43.

27 According to Janet Adelman, *Troilus and Cressida* dramatizes 'the morning-after fantasy in which the madonna is transformed into the whore'. See Janet Adelman, *Suffocating Mothers: Fantasies of Maternal Origin in Shakespeare's Plays, Hamlet to the Tempest* (New York and London: Routledge, 1992), 64.

28 See Chapter 8 in this volume on the ambiguity of the sleeve in the play, especially in relation to the staging of its exchanges.

29 Efterpi Mitsi, 'Greece "Digested in a Play": Consuming Greek Heroism in *The School of Abuse* and *Troilus and Cressida*', in *Shakespeare and Greece*, ed. Alison Findlay and Vassiliki Markidou (London: Bloomsbury Arden Shakespeare, 2017), 93–114, 104.

30 Bevington, *Troilus and Cressida*, 206, n.15.

31 Bevington, *Troilus and Cressida*, 213, nn.114–16.

32 Calvin's text was first published in French in 1543 and in Latin in 1548; it went through multiple editions in the sixteenth century. An English translation by J. Wythers was published in London in 1561 under the following title: 'A very profitable Treatise, declarynge what great profit might come to all Christendom yf there were a regester made of all the saincts' bodies and other reliques which are as well in Italy as in France, Dutchland, Spaine, and other kingdoms and countreys.' See John Calvin, *A Treatise on Relics*, translated by Valerian Krasinski (Edinburgh: Johnston and Hunter, 1854 [1543]), v.

33 John Jeffries Martin, 'Calvin's Smile', in *History in the Comic Mode: Medieval Communities and the Matter of Person*, ed. Rachel Fulton and Bruce W. Holsinger (New York: Columbia University Press, 2007), 158–70, 158.

34 Ibid.
35 Michael Neill, '"In Everything Illegitimate": Imagining the Bastard in Renaissance Drama', *The Yearbook of English Studies* 23 (1993): 270–92, 271. For Thersites' illegitimate power, see Alison Findlay, *Illegitimate Power: Bastards in Renaissance Drama* (Manchester: Manchester University Press, 1994), 233–5.
36 Along similar lines, in his assault of Patroclus, Thersites claims that '[i]f I could ha' remembered a gilt counterfeit, thou wouldst not have slipped out of my contemplation' (2.3.23–4), thus conflating the image of a fake coin with false humanity.
37 Matthew Greenfield, 'Fragments of Nationalism in *Troilus and Cressida*', in *Shakespeare's Problem Plays: All's Well That Ends Well, Measure for Measure, Troilus and Cressida*, ed. Simon Barker (Basingstoke: Palgrave Macmillan, 2005), 199–222, 199, 205, 208.
38 Northrop Frye, *The Myth of Deliverance: Reflections on Shakespeare's Problem Comedies* (Sussex: Harvester Press, 1983), 62. On the Troynovant myth, see also, for example, James, *Shakespeare's Troy*; Douglas Bruster, *Drama and the Market in the Age of Shakespeare* (Cambridge: Cambridge University Press, 1992); Greenfield, 'Fragments of Nationalism'; and Chapter 4 in this volume.
39 Bruster, *Drama and the Market in the Age of Shakespeare*, 108.
40 Thomas Nashe, *Pierce Penilesse* (1592), in *The Works of Thomas Nashe*, ed. R.B. McKerrow (Oxford: Blackwell, 1966), 5 vols, vol. 1, 181; cited in *London in the Age of Shakespeare: An Anthology*, ed. Lawrence Manley (London and Sydney: Croom Helm, 1986), 277–8.
41 See Valerie Traub, *Desire and Anxiety: Circulations of Sexuality in Shakespearean Drama* (London and New York: Routledge, 1992), 77; René Girard, 'The Politics of Desire in *Troilus and Cressida*', in *Shakespeare and the Question of Theory*, ed. Patricia Parker and Geoffrey Hartman (New York: Methuen, 1985), 188–209; and Linda Charnes, '"So Unsecret to Ourselves": Notorious Identity and the Material Subject in Shakespeare's *Troilus and Cressida*', *Shakespeare Quarterly* 40 (1989): 413–40.
42 Traub, *Desire and Anxiety*, 77.

Chapter 7

1. The author wishes to thank Nikos Hatzopoulos and Raia Mouzenidou, two of the Greek translators of *Troilus and Cressida*, who responded to questions on their process via e-mail interviews, as well as for bibliographical assistance and for access to drafts of their work. Xenia Georgopoulou and Manuela Perteghella also provided some precious remarks and valuable suggestions after reading an early draft of this essay.
2. Dirk Delabastita, 'Shakespeare Translation', in *Routledge Encyclopedia of Translation Studies*, ed. Mona Baker (London and New York: Routledge, 1998; PB repr., 2001), 222–6.
3. See Ton Hoenselaars, ed., *Shakespeare and the Language of Translation*, rev. edn (London: Bloomsbury, 2011), 216–86.
4. Delabastita, 'Shakespeare Translation', 223. There are, of course, notable instances of neoclassical translations of Shakespeare too, such as Jean-François Ducis's *Hamlet* in French (1760). For a detailed discussion, see especially Romy Heylen, *Translation, Poetics and the Stage: Six French Hamlets* (London and New York: Routledge, 1993).
5. See Juan J. Zaro, 'Moratin's Translation of *Hamlet* (1798): A Study of the Paratexts', in *The Practices of Literary Translation: Constraints and Creativity*, ed. Jean Boase-Beier and Michael Holman (Manchester: St Jerome, 1999), 125–33.
6. Jane Adamson, '*Troilus and Cressida*', New Critical Introductions to Shakespeare (Brighton: Harvester, 1987), 25, cited in Bevington, 'Introduction', *Troilus and Cressida*, 84.
7. Adamson, '*Troilus and Cressida*', 30, cited in Bevington, 'Introduction', 84.
8. Elizabeth Freund, '"Ariachne's Broken Woof": The Rhetoric of Citation in *Troilus and Cressida*', in *Shakespeare and the Question of Theory*, ed. Patricia Parker and Geoffrey Hartman (New York and London: Methuen, 1985), 21, emphasis mine.
9. See Chapter 2 on metadrama and theatricality in the play.
10. Heather James, '"Tricks We Play on the Dead": Making History in *Troilus and Cressida*', in *Shakespeare's Troy: Drama, Politics and the Translation of Empire* (Cambridge: Cambridge University Press, 1997), 85–111.

11 Jiří Josek, 'A Czech Shakespeare?', in *The Translator as Writer*, ed. Susan Bassnett and Peter Bush (London and New York: Continuum, 2006), 87.

12 See Ekaterini Douka-Kabitoglou, *I Parousia tou Shakespeare ston Elliniko Horo. Mia Apopeira Vivliografias* [Shakespeare's Presence in Greece. An Attempt at a Bibliography] (Thessaloniki: n. p., 1981), 15.

13 Xenia Georgopoulou, 'Shakespeare and Modern Greek Politics', *Cahiers Élisabéthains* 96, no. 2 (July 2018, special issue: 'Europe's Shakespeare(s)', ed. Nicoleta Cinpoeş and Janice Valls-Russell): 41–58.

14 On the *Classics Illustrated* project and for a detailed survey of Rotas's output addressed to a younger audience, see Thanasis Karayannis, *O Vassilis Rotas ke to Ergo tou yia Paidia ke Efivous. Theatro, Poiisi, Pezografia, Klassika Eikonografimena* [Vassilis Rotas's Works for Children and Young Adults: Theatre, Poetry, Prose, *Classics Illustrated*] (Athens: Synchroni Epochi, 2007).

15 *Katharevousa*, or 'purist' Greek, differed from the more absorptive and organically evolving 'demotic' Greek. In fact, it was an artificial, highly formalized language variety based on the ancient language and eschewing foreign influences, especially Turkisms. It was developed by scholars in the nineteenth century and deployed in formal writing and speech. Its use led to much controversy, especially in the first part of the twentieth century, and even language riots.

16 See, in particular: Myrto Loverdou, 'I Tychi me Odigise ston Shakespeare' [Chance Brought me to Shakespeare], *To Vima*, 12 April 2009. Available online: http://www.tovima.gr/books-ideas/article/?aid=263587 (accessed 16 February 2017); and Mairi Papayiannidou, 'Diarkis Antamoivi: O Metafrastis tou Synolou ton Saikspirikon Theatrikon Ergon Apokalyptei ti Stratigiki tis Kataktisis tous' [Constantly Rewarded: The Translator of Shakespeare's Complete Theatrical Works Reveals the Strategies for Possessing Them], *To Vima*, 25 March 2006. Available online: http://www.tovima.gr/books-ideas/article/?aid=172276 (accessed 3 December 2016).

17 Bellies in Loverdou (my translation).

18 Bellies in Papayiannidou (my translation), where he further notes how earlier Shakespeare translators, like Kostas Karthaios, were similarly reflecting the language of poets from the generation of the 1930s, for instance, George Seferis and Odysseus Elytis. Instead, Rotas chose to align himself with proponents of demoticism, like Ioannis Gryparis.

19 Vassilis Rotas, trans., *Troilos ke Hrysida* (Athens: Epikairotita, 1988), 19.

20 Errikos Bellies, trans., *Troilos ke Hrysiida* (Athens: Kedros, 2001), 11.

21 Rotas, *Troilos ke Hrysida*, 9–14.

22 Rotas, *Troilos ke Hrysida*, 172–5.

23 Susan Bassnett, 'Plays for Today', in *Reflections on Translation* (Bristol: Multilingual Matters), 100–1.

24 Bassnett, 'Plays for Today', 100.

25 George Steiner, *Grammars of Creation: Originating in the Gifford Lectures for 1990* (London: Faber and Faber, 2001), 181.

26 The press release of 5 March 2012 announcing the cancellation (including the National Theater's last minute scheduling of other performances from 7 to 11 March) is available online: http://www.nationaltheater.gr/el/news/archive/?nid=1097 (accessed 2 March 2017).

27 Nikos Hatzopoulos, e-mail message to author, 19 February and 27 March 2017.

28 Hatzopoulos, e-mail, 19 February 2017.

29 Hatzopoulos, e-mail, 19 February 2017.

30 Cf. Dryden's actions here with other similar pronouncements, for instance, in his 'Preface' to Chaucer's *Fables* (1700; included in *Theories of Translation: An Anthology of Essays from Dryden to Derrida*, ed. Rainer Schulte and John Biguenet (Chicago, IL, and London: The University of Chicago Press, 1992), 27):

> Chaucer, I confess, is a rough diamond and must first be polished ere he shines . . . An author is not to write all he can, but all he ought. Having observed this redundancy in Chaucer, (as it is an easy matter for a man of ordinary parts to find a fault in one of greater,) I *have not tied myself to a*

literal translation; but have often omitted what I judged unnecessary, or not of dignity enough to appear in the company of better thoughts. I have presumed farther in some places, and added somewhat of my own where I thought my author was deficient (my emphasis).

For detailed discussion of the changes in Dryden's adaptation, see David Bevington, ed., 'Introduction', in *Troilus and Cressida*, The Arden Shakespeare, rev. edn (London and New York: Bloomsbury, 2015), 94–6. See also Chapter 2.

31 Hatzopoulos, e-mail, 19 February 2017.

32 Hatzopoulos, e-mail, 27 March 2017.

33 Cf. choices made in the Rotas translation (1988): 'αφέντη', 'βασίλισσα', 'αρχηγός' (for instance: *Troilos ke Hrysiida*, 23, 24 and 25) and in the case of Bellies (2001), 'πρίγκηπάς', 'βασίλισσα', 'αρχηγός' (*Troilos ke Hrysiida*, 15, 17 and 17).

34 Nikolaos M. Panagiotakis, trans., *Troilos ke Hrysiida* (Athens: Stigmi), 133.

35 Yorgos Kitsopoulos, 'Troilos ke Hrysiida', *Ellinikos Vorras*, 27 April 1983.

36 Elli Avloniti, 'Troilos kai Hrysiida', theatre programme (Kalamata: Municipal and Regional Theatre of the City of Kalamata, 1991), 48.

37 Perseas Athinaios, 'Troilos ke Hrysiida', *Imerisia*, 14 August 1991.

38 Mouzenidou, e-mail, 25 March 2017 (my translation).

39 For an examination of different contexts, strategies and priorities, see Roger Baines, Christina Marinetti and Manuela Perteghella (eds), *Staging and Performing Translation: Text and Theatre Practice* (Basingstoke: Palgrave Macmillan, 2011).

40 See, for instance, Eva Espasa, 'Performability in Translation: Speakability? Playability? Or just Saleability?' in *Moving Target: Theatre Translation and Cultural Relocation*, ed. Carole-Anne Upton (Manchester: St Jerome Publishing, 2000), 49–62.

41 Mouzenidou, e-mail, 25 March 2017 (my translation).

42 Mouzenidou, e-mail, 25 March 2017 (my translation).

43 A Greek translation was published in 1993; see also his essay 'The Politics of Desire in *Troilus and Cressida*', in Parker

and Hartman, *Shakespeare and the Question of Theory*, 188–209.

44 Mouzenidou, e-mail, 25 March 2017 (my translation).

45 For an account of how her combining scenes enable this, see Xenia Georgopoulou, '*Lege me Ioulieta:* Apo ti Chora tou Shakespeare sto Vasileio tis Raias Mouzenidou' [*Call me Juliet*: From Shakespeare's Realm to Raia Mouzenidou's Kingdom], in *Apo ti Hora ton Keimenon sto Vasileio tis Skinis: Praktika Epistimonikou Synedriou, Athina, 26–30 Ianouariou 2011* [From the Realm of Texts to the Kingdom of the Stage: Conference Proceedings, Athens, 26–30 January 2011], ed. Gogo K. Varzelioti (Athens: National and Kapodistrian University of Athens and Department of Theatre Studies, 2014), esp. 271–2; the paper is a thorough analysis of all of Mouzenidou's adaptations and theatre activity up to that point. For a detailed account in English, see also, 'Shakespeare's Magic Mirror: The Work of Raia Mouzenidou', in *'No Other but a Woman's Reason: Women on Shakespeare. Towards Commemorating the 450th Anniversary of Shakespeare's Birth*, ed. Krystyna Kujawińska-Courtney, Izabella Penier and Katarzyna Kwapisz-Williams (Frankfurt am Main: Peter Lang, 2013), 173–80.

46 Several videos from these performances are available online, at *Theatro Dipylon – Entos ton Technon Blog*: http://dipylon-entostwntexnwn.blogspot.gr/ (accessed 3 December 2016).

47 See Raia Mouzenidou, *Troilos kai Hrysiida – Plano 1* [Troilus and Cressida – First Shot] (Athens: Dipylon/Entos ton Technon, 2011), 102.

48 Raia Mouzenidou, 'Anti Programmatos', theatre programme (Spring 2011), 1 (my translation).

49 For one list of such anachronisms, appropriations and relocations in recent years, see David Bevington, 'Additions and Reconsiderations: Performance and Critical History since 1998', in Bevington, *Troilus and Cressida*, 125–34, and Chapter 2.

50 Mouzenidou, 25 March 2017 (my translation).

51 See among others, Jiří Josek, 'A Czech Shakespeare?', 84, as well as Bassnett, 'Plays for Today', 98–9, for comments on how Shakespeare is modernized less for an English audience that experiences the original texts (or, such attempts may focus more

on visual aspects). Other cultures, through translation, are often closer to innovative approaches that help them more easily see Shakespeare as their contemporary.

52 Willis Barnstone, *The Poetics of Translation: History, Theory, Practice* (New Haven, CT, and London: Yale University Press, 1993), 87.

53 Barnstone, *The Poetics of Translation*, 88.

54 William Shakespeare, *Midsummer Night's Dream*, ed. Sukanta Chaudhuri, The Arden Shakespeare, Third Series (London: Bloomsbury, 2017), 3.1.109.

55 Matthew Reynolds, *The Poetry of Translation: From Chaucer & Petrarch to Homer & Logue* (Oxford: Oxford University Press, 2011), 5.

Chapter 8

1 William Shakespeare, *Troilus and Cressida*, ed. David Bevington, The Arden Shakespeare, rev. edn (London: Bloomsbury, 2015).

2 The two states also offer different titles. They are: Shakespeare, *The famous historie of Troylus and Cresseid* (London: George Eld, 1609); William Shakespeare, *The historie of Troylus and Cresseida As it was acted by the Kings Majesties servants at the Globe* (London: George Eld, 1609). The former contains a lengthy exhortation from 'A never writer, to an ever reader' on Sig. A1r–v and offers an account of the play which stresses its exclusivity and modish innovation as a reader-only text.

3 George Puttenham defines antanaclasis as 'the Rebounde' and states that it 'playeth with one word written all alike but carrying diuers sences'. George Puttenham, *The arte of English poesie* (London: Richard Field, 1589), 179.

4 There are a host of online dictionaries which could feasibly be used to pursue the same type of investigation; for example, the *Merriam-Webster* is free to access and covers word definition, meaning and pronunciation: *Merriam-Webster's Collegiate Dictionary*, 11th edn (Merriam-Webster, 2005).

5   'mastic, n.1a.', OED online (Oxford University Press). Available at: http://www.oed.com/ (accessed 1 September 2017).

6   're-, prefix. 1.'; '-ure, suffix. 1.', OED online (Oxford University Press). Available at: http://www.oed.com/ (accessed 1 September 2017).

7   See also Chapter 6 in this volume on the comparison of Cressida to a pearl.

8   Christopher Marlowe, *Doctor Faustus: A- and B- texts (1604, 1616)*, ed. David Bevington and Eric Rasmussen (Manchester: Manchester University Press, 1993).

9   For a comprehensive account of the scope of Shakespeare's education, and the likely content of the syllabus he would have been taught, see Lynn Enterline, *Shakespeare's Schoolroom: Rhetoric, Discipline, Emotion* (Philadelphia, PA: University of Pennsylvania Press, 2012), 9–32. There are a number of early modern rhetorical manuals which can be accessed on *EEBO*. Some of the most prominent include: Richard Sherry, *A treatise of schemes [and] tropes* (London: John Day, 1550); Henry Peacham, *The garden of eloquence* (London: H. Jackson, 1577); George Puttenham, *The arte of English poesie* (London: Richard Field, 1589); and Angel Day, *The English secretary* (London: P. Short, 1599).

10 Henry Peacham, *The garden of eloquence* (London: H. Jackson, 1577), sig. I3r.

11 There was a vogue for armed prologues and epilogues on stage in the late 1590s; both Ben Jonson's *Poetaster* (*c.* 1601) and John Marston's *Antonio and Mellida* (*c.* 1599) exploit the device to signal a generic emphasis on combat and military threat (satirically in the case of Jonson).

12 See Chapter 6 for an interpretation of the sleeve as a memento and mock-contact relic.

13 For a comprehensive analysis of the complexities surrounding the text of the play, see *Troilus and Cressida*, ed. Bevington, 233–464; William Shakespeare, *Troilus and Cressida*, ed. Anthony B. Dawson (Cambridge: Cambridge University Press, 2003), 234–52. See also Chapter 1 in this volume. Students interested in the textual history of the play may find the following

article of use: William Godschalk, 'The Texts of *Troilus and Cressida*', *Early Modern Literary Studies* 1 (1995): 1–54.

14 Dominic Cavendish, *Time Out*, 11 November 1996, reprinted in *Theatre Record*, issue 25–6 (2–31 December 1996), 1575–7; Benedict Nightingale, *The Times*, 27 July 1996, reprinted in *Theatre Record* 15 (15–28 July 1996): 968.

15 Charles Spencer, *Daily Telegraph*, 9 November 1998, reprinted in *Theatre Record* 23 (5–18 November 1998): 1496; John Peter, *The Sunday Times*, 15 November 1998, reprinted in *Theatre Record* 23 (5–18 November 1998): 1495.

16 Jonathan Gibbs, *What's On*, 24 March 1999, reprinted in *Theatre Record* 6 (12–25 March 1999): 335.

SELECT BIBLIOGRAPHY

Adelman, Janet. *Suffocating Mothers: Fantasies of Maternal Origin in Shakespeare's Plays, 'Hamlet' to 'The Tempest'*. London and New York: Routledge, 1992.

Alexander, Peter. '*Troilus and Cressida*, 1609'. *The Library* 4th ser., 9 (1928–9): 267–86.

Apfelbaum, Roger. *Shakespeare's Troilus and Cressida: Textual Problems and Performance Solutions*. Newark: University of Delaware Press, 2004.

Armstrong, Philip. *Shakespeare's Visual Regime: Tragedy, Psychoanalysis and the Gaze*. Basingstoke and New York: Palgrave, 2000.

Asp, Carolyn. 'In Defense of Cressida'. *Studies in Philology* 74, no. 4 (1977): 406–17.

Barfoot, C.C. '*Troilus and Cressida*: "Praise us as we are tasted"'. *Shakespeare Quarterly* 39, no. 1 (1988): 45–57.

Barton, Anne (Anne Righter). *Shakespeare and the Idea of the Play*. New York: Barnes & Noble, 1962.

Barton, Anne. 'Introduction to *Troilus and Cressida*'. In *The Riverside Shakespeare*, edited by G. Blakemore Evans and J.J.M. Tobin, 477–81, 2nd edn. Boston, MA, and New York: Mifflin, 1997.

Bate, Jonathan, and Eric Rasmussen, eds. *Troilus and Cressida*. New York: The Modern Library, 2010.

Bayley, John. 'Time and the Trojans'. *Essays in Criticism* XXV, no. 1 (1975): 55–73.

Bednarz, James P. *Shakespeare & the Poets' War*. New York and Chichester: Columbia University Press, 2001.

Bell, Robert H. *Shakespeare's Great Stage of Fools*. New York: Palgrave Macmillan, 2011.

Bevington, David. Introduction to *Troilus and Cressida* by William Shakespeare, The Arden Shakespeare, Third Series, rev. edn., 1–123, edited by David Bevington. London and New York: Bloomsbury, 2015.

Boas, Frederick S. *Shakspere and his Predecessors*. London: John Murray, 1910.

Boecker, Bettina. *Imagining Shakespeare's Original Audience, 1660–2000: Groundlings, Gallants, Grocers*. Basingstoke: Palgrave, 2015.

Bowen, Barbara E. *Gender in the Theater of War: Shakespeare's 'Troilus and Cressida'*. New York and London: Garland, 1993.

Bradbrook, M.C. 'What Shakespeare Did to Chaucer's *Troilus and Criseyde*'. *Shakespeare Quarterly* 9, no. 3 (1958): 311–19.

Bradley, A.C. *Shakespearean Tragedy. Lectures on Hamlet, Othello, King Lear, Macbeth*. London: Macmillan, 1963.

Brandes, George [sic]. *William Shakespeare*. London: William Heinemann, 1898.

Bruster, Douglas. *Drama and the Market in the Age of Shakespeare*. Cambridge and New York: Cambridge University Press, 1992.

Bushnell, Rebecca. 'Shakespeare and Nature'. In *Shakespeare in Our Time: A Shakespeare Association of America Collection*, edited by Dympna Callaghan and Suzanne Gossett, 327–34. London and New York: Bloomsbury Arden Shakespeare, 2016.

Byville, Eric. 'Aesthetic Uncommon Sense: Early Modern Taste and the Satirical Sublime'. *Criticism* 54, no. 4 (2012): 583–621.

Campbell, Oscar James. *Comicall Satyre and Shakespeare's 'Troilus and Cressida'*. San Marino, CA: C.F. Braun & Co, 1959.

Cartelli, Thomas. 'The Killing Stops Here: Unmaking the Myths of Troy in Wooster Group/RSC *Troilus and Cressida*'. *Shakespeare Quarterly* 64, no. 2 (2013): 233–43.

Chapman, George. *Seaven Bookes of the Iliades of Homere, Prince of Poets*. London: John Windet, 1598.

Chapman, George. *Chapman's Homer: The* Iliad, edited by Allardyce Nicoll. Princeton, NJ: Princeton University Press, 1998.

Charnes, Linda. '"So Unsecret to Ourselves": Notorious Identity and the Material Subject in Shakespeare's *Troilus and Cressida*'. *Shakespeare Quarterly* 40, no. 4 (1989): 413–40.

Charnes, Linda. 'The Two Party System in *Troilus and Cressida*'. In *A Companion to Shakespeare's Works, Volume IV: The Poems, Problem Comedies, Late Plays*, edited by Richard Dutton and Jean E. Howard, 302–15. Oxford and Malden, MA: Blackwell, 2003.

Cheney, Patrick. *Shakespeare's Literary Authorship*. Cambridge and New York: Cambridge University Press, 2008.
Coghill, Nevill. *Shakespeare's Professional Skills*. Cambridge: Cambridge University Press, 1964.
Cohen, Walter. 'Introduction to Troilus and Cressida'. In *The Norton Shakespeare*, edited by Stephen Greenblatt et al., 1823–32. New York: Norton, 1997.
Coleridge, Samuel Taylor. *The Complete Works of Samuel Taylor Coleridge. With an Introductory Essay upon His Philosophical and Theological Opinions*. In *Lectures upon Shakespeare and Other Dramatists*, vol. IV, edited by Professor Shedd. New York: Harper, 1858.
Dawson, Anthony B. 'Book Review: *Shakespeare's "Troilus and Cressida" and the Inns of Court Revels*'. *Modern Language Review* 97, no. 2 (2002): 390–1.
Dawson, Anthony B. Introduction. In *Troilus and Cressida*, New Cambridge Shakespeare, edited by Anthony B. Dawson. Cambridge: Cambridge University Press, 2003.
Demetriou, Tania, and Tanya Pollard. 'Homer and Greek Tragedy in Early Modern England's Theatres: An Introduction'. *Classical Receptions Journal* 9, no. 1 (2017): 1–35.
Dollimore, Jonathan. *Radical Tragedy: Religion, Ideology and Power in the Drama of Shakespeare and his Contemporaries*, 2nd edn. London and New York: Harvester, 1989.
Dowden, Edward. *Shakespeare: A Critical Study of His Mind and Art*. Cambridge: Cambridge University Press, 2009.
Dryden, John. *The Works of John Dryden*, edited by Maximillian E. Novak et al., vol. XIII. Berkeley, CA, and London: University of California Press, 1984.
Ellis-Fermor, Una. *The Frontiers of Drama*. London: Methuen, 1946.
Elton, W.R. *Shakespeare's 'Troilus and Cressida' and the Inns of Court Revels*. Aldershot and Brookfield, VT: Ashgate, 2000.
Engle, Lars. *Shakespearean Pragmatism: Market of His Time*. Chicago, IL, and London: University of Chicago Press, 1993.
Escolme, Bridget. *Talking to the Audience: Shakespeare, Performance, Self*. London and New York: Routledge, 2005.
Farnham, Willard. 'Troilus in Shapes of Infinite Desire'. *Shakespeare Quarterly* 15, no. 2 (1964): 257–64.
Findlay, Alison. *Illegitimate Power: Bastards in Renaissance Drama*. Manchester: Manchester University Press, 1994.

Findlay, Alison, and Vassiliki Markidou. 'Introduction'. In *Shakespeare and Greece*, edited by Alison Findlay and Vassiliki Markidou, 1–14. London: Bloomsbury, 2017.

Foakes, R.A. '*Troilus and Cressida* Reconsidered'. *University of Toronto Quarterly* XXXII (January 1963): 142–54.

Fowler, Benjamin. 'Culture Clash: What the Wooster Group Revealed about the RSC (and British Theater Hegemony) in *Troilus and Cressida*'. *Shakespeare Bulletin* 32, no. 2 (2014): 207–33.

Freund, Elizabeth. '"Ariachne's Broken Woof": The Rhetoric of Citation in *Troilus and Cressida*'. In *Shakespeare and the Question of Theory*, edited by Patricia Parker and Geoffrey Hartman, 19–36. London: Methuen, 1985.

Frye, Northrop. *Fools of Time: Studies in Shakespearean Tragedy*. Toronto: University of Toronto Press, 1967.

Frye, Northrop. *The Myth of Deliverance: Reflections on Shakespeare's Problem Comedies*. Sussex: Harvester Press, 1983.

Frye, Northrop. *The Myth of Deliverance: Reflections on Shakespeare's Problem Comedies*. Sussex: Harvester Press, 1983.

Garrison, James S. *Friendship and Queer Theory in the Renaissance: Gender and Sexuality in Early Modern England*. London: Routledge, 2014.

Georgopoulou, Xenia. 'Shakespeare's Magic Mirror: The Work of Raia Mouzenidou'. In *'No Other but a Woman's Reason': Women on Shakespeare. Towards Commemorating the 450th Anniversary of Shakespeare's Birth*, edited by Krystyna Kujawińska-Courtney, Izabella Pennier and Katarzyna Kwapisz-Williams, 173–80. Frankfurt am Main: Peter Lang, 2013.

Gieskes, Edward. '"Honest and Vulgar Praise": The Poets' War and the Literary Field'. *Medieval and Renaissance Drama in England* 18 (2005): 75–103.

Gervinus, G.G. *Shakespeare Commentaries*, translated by F.E. Bunnett. London: Smith, Elder &. Co: 1875.

Gil, Daniel Juan. 'At the Limits of the Social World: Fear and Pride in *Troilus and Cressida*'. *Shakespeare Quarterly* 52, no. 3 (2001): 336–59.

Girard, René. 'The Politics of Desire in *Troilus and Cressida*'. In *Shakespeare and the Question of Theory*, edited by Patricia Parker and Geoffrey Hartman, 188–209. New York and London: Methuen, 1985.

Girard, René. *A Theatre of Envy: William Shakespeare*. Oxford: Oxford University Press, 1991.
Godschalk, William. 'The Texts of *Troilus and Cressida*'. *Early Modern Literary Studies* 1 (1995): 1–54.
Goethe, Johann Wolfgang von. *Goethe's Literary Essays*, edited by J.E. Springarn. London: Humphrey Milford, Oxford University Press, 1921.
Grady, Hugh. *Shakespeare's Universal Wolf: Studies in Early Modern Reification*. Oxford and New York: Oxford University Press, 1996.
Grady, Hugh, and Terence Hawkes. 'Introduction: Presenting Presentism'. In *Presentist Shakespeares*, edited by Hugh Grady and Terence Hawkes, 1–5. London and New York: Routledge, 2007.
Greene, Gayle. 'Language and Value in Shakespeare's *Troilus and Cressida*'. *Studies in English Literature 1500–1900* 21, no. 2 (1981): 271–85.
Greene, Gayle. 'Shakespeare's Cressida: "A kind of self"'. In *The Woman's Part: Feminist Criticism of Shakespeare*, edited by Carolyn Ruth Swift Lenz, Gayle Greene and Carol Thomas Neely, 133–49. Urbana, IL, and London: University of Illinois Press, 1983.
Greenfield, Matthew. 'Fragments of Nationalism in *Troilus and Cressida*'. In *Shakespeare's Problem Plays: All's Well That Ends Well, Measure for Measure, Troilus and Cressida*, edited by Simon Barker, 199–222. Basingstoke: Palgrave Macmillan, 2005.
Gregory, Johann, and Alice Leonard. 'Assuming Gender in *Hamlet* and *Troilus and Cressida*: "Are we to assume that there were women in the audience?"'. *Assuming Gender* 1, no. 2 (2010): 44–61.
Gregory, Johann. 'The "author's drift" in Shakespeare's *Troilus and Cressida*: A Poetics of Reflection'. *Medieval and Early Modern Authorship: SPELL: Swiss Papers in English Language and Literature 25*, edited by Guillemette Bolens and Lukas Erne, 93–106. Tübingen: Gunter Narr Verlag, 2011.
Gregory, Johann. 'Shakespeare's "Sugred Sonnets", *Troilus and Cressida* and the *Odcombian Banquet*: An Exploration of Promising Paratexts, Expectations and Matters of Taste'. *Shakespeare* 6, no. 2 (2010): 185–208.

Gregory, Johann. 'Shakespeare's *Troilus and Cressida*: Visualising Expectations as a Matter of Taste'. In *Shakespeare et les arts de la table: Actes du Congrès organisé par la Société Française Shakespeare*, edited by Pierre Kapitaniak, Christophe Hausermann and Dominique Goy-Blanquet, 47–66. Paris: Société Française Shakespeare, 2012. Available at http://www.societefrancaiseshakespeare.org/document.php?id=1705 (accessed 1 March 2017).

Griffin, Andrew. 'The Banality of History in *Troilus and Cressida*'. *Early Modern Literary Studies* 12, no. 2 (2007): n.p. Available at http://purl.oclc.org/emls/12–2/grifbana.htm (accessed 10 March 2017).

Hampton, Timothy. *Writing from History: The Rhetoric of Exemplarity in Renaissance Literature*. Ithaca, NY: Cornell University Press, 1990.

Hanna, Sara. 'Shakespeare's Greek World: The Temptations of the Sea'. In *Playing the Globe: Genre and Geography in English Renaissance Drama*, edited by John Gillies and Virginia MasonVaughan, 107–28. Madison, NJ: Fairleigh Dickinson University Press, 1998,

Harlan, Susan. 'Militant Prologues, Memory, and Models of Masculinity in Shakespeare's *Henry V* and *Troilus and Cressida*'. In *Violent Masculinities: Male Aggression in Early Modern Texts and Culture*, edited by Jennifer Feather and Catherine E. Thomas, 23–6. New York: Palgrave Macmillan, 2013.

Harmon, A.G. *Eternal Bonds, True Contracts: Law and Nature in Shakespeare's Problem Plays*. Albany, NY: State University of New York Press, 2004.

Harris, Jonathan Gil. *Sick Economies: Drama, Mercantilism, and Disease in Shakespeare's England*. Philadelphia, PA: University of Pennsylvania Press, 2004.

Hazlitt, William. *Characters of Shakespeare's Plays*. London: R. Hunter and C. and J. Ollier, 1817.

Heavey, Katherine. '"Properer Men": Myth, Manhood and the Trojan War in Greene, Shakespeare and Heywood'. *Journal of the Northern Renaissance* 7 (2015): 2–18. Available at http://www.northernrenaissance.org/properer-men-myth-manhood-and-the-trojan-war-in-greene-shakespeare-and-heywood/ (accessed 22 February 2017).

Heine, Heinrich. *Heine on Shakespeare. A Translation of His Notes on Shakespeare Heroines*, translated by Ida Benecke. Westminster: Archibald Constable and Co., 1895.
Hiken, Arlin J. 'Texture in *Troilus and Cressida*'. *Educational Theatre Journal* 19, no. 3 (1967): 367–9.
Hillman, David. 'The Gastric Epic: *Troilus and Cressida*'. *Shakespeare Quarterly* 48, no. 3 (1997): 295–313.
Hillman, David. 'The Worst Case of Knowing the Other? Stanley Cavell and *Troilus and Cressida*'. *Philosophy and Literature* 32, no. 1 (2008): 1–13.
Hiscock, Andrew. '"Will You Walk in, My Lord?" Shakespeare's *Troilus and Cressida* and the Anxiety of Oikos'. In *Shakespeare and Hospitality: Ethics Politics, and Exchange*, edited by David B. Goldstein and Julia Reinhard Lupton, 17–38. Abingdon: Routledge, 2016.
Hodgdon, Barbara. 'He Do Cressida in Different Voices'. *English Literary Renaissance* 20, no. 2 (1990): 254–86.
Hoenselaars, Ton, ed. *Shakespeare and the Language of Translation*, rev. edn. London: Bloomsbury, 2011.
Honigmann, E.A.J. *Myriad-minded Shakespeare: Essays, Chiefly on the Tragedies and Problem Comedies*. Basingstoke: Macmillan, 1989.
Jackson, Ken. 'Review: *Shakespeare and the Poets' War*'. *The Sixteenth Century Journal* 33, no. 2 (2002): 501–3.
James, Heather. *Shakespeare's Troy: Drama, Politics, and the Translation of Empire*. Cambridge and New York: Cambridge University Press, 1997.
Jamieson, Michael. 'The Problem Plays, 1920–1970: A Retrospect'. *Shakespeare Survey* 25 (1972): 1–10.
Johnston, Andrew James, Russell West-Pavlov and Elisabeth Kempf, eds. *Love, History and Emotion in Chaucer and Shakespeare: 'Troilus and Criseyde' and 'Troilus and Cressida'*. Manchester: Manchester University Press, 2016.
Kaula, David. 'Will and Reason in *Troilus and Cressida*'. *Shakespeare Quarterly* 12, no. 3 (1961): 271–83.
Kaufman, R.J. 'Ceremonies for Chaos: The Status of *Troilus and Cressida*'. *English Literary Renaissance* 32, no. 2 (1965): 139–59.
Kennedy, Dennis. *Foreign Shakespeare: Contemporary Performance*. Cambridge: Cambridge University Press, 1993.

Kennedy, Dennis. *Looking at Shakespeare: A Visual History of Twentieth-century Performance*. Cambridge: Cambridge University Press, 2001.

Kerrigan, John. 'Shakespeare, Oaths and Vows'. *Proceedings of the British Academy: 2009 Lectures* 167 (2011): 61–89.

Kerrigan, John. *Shakespeare's Binding Language*. Oxford: Oxford University Press, 2016.

Knight, G. Wilson. *The Wheel of Fire: Interpretations of Shakespearean Tragedy*. London and New York: Routledge, 2001.

Kott, Jan. *Shakespeare Our Contemporary*, translated by Boleslaw Taborski, 1964. New York and London: Norton, 1974.

Kwan, Roberta. '"You Are in the State of Grace?": The Absence of Grace and Semantic Embranglement in Shakespeare's *Troilus and Cressida*'. *English Studies* 97, no. 4 (2016): 362–82.

Lamb, Charles. 'Those Big Boobies'. In *Shakespeare 'Troilus and Cressida': A Casebook*, edited by Priscilla Martin, 43. London and Basingstoke: Macmillan, 1976.

LeCompte, Elizabeth, Kate Valk and Maria Shevtsova. 'A Conversation on the Wooster Group's *Troilus and Cressida* with the RSC', *New Theatre Quarterly* 29, no. 3 (Aug. 2013): 233–66.

Leech, Clifford. 'Shakespeare's Greeks'. In *Stratford Papers on Shakespeare*, edited by B.W. Jackson, 1–20. Toronto: W.J. Gage, 1963.

Leech, Clifford. 'Ephesus, Troy, Athens: Shakespeare's Use of Locality'. In *Stratford Papers on Shakespeare*, edited by B.W. Jackson, 151–69. Toronto: W.J. Gage, 1963.

Lees-Jeffries, Hester. 'A Subtle Point: Sleeves, Tents and "Ariachne's Broken Woof" (Again)'. *Shakespeare Survey* 62 (2009): 92–103.

Leggatt, Alexander. *Shakespeare's Tragedies: Violation and Identity*. Cambridge and New York: Cambridge University Press, 2005.

Lenz, Joseph. 'Base Trade: Theater as Prostitution'. *English Literary History* 60, no. 4 (1993): 833–55.

Lessenich, Rolf P. 'Shakespeare's *Troilus and Cressida*: The Vision of Decadence'. *Studia Neophilological* 49, no. 2 (1977): 221–32.

McAlindon, T. 'Language, Style, and Meaning in *Troilus and Cressida*'. *PMLA* 84, no. 1 (1969): 29–43.

Maguire, Laurie E. 'Performing Anger: The Anatomy of Abuse(s) in *Troilus and Cressida*'. *Renaissance Drama* n.s., 31 (2002): 153–83.

Mallin, Eric S. *Inscribing the Time: Shakespeare and the End of Elizabethan England*. Berkeley, CA, and London: University of California Press, 1995.
Maquerlot, Jean-Pierre. *Shakespeare and the Mannerist Tradition: Five Problem Plays*. Cambridge and New York: Cambridge University Press, 1995.
Marsh, Nicholas. *Shakespeare: Three Problem Plays*. Basingstoke: Palgrave Macmillan, 2003.
Martin, Priscilla, ed. *Shakespeare 'Troilus and Cressida': A Casebook*. London and Basingstoke: Macmillan, 1976.
Mentz, Steve. 'Shakespeare without Nature'. In *Shakespeare in Our Time: A Shakespeare Association of America Collection*, The Arden Shakespeare, edited by Dympna Callaghan and Suzanne Gossett, 334–8. London and New York: Bloomsbury, 2016.
Minton, Gretchen E. '"Discharging less than the Tenth Part of One": Performance Anxiety and/in *Troilus and Cressida*'. In *Shakespeare and the Cultures of Performance*, edited by Paul Yachnin and Patricia Badir, 101–19. Aldershot and Burlington, VT: Ashgate, 2008.
Mitsi, Efterpi. 'Greece "Digested in a Play": Consuming Greek Heroism in *The School of Abuse* and *Troilus and Cressida*'. In *Shakespeare and Greece*, edited by Alison Findlay and Vassiliki Markidou, 93–114. London: Bloomsbury Arden Shakespeare, 2017.
Muir, Kenneth. '*Troilus and Cressida*'. *Shakespeare Survey* 8, The Comedies (1955): 28–39.
Navitsky, Joseph. 'Scurrilous Jests and Retaliatory Abuse in Shakespeare's *Troilus and Cressida*'. *English Literary Renaissance* 42, no. 1 (2012): 2–31.
Neill, Michael. '"In Everything Illegitimate": Imagining the Bastard in Renaissance Drama'. *The Yearbook of English Studies* 23 (1993): 270–92.
Newlin, Jeanne T. 'The Darkened Stage. J.P. Kemble and *Troilus and Cressida*'. In *The Triple Bond: Plays, mainly Shakespearean in Performance*, edited by J.G. Price, 190–202. University Park and London: Pennysylvania University Press, 1975.
Nuttall, A.D. 'Action at a Distance: Shakespeare and the Greeks'. In *Shakespeare and the Classics*, edited by Charles Martindale and A.B. Taylor, 209–24. Cambridge: Cambridge University Press, 2004.

Nuttall, A.D. *Shakespeare the Thinker*. New Haven, CT, and London: Yale University Press, 2007.

Oates, Joyce Carol (J. Oates Smith). 'Essence and Existence in Shakespeare's *Troilus and Cressida*'. *Philological Quarterly* 46 (1967): 167–85.

Orgel, Stephen. 'Afterword'. In *Shakespeare, Memory and Performance*, edited by Peter Holland, 346–9. Cambridge: Cambridge University Press, 2006.

Palfrey, Simon. *Doing Shakespeare*. London: Thomson Learning, 2005.

Parker, Patricia. *Shakespeare from the Margins: Language, Culture, Context*. Chicago, IL, and London: Chicago University Press, 1996.

Pincombe, Mike. *Elizabethan Humanism: Literature and Learning in the later Sixteenth Century*. Harlow: Longman, 2001.

Powell, Neil. 'Hero and Human: The Problem of Achilles'. *Critical Quarterly* 21, no. 2 (1979): 17–28.

Purcell, Stephen. '*Troilus and Cressida*'. In *A Year of Shakespeare*, edited by Paul Prescott and Erin Sullivan, 210–12. London: Bloomsbury, 2013.

Poole, Adrian. 'Relic, Pageant, Sunken Wreck: Shakespeare in 1816'. In *Commemorating Shakespeare: Commemoration and Cultural Memory*, edited by Clara Calvo and Coppélia Kahn, 57–77. Cambridge: Cambridge University Press, 2015.

Prescott, Paul. 'Review of *Troilus and Cressida* (directed by Peter Stein) at the Royal Shakespeare Theatre September 2006'. *Shakespeare* 3, no. 2 (2007): 234–8.

Raber, Karen. 'The Chicken and the Egg'. In *Shakespeare in Our Time: A Shakespeare Association of America Collection*, The Arden Shakespeare, edited by Dympna Callaghan and Suzanne Gossett, 338–41. London and New York: Bloomsbury, 2016.

Rabkin, Norman. '*Troilus and Cressida*: The Uses of the Double Plot'. *Shakespeare Studies* 1 (1965): 264–82.

Razzall, Lucy. '"A good Booke is the pretious life-blood of a master-spirit": Recollecting Relics in Post-Reformation English Writing'. *Journal of the Northern Renaissance* 2 (2010): 1–27. Available at: http://www.northernrenaissance.org/a-good-booke-is-the-pretious-life-blood-of-a-master-spirit-recollecting-relics-in-post-reformation-english-writing/ (accessed 5 October 2017).

Reilly, Kara. '*Troilus and Cressida* (Wooster/RSC)'. *Theatre Journal* 65, no. 2 (2013): 277–9.
Ribner, Irving. 'Marlowe and Shakespeare'. *Shakespeare Quarterly* 15, no. 2 (1964): 41–53.
Riehle, Wolfgang. 'Shakespeare in Switzerland'. *Shakespeare Quarterly* 31, no. 3 (1980): 423–4.
Rizi, Pervez. 'The Bibliographical Relationship between the Texts of *Troilus and Cressida*'. *Library* 14, no. 3 (2013): 271–312.
Robertson, Elizabeth, and Jennifer Jahner, eds. *Medieval and Early Modern Devotional Objects in Global Perspective: Translations of the Sacred*. New York: Palgrave MacMillan, 2010.
Ross, Emily. '"Words, Vows, Gifts, Tears and Love's Full Sacrifice": An Assessment of the Status of Troilus and Cressida's Relationship According to Customary Elizabethan Marriage Procedure'. *Shakespeare* 4, no. 4 (2008): 413–37.
Rossiter, A.P. *Angels with Horns; Fifteen Lectures on Shakespeare*, edited by Graham Storey. London and New York: Longman, 1989.
Rowe, Nicholas. 'Some Account of the Life, etc. of Mr. William Shakespear'. In *The Works of Mr. William Shakespear*, edited by Nicholas Rowe, vol. I, i–xl. London: Jacob Tonson, 1709.
Ryan, Kiernan. '*Troilus and Cressida*: The Perils of Presentism'. In *Presentist Shakespeares*, edited by Hugh Grady and Terence Hawkes, 164–83. London and New York: Routledge, 2007.
Rutter, Carol Chillington. *Enter The Body: Women and Representation on Shakespeare's Stage*. London and New York: Routledge, 2001.
Sawyer, Robert. *Victorian Appropriations of Shakespeare: George Eliot, A.C. Swinburne, Robert Browning, and Charles Dickens*. Madison and Teaneck: Fairleigh Dickinson University Press; and London: Associated University Presses, 2003.
Schlegel, Augustus William. *A Course of Lectures on Dramatic Art and Literature*, translated by John Black. London: Baldwin, Cradock & Joy; Edinburgh: William Blackwood; and Dublin: John Cumming, 1815.
Schmidt, Gary A. *Renaissance Hybrids: Culture and Genre in Early Modern England*. London and New York: Routledge, 2016.
Shakespeare, William. *Troilus and Cressida*, The Arden Shakespeare, Third Series, rev. edn, edited by David Bevington. London and New York: Bloomsbury, 2015.

Schulman, Alex. *Rethinking Shakespeare's Political Philosophy*. Edinburgh: Edinburgh University Press, 2014.
Shepard, Alan, and Stephen D. Powell, eds. *Fantasies of Troy: Classical Tales and the Social Imaginary in Medieval and Early Modern Europe*. Toronto: Centre for Reformation and Renaissance Studies, 2004.
Silverstone, Catherine. 'Festival Showcasing and Cultural Regeneration: Aotearoa New Zealand, Shakespeare's Globe and Ngakau's *A Toroihi raua ko Kahira* (*Troilus and Cressida*) in te reo Maori'. In *Shakespeare Beyond English: A Global Experiment*, edited by Susan Bennett and Christie Carson, 35–47. Cambridge: Cambridge University Press, 2013.
Sinfield, Alan. 'The Leather Men and the Lovely Boy: Reading Positions in *Troilus and Cressida*'. In *Shakesqueer: A Queer Companion to the Complete Works of Shakespeare*, edited by Madhavi Menon, 376–84. Durham, NC, and London: Duke University Press, 2011.
Smith, Emma. *Shakespeare's First Folio: Four Centuries of an Iconic Book*. Oxford: Oxford University Press, 2016.
Southall, Raymond. '*Troilus and Cressida* and the Spirit of Capitalism'. In *Shakespeare in a Changing World*, edited by Arnold Kettle, 217–32. London: Lawrence & Wishart, 1964.
Spear, Gary. 'Shakespeare's "Manly" Parts: Masculinity and Effeminacy in *Troilus and Cressida*'. *Shakespeare Quarterly* 44, no. 4 (1993): 409–22.
Spurgeon, Caroline. *Shakespeare's Imagery and What it Tells Us*. Cambridge: Cambridge University Press, 1935.
Stein, Arnold. '*Troilus and Cressida*: The Disjunctive Imagination'. *English Literary History* 36, no. 1 (1969): 145–67.
Swinburne, Algernon Charles. *A Study of Shakespeare*. London: Chatto & Windus, 1880.
Symons, Arthur. '*Troilus and Cressida*'. *Harper's Monthly Magazine* CXV (October 1907): 659–64.
Szőnyi, György Endre. 'Indecorum and Subversion of Equity in Shakespeare's *Troilus and Cressida*'. In *The Concept of Equity: An Interdisciplinary Assessment*, edited by Daniela Carpi, 209–22. Heidelberg: Winter, 2007.
Theobald, Lewis. Preface to *The Works of Shakespeare: in Seven Volumes*, i–lxviii, edited by Lewis Theobald. London: A. Bettesworth et al., 1733.

Tillyard, E.M.W. *Shakespeare's Problem Plays*. London: Chatto & Windus, 1951.
Toole, William B. *Shakespeare's Problem Plays. Studies in Form and Meaning*. London, The Hague, and Paris: Mouton, 1966.
Traub, Valerie. *Desire and Anxiety: Circulations of Sexuality in Shakespearean Drama*. London and New York: Routledge, 1992.
Tylee, Claire M. 'The Text of Cressida and Every Ticklish Reader: *Troilus and Cressida*, The Greek Camp Scene'. *Shakespeare Survey* 41 (1989): 63–76.
Van Doren, Mark. *Shakespeare*. New York: Holt & Co., 1939.
Vaughan, Virginia Mason. 'Daughters of the Game: *Troilus and Cressida* and the Sexual Discourse of 16th-Century England'. *Women's Studies International Forum* 13, no. 3 (1990): 209–20.
Velz, John W. 'The Ancient World in Shakespeare: Authenticity or Anachronism? A Retrospect'. *Shakespeare Survey* 31(1978): 1–12.
Walker, Alice. 'Introduction'. In *Troilus and Cressida*, edited by Alice Walker and John Dover Wilson, ix–xlvi. Cambridge: Cambridge University Press, 1957.
Wells, Robin Headlam. *Shakespeare on Masculinity*. Cambridge and New York: Cambridge University Press, 2000.
White, R.S. 'Troilus and Cressida as Brechtian Theatre'. In *Shakespearean Continuities: Essays in Honour of E.A.J. Honigmann*, edited by John Batchelor, Tom Cain and Claire Lamont, 221–37. Basingstoke: Palgrave Macmillan, 1997.
Wilson-Lee, Edward. 'Shakespeare by Numbers: Mathematical Crisis in *Troilus and Cressida*'. *Shakespeare Quarterly* 64, no. 4 (2013): 449–72.
Yachnin, Paul. '"The Perfection of Ten": Populuxe Art and Artisanal Value in *Troilus and Cressida*'. *Shakespeare Quarterly* 56, no. 3 (2005): 306–27.
Yoder, R.A. '"Sons and Daughters of the Game": An Essay on Shakespeare's *Troilus and Cressida*'. *Shakespeare Survey* 25: The Problem Plays (1972): 11–26.
Žižek, Slavoj. '"Wicked Meaning in a Lawful Deed": Shakespeare on the Obscenity of Power'. In *Shakespeare After 9/11: How a Social Trauma Reshapes Interpretation*, edited by Matthew Biberman and Julia Reinhard Lupton, 81–100. Lewiston, NY, Queenston and Lampeter: Mellen, 2011.

Zurovski, Andrej. 'Cressida's Children: *Troilus and Cressida* in Gdansk'. *Shakespeare Quarterly* 42, no. 3 (1991): 359–63.

Zyszet, Sylvia. 'Apocalyptic Beginnings at the End of the New Millennium: Stefan Bachmann's *Troilus and Cressida*'. In *Four Hundred Years of Shakespeare in Europe*, edited by A. Luis Pujante and Ton Hoenselaars, 196–210. Newark, DE: University of Delaware Press, 2003.

INDEX

Agamemnon, 5, 12, 44, 54
   council scene, 136–7
   as exemplar, 112–13, 123
   in the *Iliad*, 134–5, 139
   as portrayed in stage productions, 60, 72, 74, 76
Achilles, 7, 30, 33, 44–5, 82, 91, 131, 134, 143, 145, 159
   as exemplar, 112–13, 118
   killing of Hector, 9, 125–6, 149, 204–6
   link with Earl of Essex, 93, 108–9
   as portrayed in stage productions, 61, 64, 67–9, 74, 77, 79, 182, 206
   relationship with Patroclus, 140–2
   reputation, 55, 123, 137, 140
   withdrawal from battle, 8, 54–5, 139, 150
Aeneas, 6, 8, 108, 112, 119, 123, 135, 137
   as portrayed in stage productions, 58, 69, 72, 74
Alexander, Peter, 16, 88
acculturation, 168, 170
adaptation, 31, 170
   film adaptation, 85–6
   stage adaptation, 17–9, 23, 29, 56–7, 174, 180, 183, 187
   television and radio adaptation, 84
   translation, 166, 181, 184
Ajax, 9, 30, 33, 44, 55, 73, 85, 124–5, 133, 137, 140, 145, 158–9, 203
   as exemplar, 115–16
   as portrayed in stage productions, 79, 83
All's Well That Ends Well, 4, 15, 37–8, 45, 153
anachronism, 19, 21–3, 26, 60, 178, 182
Andromache, 57, 74, 118–19
appropriation, 147, 149, 158, 160, 166, 178, 183, 186
audience
   audience expectations, 6, 89, 91, 93, 98, 101, 104–5, 167
   early (Elizabethan), 3, 5–7, 42, 53, 88, 91, 100, 102, 108, 117, 140, 148, 151, 162, 168, 208
   global, 81–2, 86
   Greek, 178–9, 185, 189
   modern, 46, 60, 62, 75–6, 79, 101, 169
   Restoration, 17, 14, 57, 176

Babicki, Krzysztof, 68
Bachmann, Stefan, 76
Barfoot, C.C., 95, 155
Barton, Anne, 49, 104
Barton, John, 3, 63–5, 68, 70–1, 79, 85
Bednarz, James P., 90–1
Bellies, Errikos, 169–72, 175–7, 186
Bevington, David, 1, 14, 15, 17, 75, 94, 134, 137, 154, 155, 159, 203–4
Boas, Frederick S., 4–5, 36–8, 43, 45
body, 96, 109–10, 117, 125, 148–9, 160
   actors', 63–4, 68, 79, 201, 206
   Hector's, 58, 63
   women's, 114–15, 122, 127, 158
Bowen, Barbara, 99
Boyd, Michael, 206, 211
Bradbrook, M.C., 46
Bradley, A.C., 38–40
Brandes, George, 34–5
Bruster, Douglas, 95
Bushnell, Rebecca, 103

Calvin, John, *Traité des reliques*, 159–60
Campbell, O.J., 43, 47–8
Cartelli, Thomas, 78
Caxton, William, *Recuyell of the Histories of Troye*, 5, 131, 148
Catholics, 151, 159, 161
Chapman, George, 5, 35, 148, 173, 184
Seaven Bookes of the Iliades of Homere, 7, 109–10, 122, 131, 133–6
Charnes, Linda, 97, 163
Chaucer, Geoffrey, 5, 18, 20, 28, 92, 94, 131–2, 148, 185, 189
Cheek by Jowl (Declan Donnellan), 75, 212
Cheney, Patrick, 97
Coleridge, Samuel Taylor, 18, 25, 29
council scene(s), 9, 66, 134–9, 149, 155, 196
   juxtaposition with *Iliad*, 134–5
Cressida
   as exemplar, 113–14, 118, 207–8
   feminist readings, 50, 71, 99–101
   idealization, 120–1, 125, 154, 157, 196
   nineteenth-century readings, 28, 31, 33–4, 41
   as portrayed in stage adaptations, 58, 61, 63–5, 68–72, 75, 77, 79–82, 85, 181
   relationship with Troilus, 114, 120, 124–7, 144, 150, 153, 158, 194
   unfaithfulness, 34, 81, 114, 127, 156, 190, 199–200
criticism, critics (*see also under individual names*)
   biographical, 34–6
   character-based, 20, 23, 27–8, 30–1, 33, 40
   ecocriticism, 6, 101, 103

eighteenth-century, 20–5
feminist, 50, 99–101
German, 25–7, 29–32, 33, 36
historical, 91–4
Marxist, 95
presentist, 101–2
psychological, 25, 31, 98–101
Romantic, 25–31
twentieth-/twenty-first-century, 38–51, 88–103
Victorian, 32–8

Dawson, Anthony B., 89, 209
Davies, Howard, 70–1, 211
desire, 48, 61, 64, 69, 100, 118, 125, 151, 158, 180, 183, 195, 197
Diomedes, 10, 114, 125, 136, 190, 197, 207
  fight against Troilus, 201–2
  as portrayed in stage productions, 59, 65, 69, 72, 75, 78, 81, 83
  relationship with Cressida, 122, 156–8, 195
Dollimore, Jonathan, 95
Dorn, Dieter, 75
Dryden, John, 4, 17–19, 22–3, 56–7, 102, 176–7
Dunster, Matthew, 81, 212

Early English Books Online, 98
editors, editorial history, 3–4, 17–18, 20–4, 98, 131, 185, 203–4, 209
Elizabeth I, 7–8, 42, 92–3, 107–8
Ellis-Fermor, Una, 10, 44, 47

Elton, W.R., 88–9
Elyot, Thomas, 111
Engle, Lars, 92, 95–6
Escolme, Bridget, 89, 98
Esrig, David, 66
Essex, Earl of (Robert Devereux), 8, 44, 107
  comparison to Achilles, 7, 92–3, 108–9, 149
exemplarity, 7, 11, 108–10, 114–16, 118–19, 121–6, 136, 140, 207–8

Fenton, Geoffrey, *Certaine Tragicall Discourses*, 110–11, 117
Findlay, Alison, 133
folio, 3, 10, 16–17, 20–2, 24
Freund, Elizabeth, 167
Freud, Sigmund, 50, 100
Frye, Northrop, 45–6

Garrison, James S., 141–2
gender, 3, 6, 10, 98–9, 101, 113, 118, 147, 153, 157, 162–3
  approaches in stage productions, 69, 71–2, 74, 83, 87
genre, 2, 4, 16, 18, 21, 30, 32, 34, 36–7, 43, 45, 130, 184, 192
Georgopoulou, Xenia, 169–70
Gervinus, G.G., 31–3, 36
Gil, Daniel Juan, 99
Girard, René, 100, 163, 180
Goethe, Johann Wolfgang von, 29
Grady, Hugh, 95, 101–2

Greece, 11, 33, 131–3, 135, 137, 139, 142, 144–5, 169–70, 174, 177–8, 184, 186–7
   Greek language, 170–1
      demotic, 170–2, 178–9
      katharevousa (purist), 170, 178
   Greek plays (Shakespeare's), 132, 138
Greekness, 11, 131–3
Greeks
   and honour, 124, 136–7
   as portrayed in stage productions, 58–63, 66–7, 69, 72, 77–8, 82, 84, 207
   stereotypes in early modern England, 110, 129–34, 136–7, 140–3, 145
Greene, Gayle, 95, 98–100
Gregory, Johann, 10, 50
Guthrie, Tyrone, 59–60

Hall, Adrian, 60
Hamlet, 2, 8–9, 15, 17, 21, 25, 37–8, 42, 45, 93, 166, 173–4
Hands, Terry, 67–8
Hanna, Sara, 132, 138
Harmon, A.G., 94
Harrison, G.B., 44–5
Hatzopoulos, Nikos, 174–9, 187
Hazlitt, William, 13, 25, 27–8, 31, 104
Hector, 1–2, 9, 21–3, 27–8, 49, 55, 57, 64, 72, 92–3, 120, 130, 134, 137, 139–40, 191
   death of, 5, 9, 57, 67, 125–6, 149, 202–5
   as exemplar, 112, 118–19, 122, 124, 150
   as portrayed in stage productions, 60, 62–3, 68, 71, 74, 76, 82, 206–7
Heine, Heinrich, 26, 30–1, 33
Helen, 8, 31, 100, 108, 113, 128, 143, 150
   and Elizabeth, 122
   and exemplarity, 118, 123
   link with Cressida, 34, 71, 150, 154–5, 162–3
   as portrayed in stage productions, 59, 61, 64–5, 68, 69, 72–4, 77, 83
   worth of, 55, 119, 121–2, 124, 144, 191, 196–7
Henry V, 61, 108
Henryson, Robert, *Testament of Cresseid*, 5, 20
heroism, 3, 9–10, 30, 57, 73, 142, 144, 167
Hillman, David, 96
Hillman, Melissa, 61
Hiscock, Andrew, 96
history, 3, 7, 11, 13, 15, 26, 90, 92–3, 108, 110–13, 117, 125–6, 128, 161, 166, 169, 182
Hodgdon, Barbara, 100
Homer, *Iliad*, 5, 7, 9, 18, 27, 31–2, 33, 35–6, 62, 109–11, 112, 126, 130–6, 138–40, 145, 147, 186, 189

homosexuality, 3, 10, 63–4, 70, 99, 140–2, 206–7
homosociality, 6, 92, 99, 157
Honigmann, E.A.J., 91–2
honour, 4, 8–9, 15, 59, 61, 63, 73, 76, 82, 119, 123–4, 140, 144–5, 206
House, Rachel, 82, 212
Howarth, Carolyn, 73–4

idol, 109, 117, 122, 153, 157, 159
imagery
   animals, 42, 47, 103, 194
   disease/decay, 4, 7, 42, 47, 108–9, 125, 155–6, 162
   food, 42, 91, 148, 156, 163
   jewels, 144, 154–5, 196–7
   mercantile, trade, 9, 95, 155, 162–3, 197
   time, 1, 5–6, 10, 41, 47, 93, 127, 194

James, Heather, 7, 93, 167
Johnson, Samuel, 4, 22–3, 25–8
Judge, Ian, 206, 211

Kennedy, Dennis, 75–6
Kerrigan, John, 94
Kiernan, Ryan, 102
Knight, G. Wilson, 10, 40–1, 43, 47
Koun, Karolos, 169–70, 175
Kott, Jan, 10, 47, 65–7
Kwan, Roberta, 96

Lamb, Charles, 30
Lawrence, W.W., 42
LeCompte, Elizabeth, 77–80, 213

Leech, Clifford, 131
Lenz, Joseph, 95
Lessenich, Rolf P., 97
Lydgate, John, *Troy Book*, 5, 131, 148

Macbeth, 38, 139, 173
Macowan, Michael, 58–9, 63
Mallin, Eric, 92–3
Malone, Edmund, 24
Maquerlot, Jean-Pierre, 97
Markidou, Vassiliki, 6–7, 11, 133
Marlowe, Christopher, 48
   Doctor Faustus, 143–4
   Jew of Malta, 142–4
   'The Passionate Shepherd to his Love', 143
Martin, Priscilla, 36
Measure for Measure, 4, 15, 32, 37–8, 45
Mendes, Sam, 71, 211
Menelaus, 34, 44, 55, 112, 128, 137, 143, 157, 204
Mentz, Steve, 103
metadrama, metaatheatre, 6, 9, 90, 94, 97–8, 167, 185
Midsummer Night's Dream, A, 185
Minton, Gretchen, 98
morality, 8, 13, 18, 25, 28, 31, 33–6, 43, 80, 117–18, 142, 167, 184, 207–8
Mouzenidou, Raia, 180–3, 186–7
Muir, Kenneth, 42, 46–7
myth, mythology (*see also* Troy), 6–8, 80, 94, 112, 122–3, 132, 143, 162–3, 167–8, 179

nation, nationalism, 8, 72–3,
    78–9, 131, 147, 161,
    163, 169
neologism, 50, 166, 178
Nestor, 44, 69, 72, 111, 134–8,
    160
Nunn, Trevor, 207, 211
Nuttall, A.D., 96, 132

Oates, Joyce Carol, 47
Orgel, Stephen, 64
Oxford English Dictionary, 54,
    147, 192

Pandarus, 23, 28, 57, 100, 108,
    118, 120, 123, 138,
    141, 150, 153–4
  epilogue, 17, 57, 97, 163,
    167–8, 178–9
  and metadrama, 10, 55, 97,
    207–8
  as portrayed in stage
    productions, 58, 60,
    63, 67–71, 76–7, 81,
    83–5, 182
Papp, Joseph, 69–70, 85
Paris, 21, 119, 122, 138, 143,
    150
  as portrayed in stage
    productions, 58–61,
    65, 68–9, 71, 73
Parker, Patricia, 96
Patroclus, 33, 44, 206
  pageant/metadrama, 9, 54,
    134, 137, 150
  as portrayed in stage
    adaptations, 67–9, 71,
    78–9, 83
  relationship with Achilles,
    140–2, 159–60

Peacham, Henry, *The Garden of
    Eloquence*, 198
performance
  early theatre, 3, 22, 53–6,
    88–9
  in languages other than
    English, 65–9, 75–7,
    169–70, 177–83
  postmodern, 75–84
  Restoration performance,
    56–7
  twentieth-/twenty-first-
    century, 57–84,
Poel, William, 58
Pope, Alexander, 20–1, 25
Powell, Neil, 97
problem play(s), 2, 4, 14–15, 34,
    36–8, 40, 42, 45–6,
    48–9, 167, 183, 185
prologue, 17–18, 104, 117, 129,
    138, 148–50, 200–1
  as performed in stage
    productions, 56, 62,
    68, 73, 75, 83
props, 59, 77–9, 148, 157–8,
    201–2
Purcarete, Silviu, 77

quarto, 2–3, 10, 14–15, 17, 20,
    22, 53, 88, 176–7, 180,
    189–90, 203

Ravenhill, Mark, 77–8, 213
Reformation, 96, 151, 158
relics, 7, 11, 42, 147–59, 162–3
religion, 49, 94, 147, 151–6,
    158–61, 163
rhetoric, 11, 27, 50, 108, 167,
    176, 191, 194, 197–8,
    201, 209–10

anadiplosis, 198–200
antanaclasis, 190
ekphrasis, 8, 115–16
epideictic, 136
Ribner, Irving, 143
Romeo and Juliet, 16, 21, 61,
    152–3, 181–2
Rossiter, A.P., 48, 103
Rotas, Vassilis, 169–72, 175–6,
    179–80, 186
Rowe, Nicholas, 20–1
Rutter, Carol Chillington, 64,
    70

Segar, William, 112–13
Schlegel, August Wilhelm, 26–7,
    29, 31
Schulman, Alex, 97
Shakespeare Concordance,
    192–3, 195–7
Shaw, G.B., 34, 37, 41
Sidney, Philip, *Apology for
    Poetry*, 11, 113, 116
Smith, Emma, 19, 24
sources, 2, 14, 23, 27–8,
    33–4, 48, 93–4, 102,
    138, 168, 172, 184,
    186
Spear, Gary, 99
Spurgeon, Caroline, 42
stage directions, 203–5
Stein, Peter, 65
Swinburne, Algernon Charles,
    13, 26, 32–3, 39
Silva Rhetoricae, 198
Symons, Arthur, 39

theatre programmes, 170,
    173–4, 179, 182
Theobald, Lewis, 20–2

Thersites
    as critic and spectator, 9–10,
        33, 39, 44, 89, 100,
        207–8
    cursing, 125, 130, 135–7,
        141, 158–9
    illegitimacy, 160–3
    as portrayed in stage
        productions, 57–9, 61,
        64–6, 68–71, 73, 77,
        79–80, 82–3, 85
    as satirist, 20, 109
Tillyard, E.M., 45
Traub, Valerie, 162
translation (*see also* adaptation)
    and Shakespeare, 166, 176,
        184–5
    of *Troilus and Cressida*, 11,
        26, 66–8, 82, 84–5
    as experiment, 180–3
    in Greek, 168–83, 187
Troilus
    as exemplar, 126–7, 191,
        207
    and heroic masculinity,
        55, 123, 150, 172,
        202
    as portrayed in stage
        productions, 57–8,
        68–70, 72, 75, 77,
        81–2, 84–5, 181
    relationship with Cressida,
        124, 97, 113–14, 118,
        120–1, 124, 127–8,
        151, 153–8, 198–9,
        193, 196–7
    and vows, 12, 94, 200–1
Troy (*see also* myth)
    fall/sack of, 8–9, 43, 46, 135,
        162

in Tudor England, 7, 108, 110, 112, 161–2
Twelfth Night, 89, 131

Ulrici, Hermann, 31
Ulysses
 degree speech, 103, 124, 135, 137–8, 173, 191, 193, 199
 and metatheatre, 9–10, 54–6, 134, 140–1, 207
 as portrayed in stage productions, 58–9, 63–5, 70, 72, 74, 77, 79, 81, 85

Van Doren, Mark, 13

war
 First and Second World Wars, 34, 43, 46, 58–9
 Poets' War, 90–1
 Trojan War, 2–3, 8–10, 14, 34, 54, 63, 68, 80–2, 92, 108, 110–13, 117–19, 123–5, 128–9, 133, 139, 142, 144, 147–8, 150, 158, 181, 193, 203–4
 twentieth-/twenty-first-century international conflicts, 4, 50, 60–2, 72–3, 77, 79
Wells, Robin Headlam, 99, 149
Wing-Davey, Mark, 76
words
 coinages, 191–3
 compounds, 194–5
 morphology, 167, 194

Yachnin, Paul, 89

Žižek, Slavoj, 104

www.ingramcontent.com/pod-product-compliance
Lightning Source LLC
Chambersburg PA
CBHW052154300426
44115CB00011B/1667